HOLDING ON

This is a work of nonfiction.
I have changed the names and identities of some individuals
to protect their anonymity and privacy
or to simplify the number of characters in my life.

Sedna Marketing Partners LLC

ISBN: 0-6157-4945-3
ISBN-13: 9780615749457

HOLDING ON

a mom during war

Beth Jackson

2013

To my younger but wiser sister, Carrie.

Thank you for teaching me how to exhale.

I may still need your little reminders once in a while.

Chapters

Chapter 1 – Preparing for Battle

February 2011

We each have our own story. We brave women have each faced
wrenching challenges throughout life, and throughout history.
While each of our stories may be totally unique, the soil of
our lives is rich with despair and hope, loss and resilience, and
ultimately love and friendship. These interlaced roots are what
hold us together and give us strength. Somehow the sun and
the rain, with a little help from those industrious bees, keep us
enduring life, like a perennial returning with the spring, even
when we are ready to give up.

My story began on Monday, February 7, 2011. It, too, is a story of
returning, as a working mom of three, from rock bottom.

I was working in the headquarters of my own marketing consulting
business, a home office in truth, with a window by my desk
overlooking our large side yard. We call that part of our property
"the field," and it sits near the edge of the Sakonnet River, which
feeds the Atlantic Ocean with its strong currents just a couple miles
south. A few minutes before I was going to drive Ian to his evening
hockey practice, Colin walked into the room, quietly, with an
uncharacteristically grave look on his face.

"Beth, I have to tell you something before you go," he stammered in
a monotone. I swiveled my chair, turning my back to the window.

"My Reserve Unit called me. I am getting deployed to Kuwait
or Afghanistan. I don't know which yet. I will probably leave
sometime next month. For a year. "

Beth Jackson

My throat clenched shut. I don't remember breathing or moving.

After a few moments, I mustered, "It is fair. It is your turn. " And I meant it. I knew it was true, but I shocked my husband and myself with the ease with which the words came out. We had always known this was a possibility. Immediately after 9/11, I thought there was a probable chance Colin would be called up. But month after month and year after year passed, and after fourteen years since Colin had last served Active duty, I thought that chapter had closed. Frankly, I did not even think of ourselves as a military family; our children had never once stepped foot onto an Army base. Colin's monthly Reserve duty, always in a different state from our own, seemed like a business trip. Our lives were as "civilian" as a professor husband and marketing wife with three children could be. A girlfriend later told me she was surprised by how non-chalant I was in my response to her question when we first met about a chance of deployment. "Sure, it can happen," I had said without emotion, or even thought. I had the cocktail party line down, but the reality was I never ever thought it would actually transpire.

Until now. The reality hit me like lightening.

"That is what I first thought, too," Colin nodded. Time suspended as we locked eyes. My body slowly peeled away from its inertia and rose to a standing position, as my arms hugged my soul mate. "I love you," we exchanged.

But there was no time to talk any longer. Ian had to get to practice. Colin was taking over child detail from our nanny and staying with the other two. Later in the evening he was going to take Karl to *his* hockey practice, and I would put Ian and Thais to bed. We would likely not have time to talk again for another five hours, after the typical weeknight shuffle of children, multiple hockey practices, and staggered bedtimes.

I walked downstairs where the noise of child play and sizzle from the sautéing chicken permeated the air. Numbness had started to take over my body, like a white fluffy cloud. I was going through the motions, speaking words to Dana, our nanny, and quickly checking that all of Ian's hockey equipment was in his bag. I could see myself moving, but my mind was somewhere else, clouded by this fog.

At that moment, my precocious daughter, Thais, ran up to me and squeezed my leg tight. My eyes looked down at her chestnut brown hair as my arm reflexively wrapped a hug around her. In her hand, I saw that she held a green and pink polka dotted canvas bag. A small black and white stuffed animal kitten that Colin had given her last Christmas peered out over the corner edge. Then it hit me that Colin would miss this next Christmas.

The children had no idea what I had just learned. Looking at the three of them, my mind wondered. *How would we tell them? What would this mean for them?*

I pushed the thought away and returned to autopilot. We were going to be late for Ian's practice if we did not leave immediately. I grabbed my coat and slipped my arms into each sleeve. Ian picked up his hockey bag and lumbered outside. My right hand carried his stick. We loaded everything into the back of my car and were on our way.

As I drove to the rink, my focus kept shifting to the rearview mirror, so I could see Ian. At eight years old, he was just an innocent little boy, staring out the window as we passed a herd of cattle behind a low stone wall and a plot of land with a series of grapevines tied to wooden stakes. *How will he cope without Dad?*

I thought about him as a toddler boy who used to pretend play with yellow rubber rain boots on his feet, a wooden sword in his hand, and a red and blue plaid fleece blanket around his shoulders like a cape. Years later, his love of play had shifted towards sophisticated Lego set-ups and model-making, but his imagination only continued to bloom. My eyes studied his fair freckled face. We were so similar in appearance, yet why was he such a mystery to me? I adored Ian with his wit, sharp mind, and enchanting smile. But he was a master of one-word answers and had stopped saying "I love you" to me over a year ago.

Ian idolized his Dad; they both could be introverted and shared a passion for sports and history. Last season Ian refused me when I offered to coach his town soccer team, despite the fact I played varsity soccer in high school and was trying to spend more time with him in his world. He wanted Dad, who did not know the game as I did, or someone else's Dad. Not Mom.

Colin had the key to connect with Ian. He was the one who cracked jokes when Ian refused to do work on a school project or help around the house. "If you piss in the wind," Colin explained to him one night, "you get wet. I know how this standoff between you and your mother is going to end, and you are going to do what she asked. Don't piss in the wind. Just do it. Piss *with* the wind. " Eventually, this light-hearted advice cracked Ian's resistance, and he did his schoolwork that night. Somehow whatever I said or did was wrong.

After a recent argument over homework, which included screaming matches and slammed doors, I told Ian how much I loved him. I tried to explain that I was trying to help him avoid having to stay up until midnight later in the week when hockey practices were scheduled every night. I broke a cardinal parenting rule by venturing out to ask Ian if he loved me, but my heart needed to hear it. My personality was not one that cared much what others thought of me, but I needed to be loved back by my middle son.

"Sort of," he responded sheepishly.

I just wanted to embrace Ian after he said this, but I held back knowing he was not ready. Sadness was replaced with the need to simply accept this unsatisfactory answer, and my mouth repeated the words, "I love you, Ian. "

Since Colin was a political scientist, thousands of books occupied shelves and floor space throughout our colonial style house. Ian had read many of the military history titles and knew exactly what his Dad did as a former tank commander and now an intelligence officer. He amazed me with how much he knew and understood about past wars, especially World War II. Ian wanted to be a fighter pilot, a dream that less than perfect eyesight prevented Colin from obtaining himself.

I thought about Colin leaving, possibly to a war zone, and my mind was flooded with images of war and how I would shield the children from it all. Ian knew enough from books about the reality of war. *Would his innocence be shattered?*

Twelve minutes later, we arrived at the ice hockey rink. After Ian put on his gear, I tied his skates. As soon as he stepped out onto the ice, I found a seat on the frozen wood bleachers and lowered myself down. As I sat, my whole body started shaking.

I felt nauseous. Sick. Scared my husband was getting called up and would be gone a long time. The cold ice rink had made me penetrate that cold reality. Maybe he would even be sent to Afghanistan, an active war zone, where the insurgents killed Americans indiscriminately. Thoughts of his possible death and anxiety over our children's well-being added layer upon layer of dread. As this disorder of my brain settled in, my stomach started eating itself. This was when my body began to give way to something, a faceless dark something I had not previously met before.

Beth Jackson

My girlfriend climbed up the bleachers and sat next to me. She had no idea of the news I had just received.

After a minute of quiet pleasantries, I told her.

"Oh, Beth," she replied with a look of complete love and support. "Are you OK?"

I choked back tears and shook my head as my desperate feelings escaped my hold. I could barely feel her hand on the small of my back as a lone tear fell down my chilled cheek.

***

The next six weeks were a blur.

Colin gave me the name of Daisy, the Family Support contact of his Reserve Unit up in Massachusetts. Clueless about how to embark on this new journey, my list of questions kept growing. I sent her an e-mail asking my most important and urgent question: how does one tell children about their father's deployment?

Colin and I were college sweethearts. He was commissioned as an officer immediately after graduation and began his service to pay back his ROTC scholarship to Princeton. A year later, at the age of twenty-two, we got married, and I joined him in Germany, where he served out the rest of his Active duty time and I began my career in marketing. While I had some familiarity with the military, our peacetime abroad without children and real responsibilities felt like a college exchange program. Deployment to war with a family of three young children was now a totally new concept for me.

I did not hear anything back from Daisy, so the next day, during dinner, we just went with our intuition and explained to the children what we knew. And what we did not yet know.

"You know how Daddy goes away for a weekend every month as part of the Reserves? Well, Daddy is getting deployed and will be serving overseas for a year. We don't know exactly when he will be leaving, but it will likely be sometime next month. "

The first question from Ian was a shocked "for how long?"

"Probably for a year. "

After a short pause, Karl, the oldest, asked, "Will he leave before my birthday?"

"Maybe. We don't know. "

I looked at Karl across the table with sadness. Only ten, he was wiser and taller than his years. He aspired to be an archeologist, and to nourish his insatiable curiosity, he carried hard-covered books around with him like an appendage to his body. Beside his dinner chair, three such books were stacked on the floor. For all his knowledge, he was still just a boy who wanted to celebrate his birthday with his Dad.

Karl always wore a smile, and his first answer was always "sure. " He shared that optimism with us on a daily basis. Two years ago, he saved a young boy from drowning in our pool but then was embarrassed by all the attention the adults gave him. He just did what needed to be done. He was just brave. Like his Dad.

Within days, we found out Colin was going to Afghanistan.

Thais, just recently turned four, did not fully comprehend the details but learned to pronounce this big word, "Af-ghan-i-stan. "

Beth Jackson

The boys found it on the world map that adorned a wall of our kitchen, and they just listened, trying to absorb everything.

To me, it felt like I was preparing for battle all by myself.

As the deployment crept closer, I could not help myself in thinking of all the bad things that could happen. This was just my way - like when I had two miscarriages before Thais was conceived - the associated worry and despair of a possible third miscarriage consumed me. The gift of Thais eventually replaced that sorrow. She was born healthy, although the umbilical cord was wrapped tightly around her neck, twice. I barely touched her body before she was whisked away to the warming table to be revived. My doctor said an angel was looking over her.

With this deployment, I worried about everything. My biggest fear was the possibility that Colin would die, and the children and I would be left all alone. The news had educated me about the commonplace of suicide bombings and attacks on U. S. bases. Snipers. IEDs. Truck bombs. These visuals bombarded my mind.

One story I heard when preparing for the deployment particularly struck a nerve. A young soldier in his early twenties had lost all four limbs in Iraq and was recovering at Walter Reed military hospital. The road ahead for him would be a long one. His fiancée visited him in the hospital and decided she could not deal with this life-altering event. So she gave her engagement ring back to him, and to ensure it did not get lost, she taped it to his abdomen. Tape. Seriously? Taped the ring. *Are you kidding me?* No human deserved to be deserted like that. This young man was alive and was a human being who had truly given himself for all of us. And he still had his mind and his heart.

I then realized that while I wanted Colin to come back home safely, it was actually more important to me that my husband would come back the same person, mentally, regardless of his

8

physical state. I had heard the stories about the difficulties returning soldiers had readjusting, along with their nightmares and anger. I had heard about post-traumatic stress disorder (PTSD), and I worried. *Was this deployment the gravestone for our marriage?*

After sharing these worries with Colin, he wrote me a loving note that said he was too old and too cynical to change, even in light of suffering or absurdity. He talked about his hope of becoming a stronger and better person out of this experience. Oh, how I wished that he was right. But what was I going to do without his calming stable force to balance my frenetic nature?

If the weeks before he left were an indication of betterment, then I had reason for hope. Our priorities shifted overnight. Both Colin and I spent more time nurturing the children and our marriage. Suddenly, skipping a day of school so the five of us could go skiing was not even a question; it was a great idea. Colin also took each of the children out of school for a one-on-one Dad day. Ian and Karl each chose to go to the Boston Museum of Science. Thais chose the local zoo.

Daily sex, morning or night, became the norm. Maybe we were storing it up or just clinging onto the closeness of our bodies for the fear it would be the last time; but regardless of the reason, we both needed and wanted it.

I still had no idea what to really expect. For the children. For me. For Colin. I needed a Deployment 101 for Dummies. I was the dummy. Anger started building inside me about the difficulties in getting basic information such as deployment tips for children, medical insurance, or even what Colin's salary would be.

We already had an extremely busy life that operated at over capacity between our three young children, their myriad of activities, and our dual careers. And I worried about my business. I had spent seven long years building the client base of my consulting company, and if I let it go, if I could not keep up, I was scared that it would be gone. Forever. The economy was already tight as it was. Clients would find others to do the work. My company would simply cease to exist, and we would not be able to pay the mortgage to our house. There was no unemployment for self-employed business owners, and we had not achieved any level of savings that would cover interrupted income.

Shortly after Thais was born, we moved to Rhode Island for Colin's teaching job, but it meant travel for my work. I was often gone for several days at a time, and worked many nights and weekends in my home office to pay bills, write proposals, and file all the monthly and quarterly forms required for running a business. Colin had the more flexible schedule as a professor, so he was the super Dad of hockey and lacrosse practices.

Every Sunday night, Colin and I mapped out the schedule for the week to make sure everything was scripted to the minute, and who between the two of us, based on our work schedules, would handle getting the children ready for school, putting homework into backpacks, letting out our dog Charlotte, and feeding her and giving her clean water. Who would put the children's lunches together and drop them off at school, pick them up, and supervise their homework. Then there were their practices, games, and music lessons... and dinners to be made and cleaned up. Dishwasher to empty, laundry to do, showers to run, toilet paper rolls to replace, forms for field trips and new sports seasons to fill out, and doctor visits to squeeze in, routine and unexpected. There had always been the two of us – with some help from an afterschool nanny. But she couldn't pay the bills, and I wouldn't ask her to pick up the dog poop on the lawn. For a long time now, I had found time late at night and on weekends to keep up and catch up. I had given up blow-drying my hair years ago; those ten minutes were a waste of time, as I had too many other things to organize.

And now it was just going to be me. Our family was scattered across California, Michigan, and DC. I began feeling overwhelmed by the enormity of the change ahead and how it would impact my work and our financial security. How would I manage our logistical calendar without Colin? How would I handle the emotional side of parenting all alone?

Usually, I had confidence in myself and strove to be Superwoman in all facets of my life. In situations of stress, which admittedly I magnified by my inability to sit down, I planned and made to-do lists. I needed action. I liked control. But now as I focused obsessively on this thing called deployment, everything seemed to be outside of my control. And it drove me crazy. Literally.

The antidote to my ignorance was to build an arsenal of information. I had tried again to contact Daisy at Colin's unit, and my patience, thin to begin with, wore out. My instinct told me to Google "deployment checklists. " I did, and took action.

- Will. Updated to include birth of Thais. Changed guardians.
- Power of Attorney. Could not do that until the orders came.
- Banking. I already paid the bills. *Phew*! One less new thing to learn.
- Life Insurance. Yes, premiums increased. Colin's life was more at risk.
- Car Insurance. No need to insure his car. Changed policy.
- Military IDs. Wait. Needed orders.
- Healthcare. Something called Tricare. Could we keep our same doctors?

It appeared that the consequential effect of having a deploying family member was the addition of a part-time job "managing" the deployment, checking off the boxes of a rudimentary to-do list.

Beth Jackson

Frenzied activity gave me immediate relief and a sense of purpose, but my sleep suffered as my frustration aimed at the fact that there were not enough hours in the day to get it all done.

I kept thinking there was more I needed to know. Dental care? Colin's pay? What should we say to the children's teachers? I did not know anyone who had previously or was currently deployed to Afghanistan. How could we meet other families that have deployed loved ones, so my children did not feel alone? Was there a support group for spouses? What could we learn from them? What other questions should I be asking that I didn't even know to ask? My thoughts were urgent; my mind cartwheeling. I needed control.

I didn't know if other wives felt these same feelings of fear and anxiety, but an enormous respect for all military spouses blossomed in me. Later I learned that over two million military personnel had been deployed to Iraq, Afghanistan, or both within the past ten years, but I barely knew one.

I reached out to Meghan, the wife of this one soldier who had served in Iraq, and to Anne, the only close friend I knew whose husband was currently serving Active duty with the military, albeit not deployed, not with the Army, and they were living on the other side of the country in California. I implored the two of them for tips on how to help the children, which transferred directly onto my to-do lists; for example, put dozens of photos of Dad around the house, order a soft-sided photo book of us for Dad to carry in the pocket of his camouflage pants, and start a Daddy Kiss jar full of Hershey kisses. I executed on every single one of them.

For weeks, the anticipated but not yet actualized arrival of Colin's official orders hung over us. "Orders" were simply a page of paper from the Department of the Army that officially commanded Colin when and where to report on duty. But only official orders would give me access to check off a few more items from my growing list, and I needed that gratification of crossing something off. Was he leaving on March

15, as he was originally told? That date was creeping closer, but the orders did not come. It was the missing puzzle piece, and its absence challenged my sanity and created tension when I nagged Colin about it. When did the legal and military details have to be completed, so we, the loved ones left on the homefront, could prepare ourselves - at least on a perfunctory level?

Then I began to obsess over his departure date. Good friends offered to throw Colin a goodbye party, *phew* one less thing to do, but I did not want to schedule it too far in advance, until we knew for sure when he was leaving. Then there was a chance the date was going to be delayed two months. "NO!" I screamed inside when I heard this. After four weeks of our life being turned upside down, I was ready for him to go. The sooner he left, the sooner his hopeful return home.

A four-day business trip brought me to Wyoming the week before we thought Colin was to leave. I had stressed over its timing, but Colin still did not have his orders, and we agreed that it was better for me to go now while he was home and overnight childcare was free, in contrast to what we could expect this next year.

***

The day after I returned from my trip, Anne kindly emailed me a few thoughts.

> *It is normal for the two of you to do a lot of fighting before he leaves. It is the way both of you begins the separation process. You withdraw from each other as a way to prepare to be alone and having to be the one in complete control. Jeff and I always started to bicker more and more. Then we realized, after some of the classes we took, that it is totally normal. It helps to know this so that you don't freak out that you are fighting. Then again, you two may be special and not fighting at all...*

Beth Jackson

I forwarded Anne's note to Colin. We had been trying more than usual to be patient and supportive of each other, but we did indeed bicker. This was especially so in those last days as Colin's mental punch list and "dumping" grew.

- His car needed a new carburetor.
- Karl needed larger shin guards for hockey.
- And next Fall, Ian would need new ice skates.
- Oh, and could I send him a pillow and towels once he arrived in Kabul. (He was only being issued a sleeping bag; no, he did not yet have a mailing address.)

The list went on and on. With the wisdom that Anne had imparted to me, I simply smiled and replied, "I will add it to the list and do the best I can do." We tried not to fight. Maybe all the sex helped.

***

Colin received his orders on the following Monday via e-mail. The simple one page document began...

YOU ARE ORDERED TO ACTIVE DUTY FOR OPERATIONAL SUPPORT UNDER PROVISION OF SECTION 12301 (D), TITLE 10 UNITED STATES CODE FOR THE PERIOD SHOWN PLUS THE TIME NECESSARY TO TRAVEL. YOU WILL PROCEED FROM YOUR HOME OR CURRENT LOCATION IN TIME TO REPORT FOR DUTY ON THE DATE SHOWN BELOW.

REPORT DATE/TIME: 19 MAR 2011 BETWEEN 0800 AND 1700
PERIOD OF ACTIVE DUTY: 365 DAYS INCLUDING ACCUM LEAVE
END DATE: 17 MAR 2012
DUTY AT: AFGHANISTAN

The orders continued with his reporting location of Fort Benning, GA, for several days of in-processing, details about travel arrangements, and reemployment rights. The dates clearly read that the deployment was to begin March 19 and end March 17 of the following year. Colin printed off several copies of this one page that made everything suddenly official.

He left that Saturday.

All I remember of that last week is the five of us driving to the military base closest to us, a Navy base, to get a Power of Attorney and Colin's and my official IDs, since his status was now officially "Active" instead of "Reserve." A status change, like when I went from being "not pregnant" to "pregnant." On base, we waited in line at the one-story building, filled out forms, and signed our names over and over again. When exiting the building with the basics of my pre-deployment checklist complete, the sky unleashed its power. I gripped onto Thais's slippery hand as we sprinted through the downpour, chasing Colin and the two boys to our car. We all scrambled into the dry cavern of the metal frame and landed awkwardly onto the leather seats, totally soaked, trying to catch our breath.

I floated in that state of shallow panting, disassociated from my body, the rest of the week. I was still desperately trying to know what I was supposed to know and do what I was supposed to do. And I prayed like I had never prayed before in my life. Not in a formal Godly way, as I was not sure what I actually believed. Instead I found myself closing my eyes tight and holding my breath in an attempt to will this all to be over as quickly as possible. It didn't work.

And I can tell you that I was scared shitless...

    about Colin not coming back,

Beth Jackson

about protecting the innocence of my children,

about not being the perfect mom,

about keeping my sanity.

Chapter 2 – State of Mind

March 2011

The night before Colin left, a full moon from millions of miles away graced the sky above our home and reflected on the river below. A force greater than anything I would ever fully comprehend.

That night, we did not have sex. Colin was too distracted. It was like he was already gone. Loneliness descended upon me as I already felt a pang of loss.

My mind was a tad distracted, too. And mistakes were made. If there is just one thing to be learned from my mistakes, don't, I repeat DON'T, trim the bikini area the same day you are having an emotional meltdown. Not a good idea.

Let me back up. The morning Colin left the children and I were up at 5 to accompany him to the Providence airport and even all the way to the gate, a wonderful exception to the post 9/11 airport rules that allows family members to accompany a deploying soldier.

The departure had consumed my thoughts for weeks. Grand plans seemed to take root. We would make posters to telegraph to Colin and all the people in the airport that my dear love and the father of our children was going off to war. When I shared this plan with Anne, she told me, "No posters. Save those for the return. " Her advice gave me permission to set that idea aside and breathe a sigh of relief: one less thing to do before he left.

And Whoa Nelly was she was right. I would not have wanted to schlep posters along with my 42-pound daughter who dangled from my hip like a piece of paper that was only partially glued on.

Beth Jackson

But nonetheless, somehow I felt we needed to demonstrate our patriotism, so I brought along a four-pack of small American flags. You know, the $3. 99 cheap hand-held ones you can buy from Wal-mart.

Our goodbye was a bit awkward. Colin gave Karl, Ian, and Thais a hug, and then he looked at me. I had thought I would burst into tears at this moment, but the warm moisture stayed behind the shield of my blue eyes as we exchanged "I love you" one last time. There was nothing more to say. The night before, each of the children had given Colin a special something to bring with him in his camouflage backpack to Afghanistan. Karl gave him a black hockey puck. Ian, a white Lego soldier. Thais, thin transparent yellow shells from the beach near our house. I gave him the photo book of all of us, so he would not forget us. I think deep down, I was scared we would forget him, too. His face. His voice. His being.

My mind was filled with wishful visions of Colin looking out his airplane window, seeing us waving flags and blowing kisses until the plane pulled away and slowly crept along the path to its departure. As it turned out the plane was angled to the gate in such a way that no one but the pilots could see us. So there we sat, on the black vinyl chairs near the gate, still in a stupor of sleep, waving our pitiful flags that no one saw. Holding the flags at least gave our fidgety hands something to do in the slow motion of minutes that ticked by before Colin's plane was no longer in sight. We were able to text him during this suspension of time, and he texted back a few times. He texted that he could see the flags, so we kept waving them. Thank you, Colin, for that simple white lie.

There were two other women at the gate sending off their husbands in uniform as well. I assumed they were en route to Fort Benning for in-processing, too, but none of us spoke, so I didn't really know.

One woman was there with a little girl also stuck on her hip, much more securely than Thais. I guessed by the size of her little body that the girl was probably two years old. Beside this woman with blond hair pulled into the same messy ponytail that I threw mine up into at this wee early hour of the morning, was a man. By their similar facial features and hair color, I guessed he was her brother. They sat on seats a few down from us by the same window watching the same plane, but we never exchanged a word.

The second woman, her husband, and their infant baby hurriedly arrived at the gate after all of the other passengers had already boarded. This brown-haired, very pretty woman was crying and clinging onto her baby as she kissed her husband goodbye. My heart dipped with sadness as I watched her. She was all alone.

Without pause, a white-haired woman wearing a Delta uniform came out from behind the counter and walked up to the crying brunette to give her a hug. My body was paralyzed, watching. The brunette started to walk away, when yet another older woman who was waiting to board the next flight stood and said something to her as well. Kind words from a stranger. From yards away, I could see the tears pouring down the brunette's face. It was like watching a silent movie.

Then within seconds, the brunette was gone. She did not stay to watch the plane pull away from the gate. I did not see where she went and did not have my chance to give her a hug, too.

Instinctively, I reached out to each of my children and just touched them. They were all I had at this moment, literally and figuratively. Karl sat silently with an expressionless face. Ian's eyes were stretched wide as he soaked in the reality of Dad leaving. And my little princess just nestled into my chest as she closed her eyes to try to fall back to sleep. She didn't understand the magnitude of what was happening.

Beth Jackson

The blond woman and her brother crossed our path in the parking lot on our way back to reality. The brother drove as I peered up with a look of empathy, but still no words were exchanged. I was a little jealous, actually, that she had family nearby.

Fortunately, the children and I had next day plane tickets to Florida, a trip we had booked months before to enjoy school vacation week with my family. We had not planned this surreal timing of the trip, but the idea of a week away rather than being in an empty house without Dad was exactly what we needed. AirTran graciously refunded Colin's ticket, and Orbitz waived their change fee when I faxed them a copy of his orders.

It was the middle of March now, less than six weeks after Colin first got the call. In preparation for the beach after a long cold winter, I, for some reason, decided I desperately needed to clean up the bikini line. Unable to find my small trimming scissors with rounded edges, I instead grabbed a large sharp pair of kitchen scissors that happened to be in my bathroom from Thais' recent art project. I held those large blades and started trimming away. And then my mind starting wandering... Thinking about the plane. Visualizing Colin's face and the heavy camouflaged bags he carried. And wandering... And, OUCH, I called out loud. I had cut myself. Yes, drops of blood and all. Crying would have been too mild a reaction. Rather, I felt like I wanted to punch something, anything. *Would my body heal?* Well, at least I wouldn't be having sex for a while. And my tightened fists eventually loosened.

It was not until that night when I climbed into our bed alone, that the emotion kicked in. Out of habit, I lay on the left side of the bed, and the emptiness of the right side clung to my heart. Our dog Charlotte usually slept with us as well, but she was already at the kennel where I had dropped her earlier that afternoon in anticipation of our going away. So, there I lay in bed, totally alone. Before I knew it, a wave of sadness came over me, and this time, I did cry, the tears flowing and flowing until the pillow was soaked.

***

We arrived late in the evening to Boca Grande, a sleepy old-fashioned Florida beach town, where cocktail parties and bingo at the Inn meant Lily Pulitzer dresses for the women and coat and tie with brightly-colored dress pants for the men. Our arrival was past Thais's bedtime, and her mood was cranky. Added to that, she was unable to find PJs from her suitcase. I followed her back into the small bedroom we would be sharing and dug through the clothes convinced she had just missed them, but there was nothing. I had forgotten to pack her PJs.

Despite my best attempts to convince her that she could just sleep in the clothes she had on or one of the many other t-shirts and shorts we had brought, my overtired little girl wasn't having any of it.

"I want my jammas!" she screamed out, escalating in power as she repeated it three times. She might as well have been yelling, "I want my Dad back!" but the sobs just overwhelmed the words.

I also wanted to cry out, "I want my husband back!" But I was the grown-up after all. So I tensed up, to hold it all inside.

Ian, her kindred spirit, eventually was able to convince her to wear his old green Incredible Hulk PJs that I had dutifully packed for him. Those PJs were actually too small for Ian, but my disappointment in myself was at least limited by the thought that I had at least packed something for him. I tucked Thais in, and finally all was at peace with a beautiful girl looking like a longhaired boy as she crashed for the night.

The next day, Karl's birthday, was filled with relaxation and fun at the beach club, where we swam in the large pool and looked for shells along the beach. Through their silly games and splashing in the water, the children made me smile, even laugh a little, something I had forgotten to do since the morning Colin left.

Beth Jackson

Before Karl's birthday dinner, I went for a three-mile run, my adrenaline junky addiction to releasing all the tension I had been holding. Move leg, sweat, stress released. Move other leg, sweat, stress released. I barely noticed the sounds of the ocean waves or seagulls flying overhead. I could hear my panting and feet pounding the pavement, as this therapy for my mind and body released their toxins. My face tasted salty, like a concoction of sweat, ocean air, and dried tears.

After a warm shower, I glanced into my suitcase looking for a clean pair of underwear, but I could not find any.

They must be in here somewhere. I wore a pair yesterday on the plane (now in the dirty clothes pile), and I had packed one pair for today (the sweaty pair I just ran in). And then suddenly I understood that I had only packed ONE pair.

Now, what goes through one's head when packing? *Ok, now let's add in socks and underwear...* And then what? One is OK? Or was I interrupted mid task and forgot to add more? Yes, I was clearly distracted. And now the one store in town that stocked underwear was closed. I did call to check, of course. So that night I went buff in my white jeans while the washing machine did its magic.

In that small picture book I gave Colin before his departure, I had been dissatisfied in my search for good pictures of me. So under the Florida sun later that night, I asked my younger sister, Carrie, to do a "photo shoot" of me. I planned to send off a picture of me buff in my white jeans to Colin the next day. Maybe it would be enough to replace the *Sports Illustrated* swim suit edition surely carried by many into war zones.

That night we had a festive birthday dinner of spaghetti and meat sauce, Karl's favorite foods. We sang Happy Birthday as he made a wish and blew out the candles, and then he opened presents from Ian, Thais, my parents, sister, brother, and me. Karl did not mention Dad out loud that evening, but I think I knew what his wish was.

The following day, I actually sat down for a few moments as the crashing waves soothed my ears and my eyes scanned between the three children. Thais squealed as she jumped the first row of three-inch tall waves and sprinted back to the safety of dry sand. Karl threw a football with a friend's son. And Ian played soldier, just like Dad, a plastic white strainer balanced on his head, like a helmet. That image is forever stained on my mind. With no shirt, just his bright blue and white flowered bathing suit covering his skinny body, he held a friend's Nerf gun in his hands. While the strainer was particularly humorous, I did not know if I was proud or filled with trepidation at this sight. Probably a little of both.

Ian playing soldier

A short while later, I made a huge mistake. While the boys and Thais happily played with our friends, I offered to my mom and sister to walk the half block to my parent's house to start making lunch for everyone.

Fifteen minutes later, as I laid out the quesadillas, salsa, peanut butter sandwiches, and fruit onto the table, I could hear a curdling scream of horror. The sound got louder and louder, and I quickly ran outside to see what was happening. My daughter was screaming at the top of her lungs, while my mom was trying unsuccessfully to console her. Behind them followed my sister driving the golf cart, overloaded with beach chairs and towels.

Finally, I could make out the word Thais was yelling, "MOMMY!" over a prolonged twenty seconds. I ran to her, and as soon as she saw me, her body softened into a sobbing pile. My arms scooped her up, and she wrapped herself tightly around my body, while I reassured her I was there. Ten minutes passed before her crying subsided, and I learned my first lesson that my child who just lost her Dad to the unknown needed to see and hear Mom when I left the scene, and to know the exact timing of my return, rather than having me slip silently away.

That night I read Thais a special bedtime story called *My Dad's a Hero* by Rebecca Christiansen. We would read it often, and my heart always melted when we did. Each page of the book told what soldier Dad was doing during his deployment, like wearing a uniform or sleeping in a tent. The pages then continued explaining how Dad sacrificed time with his family to help others and defined how sacrifice meant "to give up. " Those three words always choked me up, and I could never finish the next sentence, "That is why my Dad is a hero," before silence closed my throat and tears began to flow. Thais insisted I read her the book every night before bedtime.

That night as I lay down next to Thais, I just studied her face, the beauty of which was so natural. Her dark hair, dark eyes, and shape of her face were all Colin. The only thing I could claim in the physical DNA connection to my daughter was her fair skin. But hers was still flawless, without the freckles or lines that had accumulated over time to shadow my face. Purity and the grace of innocence surrounded Thais, but with every day that passed, I felt like my ability to protect her from my greatest fears was slowly diminishing.

One of the online articles I found mentioned that children often regressed during a deployment. Potty-trained children could have accidents. Adolescents could act out. Some children held it all inside; others cried and let it all out. Tumultuous behavior was possible. *Oh great. As if this weren't already hard enough.* I hoped our children would be different.

The third night after Colin left, though, Thais had her first middle of the night accident in over two years. I heard her call out in a high-pitched cry, "Mommy!"

It took me a moment to discern this cry was not part of my dream, and I slowly pulled myself out of bed when the second cry came. Within seconds, I was at her side, as she lay in her own warm pee.

"It is OK, love," I soothed her through my exhausted patience. "Let's get you clean. "

And so began our midnight shuffle. On those nights I...
- lifted her from the wetness
- helped strip off the moist clothes that clung to her legs
- ran the warm water in the tub
- lifted her again to the potty to see if there was anything left
- balled up the soiled comforter, sheets, and PJs to wash when the sun was up
- remade the bed with whatever clean sheets or blankets I could find in my half-asleep state
- scooped Thais up in a dry towel and carried her back to the bed

Beth Jackson

- found clean PJs and undies
- redressed her
- tucked her in
- told her "I love you. "

Thais peed in her bed three nights in a row that first week in Florida. Her little body was working on overload. She was off kilter, distracted, just like I was.

***

On Thursday of our vacation week, I had to return to work. I had to complete a major report following the business trip and field research I had led just before Colin left. I had already requested extra time from the client because it was Colin's last week home. But now I had to get this important work delivered to them, so my parents and siblings offered to watch the children for the morning.

After four or five hours, the final summary was all but complete, ready for proofreading one last time. I paused to get a glass of water. Within seconds of sitting back down and placing the full glass on the counter, I accidentally knocked it over. And then I learned that liquids and laptops didn't mix.

Instantly the computer died. I jumped to action to grab paper towels to start drying the computer like a mad woman. I turned the machine upside down to drain all the liquid out. A full cup of water poured out, but after the drips slowed down and eventually stopped, nothing else happened.

The screen was black. Dead. My forefinger pushed the ON button over and over again. Nothing. No, I did not have any back-up. I had not saved my work on anything but the computer. No jump drive. I began to feel defeated.

Unwilling to give up, though, I unscrewed the back metal to remove the battery to dry out the innards. I called Apple Care, and the surprisingly unhelpful genius on the phone told me that "accidental damage" like water was not covered under warranty and that the computer was not fixable.

Now, I could not blame the fact that Colin was deploying to a war zone for a year for my klutzy action. At that particular moment, in fact, I was not thinking about him at all. I had simply been engrossed in my work and then had ruined it.

I refused to give up and continued calling around to numbers from the yellow pages to try to find any IT person within a hundred-mile radius that could help me. One of them suggested dry rice might work, so there I was moving the dry rice around the keyboard to absorb every last molecule of liquid. One way; then the other. And then doing it all over again. The computer never came back, and all my work was lost.

Trying to dry out my laptop by covering it with rice

Colin had been gone less than a week. I was with my supportive and helpful family. And yet I was already walking the fine line between organized chaos, which was normal when my husband was a present co-parent, and something new, a dysfunctional insanity, which I could already taste from my reaction that day. I was going to need more body armor to avoid falling into a dark, deep hole.

***

During the six days of in-processing at Fort Benning, Colin was able to call us a few times, which always was a pleasant surprise. Then literally overnight all of his communication suddenly became "sensitive. " He could not say when he was heading overseas or where he was going or whether he would be traveling across the Atlantic on a military or commercial aircraft, the latter of which he preferred since the accommodations (seats) and noise control (insulation) were much better. I knew the general route he would be taking from prior conversations: Fort Benning to Atlanta to Germany to Kuwait to Afghanistan. I also knew he would fly in helicopters to get to Kabul. But nothing more.

At first I was a tad annoyed he could not tell me when he was leaving. Desire to talk with him up until the moment he left was strong, but I also did not want to sit by the phone all day if he were not leaving until late in the afternoon. Then I remembered the two dead U. S. servicemen, who were shot by a gunman as they traveled on a bus carrying servicemen at the Frankfurt airport just weeks before. Oh, *that* security. Right. That was why he could not tell me.

Colin left Fort Benning at some point late in the day on Friday, March 25. And our communications abruptly ended. His cell phone service was suspended. Silence.

The first e-mail came several days later. The subject line included "unclassified," but it was very brief and to the point. There were no "I love yous" and "I miss yous" that so freely permeated his normal phone calls and e-mails. Not in that one.

But at least I knew he was alive. That was my first reaction.
- He was alive.
- He was OK (he could type!).
- He was thinking about us.

I knew our communications this year would be irregular and without substance. He could not tell us the details of his job for security reasons, and he did not want to be burdened with my stress over whether I should buy a new MacBook or MacBook Pro laptop. Decisions were now uncomfortably my own. I already missed him terribly.

But as the eternal optimist, I tried to see this deployment as a potential "broadening experience" in history, geography, and culture for our children, family, and friends. After sending various separate e-mails to Colin's family, my family, local friends, and out-of-town friends, I complied a mass e-mail list and started to send regular updates.

> *After a week of in-processing, Colin was issued four duffle bags of equipment weighing 350+ pounds and began his multi-stop journey overseas. As of this morning, he was still in Kuwait but had plans to fly out by the evening. Colin had a four-day "layover" there amidst a sandstorm. Sand is everywhere in his tent. Have your kids look up 'camel spiders,' which Colin says is a local pet...*

A friend who was in the Marines gave me wise advice, which unfortunately I ignored, "It is a marathon, not a sprint. " I was the overachiever who had already started staying up too late to send Colin daily e-mails detailing all the fun stories I could think of about the children. I had already packed two boxes of goodies and necessities to send him once I knew his mailing address. I continued searching, wanting, striving to do more. For him. And for our children.

I knew I was probably sprinting too fast, but I was scared to slow down. And so I never saw what was coming.

Chapter 3 – Dysfunctional Insanity

Early April 2011

After only two weeks without Colin, I lost it. Maybe it was the reality that he was now really in the war zone. Maybe the exhaustion was kicking in. Maybe insanity had already started to weave its way into the vacuum where oxygen vonce flowed. The concept of war had definitely sparked my nerves, and learning about deployment continued now as my second full-time job.

In fact, discovering what I needed to know about deployment had become a mission. An obsession, actually, with each new piece of knowledge reinforcing my urgent need for more. For example, Meghan told me I should have been given chain of command contact information for Colin's unit both at home and in Afghanistan, but I had nothing. I read online that there were Family Readiness groups, but I did not know where to find one. The children still did not know anyone who had a Dad who was deployed, and I worried that they felt just as isolated as I did. My Princeton education and international M. B. A. were of no help to me here. I just needed a roadmap, and I just kept searching for information, a connection, for anything.

Before Colin left, I had learned that our new healthcare provider was Tricare, but I still had no information about its coverage. No card. No customer service numbers. I looked online to see where the nearest military health facility was, and one day, while the children were at school, I drove there. I showed my new military ID at the gate, signed in at the administrative office, and waited.

Eventually, a woman called my name and asked if she could help me. When I explained why I had come, she looked at me with surprise.

How had I not known this information already? "Weren't you given a briefing?" she asked. "No," I replied with a pleading smile.

This woman hesitated a moment and then motioned for me to follow her. She asked me to sit down and then patiently walked me through everything I needed to know. What services were covered; what were not. What it meant for our regular doctors and dentists. How prescriptions would be paid. And she suggested I carry a copy of Colin's orders in my wallet at all times, in case I needed them for any reason. I was so grateful to finally have some tangible information.

Next, I arranged time to meet with each of my children's teachers to share what sparse information about deployment and children I had found online. Not knowing how the children were going to be over the next long year, I wanted their teachers to be prepared and supportive. I needed their help. I had heard a story in another town about how a classmate told a boy whose Dad was deployed to Iraq, "If Bush wins the election, your Dad will stay in Iraq forever. " Children often had no idea how hurtful their words could be, and I so badly wanted to protect my children from more worry. And most importantly, I wanted to shield them from any news about Afghanistan.

Somehow I also felt the need to protect Colin, too. From the reality of our life that was already beginning to spiral out of control life. From the stress when all three children would argue and fight. From my gripping fear of losing him. But I did not tell him this. I accepted that he was doing his job, and I was damn well going to try my best to do mine and hold down the homefront.

***

As the days and nights passed, Thais's bed wetting accidents continued. At one point, I bought some older child overnight pull-ups but she refused to wear the "baby pull-ups. " All I could do was hope this would be a short-lived phase that would end soon.

Then Charlotte, our well-trained thirteen-year-old Vizsla, introduced her own version of the middle of the night shuffle. Usually, her whines to be let out started an hour or two after Thais's accidents. I then...

- got up
- opened the bedroom door
- walked downstairs
- unlocked the front door
- let Charlotte out
- stood by the door ready to turn on the lights and scare off any hungry coyote (one had attacked our neighbor's dog a few months before)
- waited for her to come back inside
- locked the door
- walked upstairs
- waited for Charlotte to come back upstairs
- closed the bedroom door, so it did not knock in the wind
- climbed under the covers
- tried to fall back asleep

My sleep was no longer sleep. It had become catnaps bookended by cleaning the latrine.

Between my obsession in managing the deployment and the interrupted sleep pattern, I urgently needed more information about what was happening around Colin. I found myself checking the news online each night, in the privacy of my home office when the children restlessly slept. I would close my eyes for a second before reading the headlines. As my eyes opened to scan the typed letters, I pleaded with the screen not to include the word "bomb," "killed," and "attack. " I was disappointed most of the time.

Beth Jackson

Like a crack habit, though, I signed up for Google alerts to receive a daily e-mail with the top headlines around the term "Afghanistan." I wanted to know what was happening, even though this obsession caused me pain every time I read them. And thus began my love-hate relationship with the alerts. In the year of 2011, we lived in this uber-connected world, which facilitated amazing transfers of knowledge around the globe. But we could not hide from knowing things, even bad things.

source: Google alerts, April 16, 2011.
Google and Google logo are registered trademarks of Google Inc., used with permission

Very soon, the novelty of this broadening experience was no longer interesting or funny. It was horribly worrisome. Colin was on a base in Kabul working in a military intelligence staff position, not necessarily on the front line. But I also knew he carried a pistol at all times, and that he was issued body armor. And it appeared that this was a war with no front line.

One of his e-mails captured this paradigm perfectly, as he asked me to send him books he had taught as a professor as well as a plastic pistol holder that would put his gun closer to his chest.

> *They said it takes 2. 5 weeks to get things here. If you could send me a couple of things soon that would be great. Any Army PT shirts and shorts you can find. The Army shirts have to have the big A stamped on the back. I need a big book, a reader on* Corruption, *which is sitting on the floor of my office; I also need a red hard cover entitled* Politics and Order in Changing Societies *- also in office. There is a book on the top shelf of the bookshelf entitled* The Other War *by Ron Neuman that would be great as well. On the book shelf in the office is a book on tax structures and state formation. Let me know if you have trouble locating any of these - you might want to take a photo of the bookshelves and e-mail it to me, so that I can reference them.*
>
> *I also need a plastic holster paddle that is in an open cardboard box to the right of my desk. It is U shaped, 4-5 inches long, and is in a box of various other plastic holster pieces.*

***

The nightmares began shortly after Colin arrived in Afghanistan. The scenery was vague, but it included trails and a vast expanse of the outdoors with no buildings in sight. And it always started with Colin running. "They" were running after him. I was not sure who "they" were, but he was running for his life. The scene then went black and silent until I heard the knocking, and two faceless men were at the door with news. The one kind of news a military wife never wanted to hear.

These nightmares visited me often. Not every night. But most.

Beth Jackson

I feared that knock at the door by a stranger. However low the probability, the very thought of such a visit upset me terribly. In my imagination, such a dreaded call would be made by Colin's Army Reserve commander. I only learned his name after he called Colin to tell him about his deployment. I didn't know what the man looked like or what his wife's name was. I didn't know how to reach him in case of emergency. I did not even know where the base was, only that it was hours away in another state. Would they know how to contact me if Colin were injured or killed?

I knew the name of Colin's commander in Afghanistan, but I didn't know what Active duty unit he was linked to back here in the U. S. or how to make contact over there. I was only on the receiving end whenever Colin initiated contact via e-mail, phone, or Skype. I didn't even know the name of one serviceperson serving with Colin. There was no Family Readiness Support Group that I knew of. And I still had not heard back from Daisy. I felt invisible.

In my nightmares, I was always alone when the knock came.

***

So after just fifteen days of deployment, I totally lost control.

We were just at the end of a long day of two lacrosse games and Ian's ninth birthday party, which was held at a bowling alley. I tried to capture photos and video with our digital camera, with plans to download and forward the pictures to Colin later that night. I wanted to share the images of Ian with his twelve friends bowling under funky lights along with the pizza and cake, so he would not miss out.

We waited until we returned home for Ian to open his presents. Then among the torn paper and empty boxes in the living room, Ian happily played with his new toys. The wooden toy bow & arrow set was one of Ian's favorite gifts, but it struck me as something that could cause problems. *Oh-no.* As expected, Karl wanted to touch it and just "try it out. " As Ian was intently putting a new Lego set together, Karl slowly picked up the bow & arrow and starting aiming it around the room.

Calmly, I requested, "Please don't use that inside. "

Karl ignored me and kept playing with it, so I repeated myself, more firmly. "Please don't do that. "

Then, suddenly, as he was aiming for Ian's new toy dragon, Karl pulled the bow back a few inches and released the plastic and rubber-tipped arrow, which sailed directly into Ian's jaw instead.

Ian did not see it coming and immediately grasped for his face and cried out in pain.

And I lost it. **"I SAID DON'T USE THAT INSIDE. DON'T AIM AT PEOPLE!"**

My voice was louder and more intense than I had ever heard myself yell before. It was purely primal, like an eruption of some uncontrollable thing inside me. I saw this wild shrieking lady from outside my body, but I could not stop her. This delusional lady yelled it again, but I was paralyzed as I could only hear the echo of my voice. Karl ran out of the room as quickly as he could to escape up to his bedroom.

My body finally came unstuck, and I went to help Ian. But his gestures clearly indicated that he was not in any real pain. My hand pulled out ice from the refrigerator for him to put on the bruised area, and then I took a few quick breaths to recover my equanimity before walking upstairs to Karl's bedroom, where I knocked on the door and turned the handle. He sat on the floor leaning up against his bed with his knees bent up towards his chin.

Beth Jackson

First, I asked that he apologize to Ian. Then to me for not listening. He stood up and looked at me as he said, "I am sorry. "

I paused for a few seconds, and then I apologized for yelling.

"Like a maniac," Karl added with consternation. As I looked into Karl's eyes, I saw an eleven-year-old boy standing up tall. Already five feet and three inches tall, he was holding his own with me and, frankly, holding onto his sanity far better than I was. I reached out tenderly to give him a hug, and he shared back. A teardrop swelled as I explained that I was scared, how I didn't want anything to hurt him, or Ian, or Thais.

Frankly, I was more than scared. I was terrified. It wasn't until a few days later when I shared this story with a girlfriend, who insightfully shared, "You were not yelling about the bow and arrow. " She was right. Anger had masked my desolation, the total loss of control that had become my life.

Several days later, Colin sent each of the children a touching e-mail expressing his love and pride of them. The bow and arrow incident notwithstanding, I told Karl how proud I was of his maturity and helpfulness, especially since Dad had left. "I know," he replied modestly but then paused, "But I still can be mischievous, right?"

"YES, of course," I quickly replied. "Your Dad is still mischievous, and he is forty!"

It was a reminder to me that the new "man" at our home was indeed only just eleven, still just a young boy.

Our life did not slow down long enough for me to think much about this first real failure, although I was disappointed in myself. But I had to keep moving. My days were filled with work. My mornings and evenings were filled with my children and the household chores. My nights were filled with laundry, bills, e-mails, and my incessant and often torturous quest for information. Sleep was the only reservoir of time, so I continued to steal from it to do everything else.

***

Weeks before Colin got the call, I actually ventured to say out loud, "Our life is good. " It was. We had lived in Rhode Island for over four years and had a solid group of friends. I know that to some, our overcommitted work schedules orbiting around the children's multiple sports teams, piano lessons, and academics might have seemed a bit much, but to us it was perfect. We loved the buzz that permeated our household, the physical activities that helped build our social life, and the engaging work that completed our identities. Colin was just told he was being promoted, and my own consulting business had completed another good year. We were comfortable and happy.

And then the call came.

Now, I would not consider myself a religious person. In the past four years since we had moved here, our family had become holiday churchgoers. Ice hockey, with its many Sunday morning games and practices, became our religion of choice. And sometimes, we just wanted to sleep in.

Raised in a Protestant church-going family, I volunteered as a teenager in the children's room, but I did that mostly just to avoid having to attend the actual church service itself. As an adult, Colin and I only went to church to get married and have our children baptized. We were not regulars.

But now, somehow, I felt an invisible tug pulling me back to church. I was so scared for Colin's well-being, I asked him to have a blessing before he left. I don't know exactly what I was looking for with this

Beth Jackson

event, but somehow it seemed urgent. The only times before that I
had asked a priest for a blessing were after each of my miscarriages.
I still remember, after learning of the second miscarriage,
sprinting over three miles from our previous home in Dedham,
Massachusetts across a highway to the Episcopal church. In salty
sweat, heavy panting, and tears, I sobbed and sobbed on my knees at
the church, as Reverend Michael read out loud from a prayer book.
I did not even hear the words he said, but his soothing voice in
the walls of the darkened church brought me comfort. It was that
abstract comfort that I was seeking with church again.

Here in Rhode Island, however, Reverend Chris barely knew my
name and did not know Colin's or the children's names when we met
with him in the small stone Episcopalian church closest to our home
that we had only attended a couple times at Christmas and Easter.

During this private ceremony, Colin shared with each of the
children, "I love you more than life itself. " He wrote that phrase
again on each of the e-mails he sent them the day he left American
soil. On the surface, I thought it was an incredible thing to say and
then repeat. But deep down, I hoped his words did not forebode my
greatest fear.

As the weeks of the deployment ticked by, I found myself wanting to
take the children to church as well. Maybe I was looking for a sign of
faith. I just did not know where to find it. I was out of practice.

***

Colin e-mailed us a picture of himself in a soft green tent, where
he had spent several days waiting for a seat on a flight to hop into
Kabul. His charming smile stood in start contrast to the gritty sand
that was visible on the sleeping bag and floor. I printed out copies
for each child to bring to school.

That night while washing the dinner dishes, I asked Karl if he had shared the picture with his friends.

"They were not really interested," he replied dryly.

"They don't understand," he added. "They don't know how lonely it is. "

My head turned away from the sink to look at him, my heart was crushed. Such honest sadness from a son who loved his father dearly and missed him greatly. We were only a few weeks into this journey, and I was saddened by the absence of a father for my dear son.

My eyes shimmered with moisture as I simply replied, "I miss him, too. "

The next night, I helped Karl put a photo taken of him with Dad at the beach into a dark wooden frame - the one that he had received as a birthday gift. I also noticed that the picture of Dad in his tent was taped up with wide blue painter's tape at a slight angle on the wall next to his bed. He wanted to have Dad close.

Picture of Dad next to Karl's bed

Beth Jackson

Colin also sent me an e-mail telling me that, as part of the government shutdown in early April 2011 when Congress had not yet passed its spending bill, he and all federal employees would not get paid. A pit in my stomach immediately took hold. My husband was at war fighting for our freedom, but he was not going to receive his paycheck.

This was a road we had been down before, both of us losing our jobs within two weeks of each other. It was November 2001 in Houston, Texas. My dot-com imploded. I was pregnant with Ian, due in four months; my large belly a warning to potential employers not to hire me. Colin had been with Enron. His job was wiped out, along with thousands of others, without severance or health insurance. We immediately stopped going out to eat. We cancelled our $15 a month Netflix subscription. We let go our cleaning lady and started drawing down our small "rainy day" fund until it hit zero. And a month after Ian was born, we sold our house and moved in with Colin's dad and stepmom in Washington, D. C. for three months as Colin got a temporary job at the Pentagon and I was looking for one.

The vacuum in my stomach was knocking again now in the spring of 2011. After reading Colin's e-mail, I checked our bank balances and when the mortgage payment and American Express bill were due. I had two outstanding client invoices that had not yet been paid. I sent an e-mail to each of those clients checking on when I could expect payment.

We were okay for the next week, but I would have to draw from our modest savings account the week after.

Eventually, the politics concerning the government shutdown were settled, and Colin, along with the other 100,000 soldiers currently serving our nation at war, was paid. Albeit, late.

Chapter 4 – My One True Love

Mid April 2011 (with flashbacks to 1991-1996)

Colin left his nice watch, a Breitling that I gave him to celebrate completing his PhD from MIT, on the top of a dark wood dresser in our bedroom. Shortly after he left, I saw it lying there, and I carefully picked it up and placed it into the top right drawer where his cufflinks and bowties rested from our younger days of college parties and weddings.

I felt Colin's absence everywhere I looked. He had been part of my life longer than most of my memories.

Spring of 1991. Colin and I first met in a Sociological Research Methodology college class, when I sat next to his cute best friend. A few months later, out of the blue, Colin asked me to be his date to House Parties. House Parties at Princeton was a three-day extravaganza that included a black-tie dinner dance, casual dinner dance, and a champagne brunch.

I was impressed when Colin arrived at my dorm room for the black-tie party holding two dozen red roses in his right hand. Wow! No guy had ever done that for me before. In the other hand, he carried a bottle of expensive scotch that his father had received from a colleague. Colin generously shared his scotch with all my roommates' dates, and only years later did I learn that Colin and the scotch suddenly parted ways into the toilet at some point that evening. I partially recall that I had consumed too much wine that night, too, so I guess there was a reason I did not notice.

I do fondly remember that Friday night, however, when Colin, President of his eating club, stood up on his chair in the formal wood-paneled dining room before anyone began eating. He invited all of us to stand, as he did, which I obligingly did, despite my high heels and without a clue why. Then suddenly, Colin began belting out the *Star Spangled Banner* with a perfect baritone voice. And the entire dining room of several hundred joined in. All standing on chairs.

Now, honestly, I knew most of the words to our national anthem, but I surely would have missed a few if I had to sing it by myself. And while I had dreams of stardom as a child, I knew my voice was usually a bit off key. But as part of the group standing on chairs that night and with a few glasses of wine pumping through my veins, I was thrilled to sing along and hum when I forgot a word. Little did I realize then the role Colin's patriotism would have in my life for decades to follow.

Later that evening, as my roommates retell the story, Colin and I were kissing on the dance floor. I guess we were having a good time indeed. Once the band stopped playing for the evening, Colin walked me the mile back home to my dorm and said goodnight at the door. I don't even remember if he kissed me then or not. But there was no awkward goodnight. Just the wonderful end to a first date.

Thirteen months later on the night before graduation, Colin proposed to me, and I married the man I loved. But I did not choose the military. Had I known then what I know now, I still would have married Colin, but I wish somehow I had been more prepared for what it really meant. For instance, three months after we set our wedding date in my Michigan hometown, we learned the date conflicted with Colin's armored unit's tank training at the range. And one did not negotiate with the Army. So we changed the date for the church, reception, band, flowers, cake, rehearsal dinner... you get the picture. I guess I should have known.

After serving his Active duty time, Colin left the service to attend graduate school and work in finance and then academia. But he remained in the Army Reserves. I still don't know exactly why he first joined the military, the only one in his family, but somehow it was just core to who he was, his essence. The years passed. After 9/11, when we had our first child, I casually asked Colin to get out of the military, even though I already knew the answer. I never asked again. He believed serving one's nation was more important than anything else, even his own life.

***

When I thought about Colin, I felt safe. Physically safe. Emotionally safe. This feeling began way back when we were first dating.

Summer of 1991. That first summer after we began seeing each other, I had an internship in Paris, and Colin did his summer ROTC training in Seattle, Washington. Before the time of e-mail, Colin and I sent good old-fashioned love letters to each other. We communicated via snail mail and arranged that Colin would come visit me in August. What a dream. We had plans to go hiking in Switzerland, after spending a week in Paris together.

I tended to be a very focused person, which also meant I could be a bit oblivious to things around me. Well, one night as we were trying to find a restaurant off some side street in Paris and my eyes scanned for street names and building numbers, I guess I walked right into the middle of the street with cars and taxis zipping by. Colin lovingly but quickly reached out to put his arm in front of me, to slow me down, and guide me sideways in a safer direction. Not a word, just a small gesture.

The following week when we were hiking in St. Moritz along with a college friend, we encountered an impasse. A cold fast-moving river impeded our path. After searching for over an hour for alternatives, we found the narrowest ten-foot width of the river. Standing in the freezing glacier water without his boots or socks on, Colin held first onto our classmate's hand and then onto mine as he helped us hop from rock to rock safely across the river.

Now, mind you, Colin might not have always felt physically safe around me. Once when falling asleep, I inadvertently whacked him on the head with my arm. And a loose pen in my hand has occasionally taken flight during one of my grand gestures, so over the years, Colin learned to dart sideways to avoid loosing an eye. But he married me anyway.

1993. While Colin served Active duty in the Army and I began working in marketing at Procter & Gamble, we lived outside of Frankfurt and travelled on weekends to every country that bordered Germany. That first New Year's weekend, we ventured to Alsace. It was the perfect city for me because I tended to mix my foreign languages together, and there I fearlessly carried on conversations because the locals understood both French and German. In the middle of a tour of historic churches, as our necks arched backwards to look up and admire some ancient stained glass, the blood rushed out of my head and I collapsed to the floor. The next thing I remembered was Colin scooping me off the ground and carrying me in his arms to move me safely to the side.

1996. When we moved to Baltimore after our return from Europe and Colin's departure from Active duty, we chose to rent a newly renovated Tudor townhouse. During our house-hunting trip, the real estate agent had driven us through this picturesque neighborhood with manicured lawns and lovely old restored homes.

On moving day after a huge truck had deposited our life's possessions, however, we drove out the other way. What a shock! Windows were boarded up with wood. Graffiti was everywhere.

There were more lawns covered with weeds than grass. We noticed that our neighbors not only all had one dog, but often two, and that they were pitbulls and other breeds known for their protective and aggressive instincts. Baltimore was known at the time to be patchy, and we were on the tip top corner of a patch to a high-crime neighborhood.

In my usual attempts to make the best of any situation, I unpacked all the boxes with our wedding china and crystal and tried to make our new house feel like home. I was a little worried, but I felt that it was nothing we could not deal with. We could get a dog and an alarm. I could take a self-defense class.

Then one night a week later, Colin said to me, "When I married you, I took on the responsibility to protect you. And I cannot protect you here. I think we should move. "

With my new job just starting, I had neither the time nor energy to take on another move. So Colin found us a new place a few miles away and packed up everything, with my help in the evenings. He rented and drove the moving truck. And he and his Dad moved every single heavy piece of furniture out of that house and into the new one. Colin's dad, understandably exhausted at the end of that very long day, stated the obvious, "You have too much stuff to do a self move again. "

So what did a spouse do when her protector and bodyguard was gone? The deployment materials I found online talked about personal safety.

- Leave the husband's car in the driveway, so it looked like he was home.
- Don't tell too many people he was gone, so I would not be a target of robbery or worse.
- Walk that fine balance between showing patriotism and telegraphing that there was no man in the house.

Beth Jackson

But our American flag was now out every day and night. And I
hung a small deployment flag with a single star in our front window.

Deployment flag in my front window

All of our friends and neighbors knew. How could I hide it? I didn't
want to hide it. Well, it helped that Colin and I played ice hockey
with our town's police chief. I asked if he would have his guys drive
by our house a few extra times when they were out, and he said of
course they would.

But that did that not make me feel any better in the middle of
the night when I heard a strange noise from downstairs. Once, I
thought maybe one of the children had gotten up. Lying in my bed,
I waited until I thought I heard the noise again. Slowly getting up
and quietly walking down the wooden floored hallway, I checked on
each of the children. They were fine, and the noises did not return.
I did not go downstairs to investigate, but I did put a second phone
next to my bed, just in case.

I was scared and glad to have our dog. To help relieve stress, I ran
around my neighborhood with her every few days. But that did not
prevent the fear without Colin from mounting.

Now, don't get me wrong. Our marriage was solid, but neither Colin nor I were perfect. We had our fair share of arguments. We were both extremely stubborn. Colin had a short temper, and I was short on patience. He liked his cave, focused single-mindedly at one task at hand; I was a multi-tasker who could be bossy. We also had a knack for arguing over directions. Usually when he was at the wheel and I was the backseat driver.

Oh, how I missed him dearly.

I chose to marry Colin, but our children did not have a choice. And now that their Dad was taken from their lives, I could see the vast disruptive shock and loss in their eyes. Pictures of Colin, alone and with each of them, adorned the large wood-framed front hall mirror and the window by Colin's chair at our dinner table. I hoped we would remember his face. I worried most that Thais would forget him. Really. How many memories do you have from when you were four? I don't have many, if any. But I hoped the pictures would help keep him current in her mind.

One day after school, Thais had a meltdown at the dinner table specifically about missing Daddy. It had been a week since we had spoken with him on a coveted Skype video call, and we did not know when the next one would come. She was inconsolable, wailing that even when she could talk with Dad, she could not play with him. That he could not lift her up to touch the ceiling, one of her favorite games.

That night, Thais brought an armful of pictures she had plucked off the front hall mirror up to her room, like she was hording them in her safe space. Or maybe she was trying to snuggle with the pictures and imagine Daddy's big embrace. She taped one next to her bed and one in the bathroom next to the sink and left the others scattered on the bed and floor. Maybe the plastic feel of a photograph lacked the same warmth and response as a real hug.

Beth Jackson

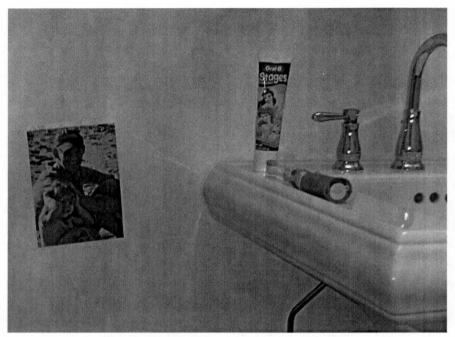

Picture of Dad and Thais by the sink in her bathroom

A year was a concept too hard for a young child to understand. Based on Meghan's advice, we started a Daddy Kiss jar to help give Thais a tangible cue. Basically, every day Daddy was gone, at any time of day, Thais got to take one Hershey kiss, a "Daddy Kiss," out of a jar. Yes, that included at 7 in the morning before she had eaten breakfast. Or at 8:30 at night after she had brushed her teeth and just remembered. So we got to brush teeth twice those nights, when I had enough energy for the follow through on that one, which often I didn't.

Almost daily, Thais asked me, "When will Daddy be home?" I pointed to the jar. "After Christmas" became my other answer to convey time. I made that one up. It was sunny spring at this point, and snow was a long way away. The names of the month did not mean anything to her. What Thais did not know was that the glass jar, actually a tall cylindrical vase, only held about 70 kisses. And neither the boys nor I liked chocolate, so this treat was just for

Thais. But every couple of days, I topped the jar to keep it full. The vase would have to be extremely large, and frankly it was too much emotionally for me to see, to hold 365 kisses.

Thais learned to say to her friends and teachers, "He is taking turns. He had to go so another Daddy could come home. " That phrase suggestion also came from Meghan. You military wives are incredible; your wisdom so keen. Oh, I guess I was now again a military wife, too. I forgot. I was still getting used to that phrase.

The two times that Thais had been able to Skype with Dad, she monopolized the screen, refusing to let her brothers invade her view, which in turn caused more strife. She talked incessantly about everything and nothing and did not want to stop. At one point, the video went blank, a common occurrence in the imperfect technology of communication, and worry overcame Thais. Where had Dad gone? She could hear him but not see him. And then when the call ended, he was gone again and her tears would return. While I was grateful for any sort of communication we had with Colin, Thais was confused and distraught by its unpredictability.

Consequently, Thais became more and more attached to me. School drop-off became tearful as she clung to my leg. Forever, I will be grateful for those loving hugs and gentle distractions that Thais's nursery teacher gave her each morning as I peeled away to go work. How does one carry on in a situation like this? Her teacher not only mothered Thais; she mothered me. I still remember those mornings when she just wrapped her arms around my shoulders and let me cry.

Saturday soccer at the YMCA also brought out a new shyness in Thais. She would only go on the field with me shadowing behind her. All of the other four and five-year-olds dutifully stood in line waiting for their turn to kick on net, while Thais stood with her Mom. Eventually, once the actual games started, I was able to slide over to the sidelines to watch. I wondered, was I right to have gone on the field with her, or should I have insisted she go alone? Should I have had her quit soccer and just wait for the following year? I did not have any of the answers, but I knew that when Thais cried for me, I needed to be at her side.

***

The despair in wanting to know more and feel connected to a community that could understand me continued to eat away at my body. I did not own a scale, but I had already lost enough weight to drop a size. My clothes just sagged off my already thin frame.

Daisy, from the Family Readiness Group, finally replied to the first e-mail I had sent two months earlier. She told me that there were very important benefits and family support contacts that she was going to send me. Information about health care. Information about Colin's pay. Information that would help the children. I was thrilled and anxiously waited for the arrival of the package.

Chapter 5 – Failing as Superwoman

Late April 2011

My life had become a sifter of sand, as I watched thousands of sand particles fall through the small holes, leaving behind a few small rocks on top. There were thousands of things to do, but every time I successfully scooped up a few rocks, other things fell through the cracks.

Still, I tried to be Superwoman. At home, I was protective mom, trying to know and anticipate everything my children needed. At work, I was a focused professional, escaping all other responsibilities. In the evenings, when I should have been sleeping, I was an uneasy wife feeding my unbalanced mind. The terrors that were suppressed while I worked or actively cared for my children came back every night as I checked the Google alerts and thought about possible disasters. Then each night I continued to feel the compulsion to send pages of e-mails to Colin describing in detail the life he was missing. After all, he was the one in a war zone, so I needed to take care of him, too. What I did not write him was the angst that occupied my mind. I was trying to protect him from me.

But in all of this, I forgot about myself. My sleep continued to be fitful. I actually started to look forward to my next business trip, so I could get a full night of sleep. No lunches to pack, dishes to wash, bedtime rituals to oversee. No dog. No 2 a. m. wake-ups when Thais's comforter fell off or she had a potty accident.

Wouldn't it have been ironic if the only way I could have truly taken care of myself this year would be to go on a business trip? The truth was I didn't like travel anymore. A decade ago, before children, I used to enjoy the novelty of fancy food and new places to see. But now, I didn't want to miss anything. And I knew the children missed me. But the elusive one night of uninterrupted sleep sounded irresistible.

Then I left for my first overnight business trip to New Jersey. My client had insisted we meet on that particular day based on when an industry expert was available to join us, and in the world of client service, their needs reigned above all else.

This new client did not know Colin was deployed, and nor did I tell them. I usually had projects lined up one to two months out, but there was a lot of uncertainty to the workload and pay in my business, and I did not want to lose this potential, and at the time, only income stream. I asked Colin about this trip to New Jersey before he left. He supported my decision that I needed to go. We had bills to pay.

I arranged for Dana to spend the night. She had been our nanny for almost two years, and she was like a part of our family. She would get the children off to school, and then she would pick them up after school as she always did, but she would also stay until I returned home late that next night.

The hand-off of co-parenting responsibilities worked just fine that first night. I hit the road at 8 p. m. with a full belly of take-out pizza and full tank of gas. Arriving at my hotel in New Jersey around 1 a. m. , sleep enveloped me as soon as my head hit the pillow.

In the middle of the night, however, a rattling sound startled me awake. It sounded like Thais's underwear drawer opening, the common sound after a pee accident, so I instantly popped up ready to go help.

As I sat up in bed, I saw that I was in a hotel room. The sound was an alarm clock, coming through the thin wall that separated me from the guest next door, who evidently happened to have a much earlier wake-up time than I did. Sleep easily called me back, but my quest for six or more straight hours of sleep still evaded me.

Then something weird happened to me on my drive back later that day. I stopped for gas, and a cute forty-something man flirted with me. Outright glancing, flirting of the eyes, a warm smile, and even a short greeting. I remember standing with the gas pump in my hand and, after the initial shock, thinking that it was the first time a stranger had paid such attention to me in a really long time. I laughed it off, but I admit it did feel good in my loneliness to know I was still somewhat attractive.

***

Many of the initial adjustments to our new life had started to settle into place. The children were now actively into their spring sports calendar, and I had identified potential carpool friends. The children started earning an allowance as an extra incentive for performing additional chores on their job charts. School and homework routines filled in the hours.

I had given the boys cell phones to preempt the latch key situation or inevitable delay from school or the sports field, as I darted back and forth between their activities. The phone gave the boys independence and me peace of mind.

I was also feeling better now that at least the start-up paperwork for all the changes in our lives was under control. I understood how Tricare worked, and CVS had already processed its first prescription drug co-pay. I had copied the Power of Attorney for our bank and the home, car, and life insurance company. We had mailed off packages to Colin every five days or so. They were filled with dried fruits, granola bars, gum, notes from the children, and more pictures of all of us. Just little tidbits of our every day life to share, so he knew we loved him.

One day after school, I asked Ian how he was feeling, and, like Karl had, he simply shared, "I miss Dad. "

I knew his feelings about his dad's deployment were more profound than that, but he did not elaborate and I did not probe. Rather, I saw his feelings through his actions.

Just as Thais and Karl had moved pictures of Dad to special places, Ian had taped up Colin's picture just above his bed next to a poster. The picture lined up next to the images of seven WWII soldiers. He thought of his Dad as one of them.

Picture of Dad, next to other soldiers

The other night, when Ian was drawing one of his elaborate D-Day scenes with detailed battles and explosions, I asked what he wanted to be when he grew up.

"An Army paratrooper," he replied without hesitation. A box Colin sent the children had just arrived the day before, and an Army paratrooper coin was a gift for Ian.

I asked, "What about a pilot?" which for several years had been his career of choice.

"They get shot down too much," he replied.

***

At first, I actually enjoyed the shocked reaction when someone would casually ask where my husband was, and I would say "In Afghanistan, for a year..."

Before Colin left, we shared an observation about our predominantly "civilian" friends and acquaintances when they heard about his deployment. We noticed two very distinct reactions, and in the unscientific sample of our life, they fell across socioeconomic lines. From our white-collar friends, the very first reaction was typically **"I am sorry. "** From our blue-collar friends, the very first reaction was universally **"Thank you. "**

Why the difference? My hypothesis was that most higher income people in our society had no direct knowledge or relationship with the military. Growing up in the conservative, affluent suburb of Grosse Pointe, I was like this, too. Until I met Colin, I did not know anyone who served in the military. My limited knowledge came from what I saw on the television show M*A*S*H. And our life for the fourteen years since Colin had left Active duty was just as civilian as my upbringing.

Most of our friends and family had no way to know what military life was like. With this deployment, they simply knew that Colin would be gone for a while and would miss out on all the activities and experiences of our life. They knew it would be hard on our children and me, and they imagined that his accommodations for the year would roughing it, rather like a stay in a low rent motel, which was reason enough for pity. They actually had no idea that my professor husband with four graduate degrees had to check the latrines for snakes before he went to the bathroom. They were sorry for all they could not imagine. These wonderful friends then also said "Thank you" and how much they appreciated what Colin was doing, but that was the second thought. Their reactions came as no surprise, and I never judged them; after all, less than 1% of the population was in the military. The vast majority of Americans have no idea about the sacrifice of military people, or their pride. It was a job most of us simply took for granted, including me - before the call came.

I have to admit; I did indulge a bit in the pity factor of "I am so sorry," but I so much preferred the "Thank you" reaction. It suggested gratitude to Colin and to our whole family. It was an acknowledgement of the incredible selfless service military families routinely make.

One of the most insightful notes I received was from my wise friend Meghan. On the day the children and I took Colin to the airport to send him off, she left a bottle of wine on my front step with a note: "Today is the day you start your journey up the hill..."

Most other people did not know what to say during this experience, and many said things that unintentionally caused me extreme pain.

"How are you?" was their most common question. I started to feel annoyed, however, because I never knew whether it came from a sincere desire to know how I was coping or was just an empty pleasantry. I wanted to scream back at them, "DO YOU KNOW MY HUSBAND IS AT WAR IN AFGHANISTAN? I HATE IT. I AM REALLY, REALLY SHITTY RIGHT NOW, THANK YOU VERY MUCH. SO PLEASE GIVE ME A FUCKING BREAK."

I wanted to wear a D for Deployment, like the Scarlet letter, so people would understand why I would cry on a moment's notice and would occasionally demonstrate signs of insanity. I felt unsuited for public consumption and avoided anything more than superficial interaction with all but those who were closest to me. In time, when people asked, "How are you?" I learned to reply more civilly, by rounding up the edges of my lips. I would not call it a smile, but it appeared to others as one. Or I would answer with something that did not actually answer the question - sharing a tidbit about Colin or saying the children were really strong. I was too proud to share the loneliness and fear I felt inside.

"Are you scared he will be killed?" YES, of course I was. I wanted to say, "I work hard every day to try to keep that fear out of my every thought, but thank you so much for bringing it back to the foreground. " But I just stayed silent. This question was asked of me several times. Maybe next time these people can go ask someone with cancer if they are scared of dying. I'm sure that people don't realize these are hot button issues for any family back home. Maybe they are simply articulating their own fear or believing they are somehow being helpful. But most of us just don't stop to think how the words we say make *others* feel.

"How much longer does he have until he can get out?" This question, asked of me often, showed a fundamental lack of understanding about those who served. Most servicemen were not counting the days until they could "get out. " Most served because they believed in a greater good, and volunteered again and again to keep us all safe. They put country above all else. Even if Colin survived this deployment, I knew he was not "getting out" anytime soon, if ever.

"My husband had to go on a business trip for two weeks. I know how hard it is to juggle. " Many friends and acquaintances said this to me, trying to empathize. I understood people were trying to somehow understand what I was experiencing and connect it to their context. But a business trip was hardly the same as a deployment to a war zone. My husband was sleeping in a sleeping bag. And there were people out there trying to kill any American in sight. Juggling life as a single parent was the easy part; my constant gnawing fear was something most people would never fully comprehend.

From my hypersensitive experience of this deployment, I have realized that I have said similarly ignorant things before, with the intention of showing sympathy to a friend. I wonder if I may have unintentionally caused pain. If so, I am truly sorry. And it has become clear to me the difficulty to demonstrate true empathy absent the credibility of having had the shared experience.

"Well, my nephew was there and has shrapnel in his neck from an IED. He will never be the same," a neighbor told me one day. What did she intend by sharing this story with me? Was she trying to show her fortitude by having gone through what I feared? Or was she just doing the typical "my labor lasted eighteen hours" one-up game that women often did when comparing birthing stories, often in front a newly pregnant woman? Well, all I can say is that my neighbor's comment caused me pain and brought visual images that only fed my worried mind.

"Well, he signed up for it. " Another neighbor said this to me, unintentionally twisting the knife as it dug into my chest. Yes, I thought, he did sign up. Each and every day, he was protecting your ignorant ass to make stupid comments like that.

"Well, in my opinion, we shouldn't be there anyway. " While everyone is entitled to their personal political opinions, I had no mental energy or desire to get into political discussions. Those comments simply devalued the incredible sacrifice my husband was making. He signed up to follow orders. He did not make them. Nor did I.

"I don't know how you manage. I don't think I could do it. " This was often said to me, intended as a compliment, but really it wasn't. Although I was trying, I was not the brave Superwoman everyone thought. I was the anxious lady who carried her cell phone everywhere, even to the bathroom, so not to miss a call from my loved one. I simply had no choice and had to be strong for my children. People saw the hardened shell I put out for them, but inside I was a mess.

"Well, my brother was a conscientious objector in Vietnam because he could not hold a gun and shoot someone. " What? Were you insinuating my husband wanted to shoot someone? Enough said, but comments like this enraged me.

"Your Dad is in combat. " One spring afternoon after Colin had reached us on my cell phone as we sat on the sidelines of Ian's lacrosse game, a woman next to us started asking questions. When Karl explained that his Dad was in Afghanistan, but "he is not in combat," the woman shot back argumentatively. "Well, yes he is! Anyone over there is in combat!" I was so shocked by her comments and rude ignorance of her audience - Karl and Thais were just children - that I just froze. Thank you, not, for fueling the fear my children already felt. I only regret today that I didn't tell her off then.

On the other hand, there were people who knew instinctively just what to say and do. They have taught me the consoling and strengthening power of words and friendship.

> *Hi Beth,*
> *I know my husband would really appreciate hearing about Colin, as I would, too. Hope you are doing well. If Karl ever needs to get out with a friend, feel free to call us and ask; we all get caught up in busy-ness and relaxations but would always enjoy having him over...*
> *A classmate's mom*

After my ice rink friend heard how Ian was nearly stranded at the soccer field one night after dark when a fellow teammate's parent forgot to drive him home, she e-mailed me.

Beth Jackson

*Please let me know if Karl ever needs a ride. And while we don't
have anyone on Ian's team, my daughter has practice on Friday nights
and one of us could always give him a ride home.
My ice rink friend*

I remembered back also to when I had those two miscarriages six
years before. Only a few people really knew what to say or do; most
were unsure and said nothing. But a close friend with same-aged
children called me the morning of my D&C. "Beth, I am going to
come pick up your boys at 3 p. m. this afternoon to take them to the
playground. I hope you can use a few hours for yourself for whatever
you want. " She did not put the typical and well-intentioned onus on
me with the offer "Let me know how I can help. " Rather, she knew
and just did.

My older brother's wife sent me a dozen white roses after my first
miscarriage. And again several months later after my second.

And now, just the other day, she mailed the children a framed photo
of Colin in uniform. Handwritten with a metallic sharpie pen on
the four panels of the black wooden frame read:

*If you don't believe in Super Heroes,
you have not met my Dad.*

I put the frame in the kitchen, so the children could see it every day.
She, too, knew and just did.

***

As I tried to hold onto my emotions and carry on each day, the
American flag took on a whole new meaning for me. What a
symbol of pride and freedom, and all the wonderful associations we
had with being an American.

When Colin first left, I pulled out the flag, which had been stored away in our front hall closet since Fourth of July. I paid a handyman to install a permanent flagpole holder on the weathered shingles between the two white garage doors. Within a day, though, I learned that our flag could twist in the wind, wrapping itself around and around the pole. I learned a new word: furl. The flag seemed to have a mind of its own.

A girlfriend went out and got me a non-twist heavy-duty plastic sleeve to put over the pole to prevent the flag from furling. She and I spent an hour trying to interpret the crude instructions and put the various plastic rings, grommets, and sleeve correctly over the pole, a design so the rings would rotate in the wind rather than the flag. Reaching up high as she held the ladder steady, I screwed the pole back into place as sweat dripped into my bra. I hoped the non-twist claim was real.

All I wanted was for my flag to fly high. To show my pride.

And still, I waited for information, and just recognition, from the institution called the Army. I anxiously waited for that package from Daisy to arrive, and my expectations grew about what it would contain. Little did I know at the time that the package was never and would never be sent.

Chapter 6 – Hanging On

End April 2011

One week, I had two different business trips. My work somehow had ramped up without me noticing. Maybe I wanted it that way, as it was a distraction from my worry. But I was moving too fast to think much about it. My mom came to stay for the first time during the deployment to help with the overnights; both to give me a hand, and to help us save money on childcare.

The first trip was to North Carolina, a follow-up to the Wyoming trip and the disastrous waterlogged report in Florida.

My Monday flight from Providence left several hours before my mom arrived. This was my first business trip I was taking by air since Colin had left. As the plane prepared to depart the gate, I instinctively pulled out my phone to text Colin, as I always did, the name of the carrier, destination, and hotel, so he knew of my whereabouts if the plane crashed.

Then I realized Colin could not receive my text on his dead cell phone. So I texted my sister, Carrie, instead. With my need assuaged, I felt momentary peace of mind and started to turn off my phone.

Suddenly I remembered that Karl lost a tooth at breakfast that morning. I told him to put the tooth under his pillow and had intentions for the tooth fairy to visit before I left for the airport. But I forgot! Yikes. So I quickly texted Dana to please put $1 under the pillow as discretely as possible while he was still at school lacrosse practice. In case you did not know, the tooth fairy has come during the day, too. I didn't question it. At any other time, as

Beth Jackson

a typical busy working mom, I would have sloughed off the omission with a laugh, especially for my oldest who did not believe in the tooth fairy anymore, but during this deployment year guilt and negligence just seemed to weigh me down even more.

Once my mom arrived, she and Dana worked as a tag team. Dana went to get Ian from soccer and pick up pizza for dinner that first night. My mom bathed Thais and put her to bed, while Dana cleaned up. My mom got the briefing from Dana on the morning and school drop-off routine.

Tuesday went smoothly as well, as far as I heard. After school, Karl rode the school bus to and from his lacrosse game in Providence. Ian completed his homework before going to his lacrosse practice. Dana did the driving, and my mom made a spaghetti dinner.

I called from the Atlanta airport again before boarding my connecting flight back, and said goodnight to the children. We blew kisses over the phone. And my mom gave them hugs in bed.

Just past midnight on Tuesday night, I returned home. Coming through the front door, I was ready to put my head on the pillow. I instead stopped and just stared at the scene. Piles of shoes and gloves adorned the entire front hall floor. Running shoes, dress shoes, rain boots, cleats, winter gloves, and hats. My shoes, Karl's shoes, Ian's shoes, and Thais's shoes. I had already put away all of Colin's shoes into a closet shortly after he left. But dozens of our pairs were lined up next to one another, bordering the entire 20x8 ft long room. A pile of unmatched shoes rested on top of each other in a pyramid. There was even a pile of dirt the size of a baseball neatly resting on the floor. Moved to a pile, but not scooped up. Just left to be.

When I left the house the morning before, the shoes and gloves were hiding neatly in three wicker baskets by the door. But now the baskets were empty, and the shoes in total disarray.

I was immediately reminded of the story Meghan told me when her mother came to help during her husband's deployment. It was seven or eight months into their year apart, and her patience was wearing thin. She had an all out yelling fit at her mother for replacing the batteries of a stopped clock in the kitchen. Her mom was only trying to help, but Meghan did not want it fixed because the clock never synched up with the other ones she actually looked at. Silly perhaps, but not unusual. I had heard that one of the biggest fights between spouses took place when the deployed husband or wife came home and couldn't find the remote control - or some other essential household item that had innocently been moved or relocated. Or fixed.

I felt the same way when I encountered my mother's half-finished attempt to organize my shoes, which were never an issue for me before. I just wanted to tell her as emphatically as I could, "Please don't fix anything. My life is not broken!"

Let me tell you, when my husband suddenly got yanked out of my life, I could not do a thing about it. When the exact timing of his departure was up in the air until five days prior, I had to let go and begrudgingly trust that I would know the details as soon as the "system" arranged everything. When I learned the full duration of his absence was a vague "year," give or take a few weeks or even months, I just had to let go.

I HATED letting go. Ok, there, I admitted it.

In this context, I had a visceral need to control whatever space in my life was available to control. For me, that was my home, including those shoe bins. I had already taken on minor projects around the house to put things in order the way I wanted them. Fixing a picture with a loose metal hook that showed on the blue matting. Buying new bathmats to replace the shredded aging ones. But my house was completely off-limits to even the most well-intentioned mom. So at the wee hours after returning from my business trip, the last thing I wanted was a messy greeting that required me to make decisions or take more action.

In frustration, I threw the shoes back into the baskets, so I did not have to look at the mess any longer. One after another. My throws became stronger each time. I then walked into the kitchen and saw the mail on the counter. As I quickly scanned through the junk and the bills, I felt a strange warmth on my back. It was a gradual warmth, but noticeable enough to draw my body to turn around.

Right in front of my eyes, I found myself staring at the oven. I looked up at the dials, and the upper oven dial was on BAKE. Adrenaline suddenly pumped through my veins as my heart beat like a hundred drummers. I was no longer tired, but wide awake and furious. My mother had forgotten to turn off the oven from when she made dinner six hours before. The house could have burned down.

I quickly turned the dial to OFF and took a shallow breath. I opened the door to check that there were no pans or extra crumbs of food inside. Seething, I finally walked upstairs.

First, I checked in on each of the children, and then I gently lifted Thais to the bathroom and helped her go, anticipating that I might successfully head off a wetting accident for at least one night.

Half asleep, she mumbled, "Tell me when my Mommy is home. "

I replied, "It is me, Mommy. " She opened her eyes for a second and gave me a big hug as she sat on the toilet and loosened her muscles.

I carried her back to her bed and snuggled with her for a minute until she fell back asleep. I heard my mother breathing in the guest bed, which was tucked in the nook of the laundry room, which had no door, as I walked down the hall. Then I arose the dog from my bed, walked back downstairs, and let her out to potty as well.

After finally climbing into my bed, I texted Carrie to tell her about the oven. My mother had left the oven on before in her own home. I had been concerned then, and it really upset me that it now had happened in my house. My eyes fell into slumber within minutes of my head hitting the pillow.

When I woke in the morning, I read what my sister had texted back.

Deep breaths. Practice forgiveness. It could have been worse.

I was grateful for her sanity.

I knew there was a school concert on Thursday night of that week, but I had never had a fifth grader before and had no idea Karl was singing in it. Unfortunately, I was leaving for the second business trip of that week. I felt guilty but was so terribly grateful that my mom would be there for him. Life, I was learning, was accepting imperfections, mine and other people's.

The day my mom was leaving, she took Colin's car to the mechanic to get the starter checked after it had stalled several times during her weeklong visit. As she was pulling out of our driveway and waving goodbye, Thais burst into tears. Big alligator tears. Later that night when my mom called to say she had arrived home safely, she added, "Wasn't it so adorable that Thais cried when I left? I kept blowing her kisses, calling out that I would be back soon. "

I decided in that moment to share the truth of my daughter's reaction. "Mom," I paused, "Thais was crying because she thought you were stealing Colin's car. "

My mother-in-law came in town the following week, and the stream of "help" continued. Both my mom and mother-in-law had lots of suggestions about what I could do to "fix" my life. Thais's hair needed more attention. The boys' homework should be done in a particular chair in the kitchen. I should make more personal time for myself. The children would enjoy a particular camp or should come to visit this summer. Honestly, I could barely think a day in advance, let alone plan something months out. Their suggestions just overwhelmed me.

"You should, you should, you should. . . " That was all I heard before I just tuned them out. I was proud of the reply I invented to shut down most of this unsolicited advice. "I will add it to my list. I think this is number seventy-two. And I am only on number eight at the moment. "

My unspoken appreciation was enormous for the moms' extra set of hands and the company of a loving relative. But my selfish analysis at the time began considering whether their help was actually more work for me than not. Maybe I needed a screener for all out of town guests who came in town to "help. " Only all YES answers allowed one to enter inside the front door:

- Will you help without judgment or suggestions?
- Will you drive over the bridges? (*we lived on an island, and yes, both moms adamantly refused!*)
- Will you fend for meals for yourself?
- Will you not only wash your sheets but also remake the guest bed?
- Will you go home soon? Please!
- And most importantly, will you read my mind? (*because I won't tell you any of this!*)

My unhappiness and anxiety clouded my gratitude, and it would be more than a year before I fully realized how resoundingly unappreciative I was to both my mom and mother-in-law for the love and help they tried to offer me. There was no one to blame for the situation in which I found myself, but nevertheless, I often unjustifiably vented my frustrations out on them, sometimes out loud but most times silently, like virtual punching bags.

While the moms were each in town, I was actually able to go to the store alone, attend a curriculum parent's night at the children's school, and attend a late book club evening with several of my girlfriends. I had actually been able to be alone for an hour or two without the children or work, something that had been missing since Colin had left. But I did not see or appreciate this at the time.

***

A few days later I got a surprise late night chirping sound of an incoming Skype call. Colin never called at night. But at 9:30 p. m. my time, 7:00 a. m. in Kabul, he had just returned from escorting a colleague to the airport. He wanted to show the boys what his body armor looked like and asked me to wake them. The boys were thrilled to see their Dad like this. I, on the other hand, was horrified. It was the first time I saw Colin dressed for war, with weapons adorning his full body. After the boys returned to their rooms, Colin casually mentioned how an Afghan man had jumped onto their armored SUV when they stopped at an intersection on the way. That sent my mind racing.

Colin in body armor, photo taken of the Skype screen

Beth Jackson

I took this picture off the image of my computer and forwarded it to my friends and family e-mail list. I wanted to tell them, "This is why I am SO FUCKING SCARED," but instead I just evenly stated the facts.

Two e-mail replies captured this ying-yang of everything I was feeling.

> *We are all safer because of what Colin is doing. And his kids are and will be super proud for the rest of their lives.*
>
> *And I like that they are keeping him safe with that uniform!*
>
> *Love, a childhood friend*

The second one read...

> *Love the getup. Like hockey goalie gear, more IS better. . .*
> *Funny, I don't recognize him in this picture, nor the last. I realized I'd never seen him without his glasses on, nor with body armor.*
>
> *We're playing lacrosse Saturday against Ian's team, right? 10:30 at the Glen? Do you want to send Ian home with us afterwards for a playdate w/ Ben? I know you tend to have pretty busy weekend schedule, but I thought I'd float it out there. Hopefully I'll see you Saturday, hopefully it'll be nice weather!*
>
> *- Molly*

I have to admit, I still liked receiving e-mails that acknowledged my fear that Colin was in a war zone and could be shot at any time. But the other type of e-mail made me smile and kept things light-hearted.

Colin's dad, also known as Gramp, shared in my feelings. After I told him about my nightmares and stresses, he replied.

Beth,

*My rational side tells me that Colin will return home without a
scratch, but my irrational side contains all sorts of groundless fears.
Guys don't get to cry but I get right to the edge all too frequently. Can
I join your club?*

*I think keeping a journal makes great sense, especially ten years from
now when everything has long since returned to normal.*

*Love
Gramp*

***

The second full moon since Colin had left was now gone. In my
effort to make the upcoming Easter holiday as special as ever, I
bought $75 tickets to the Rosecliff, one of the spectacular marbled
Newport Mansions on Bellevue Avenue that hosted an Easter
brunch and egg hunt on the Saturday before the holiday.

Of course, the day greeted us with monsoon-like rains and thirty
mile per hour wind gusts. Our dress-up clothes turned into muddy
mops, and the umbrellas inverted themselves in the wind. But there
we stood, at the starting line, a rope keeping the hounds, oh I mean
kids, behind the line until the whistle blew. To give the little ones a
chance, they split up the children by age - under six on the left and
over six on the right. I stood with Thais, while the boys stood on
the older side. Eggs were strewn over the enormous lawn, which on
any other day would have boasted gorgeous views of the Atlantic
Ocean. But today all eyes were kept down, to avoid the pelting rain.
The children were freezing and wet but all ready for the hunt.

It was over in less than thirty seconds. Thais scrambled and slipped in
the grass. Her cry was dwarfed by the rain. As a momma bear would
protect her cub, I grabbed two eggs before another child reached for

them, so at least Thais would get two. And those two were the only ones she got. It was like a scene from *Lord of the Flies*. In the rain. And mud. And cold.

Not what I had expected, but oh well, at least I tried. Little did I envision that this event would become the metaphor of my life.

***

We enjoyed a simple act of kindness from a true stranger on Easter day, which was warm and sunny unlike the day prior.

The children and I made an effort once again to dress in nice clothes, with fancy shoes, and groomed hair for church that Sunday. Not a normal feat these days. Karl wore Nantucket Red cotton pants, which I belatedly noticed were getting a little short for his growing body, a navy Brooks Brothers blazer, a white button-down, and a striped tie. Ian wore khaki pants with otherwise the same uniform. Thais was dressed in a blue and white smocked dress with a bow tied in back. Patent-leather black shoes covered her tiny feet. I don't really remember what I wore, as I only looked out at others this year. I had already forgotten about myself.

As Thais held my hand, we all walked together towards the small stone church where we greeted an interim priest at the door. Reverend Chris, the priest we were just getting to know, had left for a new position in Virginia. Inside the church, there were no pews, just individual chairs with woven seats and red velvet cushions underneath.

After the first hymns and prayers passed, Ian started to fidget. First his finger discovered how to make a pinging noise on the radiator next to his chair. "Shush," I whispered in his direction. He stopped moving his fingers.

Soon a short ringing sound filled the quiet air. *Was that his cell phone?* I had explicitly told the boys to leave their phones in the car. Was he playing a ringtone, like a mini five-second boom box? I bent my ear toward him and listened intently.

Yes, it was Ian's cell phone. I was not sure if he was just checking something or turning it on, but the noise was audible nonetheless. In addition to a second shush, I whispered that he was supposed to have left the phone in the car. I was reminding him to make the point, but really I secretly just wanted the people behind him to hear that I had tried to be a good parent, although clearly my rules were already not followed.

A few seconds later, another sound echoed off the walls. I was mortified. The church was in the midst of a silent prayer. Ian was simply turning the phone off, but as we all know, there are sound cues built into our phones just so we know they are actually turning off. Yep, there it went again.

Then Thais joined the boredom club. She became fascinated with the coat of the woman in front of her and reached out to pet the flowing black fur collar with hanging pom-poms. I was relieved that the women never noticed.

Halfway through the service, we got to the Prayers of the People. I had already seen that Colin's name was listed, as I had requested, in the program, but the children had not yet noticed it.

As the priest began, I pointed to the words, and suddenly they were mesmerized. The priest read twenty or so names on the prayer list for sickness or other needs, and then he read, "For Mike Silvera, John Rippa, Colin Jackson, and for all who are serving, and for all who are living in arenas of war. "

I looked over at the boys. Ian was quiet but attentive. Karl reached for his left eye and wiped away the moisture of sadness. Teardrops

75

welled up in my eyes as well as I whispered to myself, "Please protect Daddy, and us. "

I did not know Mike or John, and I did not know if they even lived in Rhode Island, or if someone in the congregation just added them to the prayer list as many of my parents' friends in other states had for Colin. All I knew was that I did not see any other mom alone with her children at this church that I could seek out for company.

The moment quickly passed, and the children's boredom returned again. Thais started resting her head on Ian's lap, even while the rest of the congregation stood. They were both quiet and happy, so I let it go. A moment of peace. Or so I thought. No sooner was the calm broken as Thais jumped up to give Karl a wet willie, just the thing Ian had been doing to her in relative quiet. A wet finger in one's ear. Gross. As Thais unsuccessfully reached for Karl, she stumbled on the chair, and it toppled over backwards into the lap of a man and woman, two adults without children, I will mention.

I apologized immediately, pulled the chair up, and gently but firmly admonished the two of them. "Respect," I lectured. "Quiet," I whispered.

Finally the service ended, and I turned to apologize profusely again to the couple behind us. I expected the fake response of "Oh, it is okay," but instead, I heard, "I am in awe of you. Three adorable children. "

I almost started to cry. I didn't care if the man really meant it or if he was just being nice. He did not even know my husband was in Afghanistan, and I was about to tell him, but I stopped and just smiled.

"Thank you," I said. Thank you for being a kind stranger and making me feel so much better than I could have otherwise. The children and I were holding on to our chaotic life by threads, but thank you for accepting us for who we were. If only he really knew.

***

Three days later, my best friend from childhood, Jen, e-mailed me to check in on Colin.

> *Beth,*
> *Saw the news this am, just wanting to check that Colin is ok.*
> *Hope you had a great Easter!*
> *Love,*
> *Jen*

She had seen the news. I had not. *What news?*

Panic set in. So I quickly typed in cnn. com and found the story about an Afghan military pilot opening fire at the Kabul airport, killing six U. S. soldiers.

Well, no, I had not heard from Colin that day. I also had not received a knock at my door. Yet. Colin was in the ISAF headquarters compound in Kabul, not the airport, as far as I knew. But I knew he had escorted someone to the airport just the week prior, when he asked me to wake the boys. Had there been additional airport runs I didn't know about?

My heart started racing as I told myself he must be OK. But I was still holding my breath.

A friend whose husband recently retired from the Navy e-mailed me later that morning.

> *Hey there, just checking-in.*
> *Have all the calls, texts, and concerns started about how unsafe it is in*

Beth Jackson

> *Afghanistan? Duh! Let's do lunch. Pick a day and I am yours to vent at, problem solve, or whatever.*

Her e-mail put a smile on my face. Friendship. Company. Understanding.

Meghan, the friend who yelled at her mom over the clock, sent me this funny one later that night.

> *Beth, a really brief note from me ... but I really need to go to sleep. . . .*
>
> *But first, really, don't watch the news. Listen to music. Read fiction (light fiction).*
>
> *If you want, I'll listen to the news and let you know if anything really important happens. (Let's see, there were tornadoes, bad ones, down south; and Obama was actually born in the United States, I've seen the birth certificate; and bad things are happening in Syria and Bahrain; and Panetta's going to take over Gates' job; oh, and some royal people are getting married tomorrow but that would be really light, so go ahead and watch that though you'd have to get up really early; that probably qualifies as fluff!)...*
>
> *The news they report never provides any basis for real understanding, there's no scope or perspective. . . . and when your brain is focused so specifically on one person whom you can't contact, the news just wrecks you.*
>
> *Hang in,*
> *Meghan*

She was right. But it was impossible to turn off those texts from my friends and the Google alerts. I was a wreck every time I learned of another fatality. The news media always knew the story before the families did.

Late in the afternoon on the following day, Colin e-mailed me. He was OK. I let out an audible sigh.

A friend e-mailed me the serenity prayer:

> *God grant me the serenity to accept the things I cannot change;*
> *courage to change the things I can; and wisdom to know the difference*

I really wanted to feel the meaning of those words, but honestly, I was not sure there was a God. I knew I was still desperately trying to control what I could not, but I had not really let go.

Chapter 7 – Invisible Connection

Early May 2011

My search for how to cope during Colin's deployment continued. I was still obsessed with needing more information, my search keeping me tied every night to the computer, sometimes for hours, going from link to link. I was too stubborn to give up. And I still had not received that package from Daisy.

What I really wanted was to learn about any military programs in Rhode Island or Massachusetts that I could do with our children. A movie night with others? Meet at a playground? Materials that would be helpful for the children? Anything? I craved a sense of connection.

So I continued looking myself. After many hours of clicking through virtually every page on the militaryonesource website, I finally found a link to Youth & Child Services. I was surprisingly pleased that there was actually a contact e-mail listed. So I sent the Director of Youth & Child Services, who was somewhere in Virginia, a note asking if he could so kindly send me any specific contact information of anyone who had any information for the children of military servicemen here in Rhode Island.

Within a day, I heard back. I was referred to Pamela Martin, who ran Operation Military Kids in Rhode Island. I had never before heard of Operation Military Kids, but I loved the name. She, in turn, also replied immediately, sharing information about local events and names and numbers of other military spouses who had experienced deployments before. Unlike Daisy, whose job was to support our family, Pamela became my go-to source of helpful knowledge and caring support, communicating with me almost daily.

Pamela first mentioned "Hero Packs," which were donated and stuffed by volunteers to thank children for being a hero, too. Within days, three arrived for my children. She also sent me information about a free Family Camp at the University of Rhode Island in July to celebrate the kids with fun activities like rocketeeering and Lego-building. With the hope that our children would find a connection with others going through the same separation as they were, I signed us up on the spot. Just having the camp on our calendar suddenly meant so much to the four of us. The children were so excited; they could not stop talking about it.

Finally, I felt I had some traction. I felt my hours of searching to the trade-off of sleep were not for naught. I was so grateful to Pamela, a total stranger, for the personal interest she took in my children and me.

Oh, and did I mention the kindness of the Middle Eastern man who ran the convenience store next to our favorite pizzeria? One night I took Ian for a rare one-on-one Ian and mom outing to have pizza and listen to his guitar teacher perform live, while Dana babysat Karl and Thais. Afterwards, we stopped by the convenience store, so Ian could buy Colin some fun snacks to put in a care package. When Ian chose some cappuccino shot energy drinks, the store owner added a free one "for your Dad. " The kindness of strangers, when I least expected it, had continued. When someone offered to hold the door, when a stranger just smiled, or when a friend sincerely asked about Colin, my throat hardened. And yes, I wept. Every day.

***

Ok, I will admit here that in my first couple months of deployment, I had been wallowing in bitterness and self-pity about my situation, until a turn changed my view of my new life. Two things struck me, both within the same day.

First, I learned of a Connecticut family with a deployed Dad who lost their house to a tragic fire. The mom and their four children, ages eighteen months to fourteen years old, survived unharmed but were in desperate need of items to restart their entire life - everything from children's clothing to household appliances, furniture, kitchen items, and linens. I immediately began stuffing the back of the car with six huge bags of children's clothing, hard cover books, wooden puzzles, curtains, and a bicycle my daughter just recently outgrew. Each of the children donated some of their treasured belongings as well. They knew why.

I told myself to forget feeling sorry for myself; this family had experienced far more hardship than I ever had. Hopefully they were now feeling the love of the entire military and civilian community around them. I learned about this family through an Operation Military Kids e-mail. And when I spoke with the soldier's Lieutenant Colonel about where to drop off my donations, he was enormously grateful for our help. Maybe helping others was what kept me going.

Second, I heard from Colin that he got another roommate. Now there were three grown men living in a windowless room the size of a walk-in closet. And this new roommate, a contractor not a soldier, had a breathing machine, making it impossible for Colin to sleep with the horrible whirring sound. It took over a week before Colin was able to extricate himself and take a newly empty bunk in another closet with just two beds. I, on the other hand, slept on a firm king-size mattress with a dozen pillows and a down comforter.

This new roommate of their double immediately became one of Colin's closest friends. Colin's stories about this roommate's last tour in Iraq, however, gave me no peace. Especially the one about him being splattered with other people's blood during an explosion that killed dozens in a marketplace. This was another image that became imprinted in my mind.

These things made me realize I had to be strong and just keep going. But it also meant I hardened more, too. My weariness and the growing mental turmoil did not go away; rather, I felt that I had to hide them. As I had discovered as a teenager, I was actually quite good at deception. Back in high school, I hid my anorexia while losing twenty pounds in one month by skipping breakfast, eating a salad of undressed lettuce at school, and then having a normal meal at dinner. With my loose clothes and rolls of quarters in my pockets when my dad weighed me, no one was the wiser. Again now, I just hid behind my smiley face and extra layers of that fluffy white cloud that had become my shield.

***

As we adapted to our "new normal," I started referring to our bedroom as "my bedroom" and had stopped picking up five forks to set the table. The children and I had somehow figured out the logistical aspects of our life without Dad. And their independence gradually grew out of necessity. We needed to rely on others to help with carpooling, but occasionally either boy took on the responsibility of babysitting a sleeping Thais for fifteen minutes while I drove to the field to pick up the other brother.

I felt I had been successfully sheltering our children from the worst news coming out of the war zone, and they had never seen me cry. But without any prompting, the children started asking hard questions about death.

"Mom, what is a will?" Karl asked out of the blue one afternoon.

I answered him with a simple explanation.

At dinner a few nights later, Thais asked me, "Mom, where are children buried when they die?"

"What do you mean?" I asked.

"Do they go in that thing that Aunt Lil went in?" Thais was referencing the coffin she had seen the past winter for Colin's great aunt who died at the age of 94.

"Well," I responded. "Aunt Lil wanted to be buried in a coffin. I personally just want my ashes buried by some nice tree. "

"Why don't you want a coffin?" Karl piped in, clearly overhearing the conversation.

"I don't want my body to rot underground," I blurted out with honesty unfit for my audience. I immediately felt guilty about my choice of words, as I knew the children had likely heard Colin, a Catholic, say how he wanted a coffin.

"Me, too," Thais agreed. "I don't want a coffin. "

Just as quickly as the answer was posed, the conversation moved on. But clearly, these were not just stray thoughts; they were connected to other questions pulsing through their heads.

The same thoughts went through my mind. Before Colin left, in private, we talked about living wills and our last wishes. I had asked him if he were to die, where he wanted to be buried. His "I don't know" reply left me unsettled. I did not want to be responsible for such a decision. Would he want to lie next to his beloved grandmother in Princeton, where his mom grew up and where he and his dad went to school? Would he want to lie in Arlington National Cemetery, in recognition of his service to the country? Or would he want to lie in a small plot in Rhode Island where we now lived? I was angry with him that he left that question open.

Thoughts of his possible death loomed over me. If Colin died, what would the funeral be like? Who would be the pallbearers? Most often I thought about the eulogy, and what I would say. The two messages I would share were already well crafted in my mind. One was about Colin's bravery and selflessness. The second would be a request to all men in attendance to be a presence in my children's lives. I could try to be Supermom, but I could not be Superdad. I even thought that, if I were too choked up to actually speak at the funeral, I would ask my older brother to read the words for me.

When I shared these secret plans and worries with two friends, each confided in me that they, too, had similar thoughts. When one friend had cared for her ailing elder parents, she would think about what her children would wear to their funerals. When the other friend was caring for her husband, whose life was saved by emergency surgery, she also thought about the eulogy. We women don't talk about these things, but we all think them.

***

One day the *Warrior Citizen* magazine, an Army Reserves publication, arrived at our house in the mail. I had never before taken notice of this publication, as I typically threw it into the recycling pile along with the junk mail we got each day. But this time, after seeing Army soldiers on the front cover, Ian began flipping through the magazine. And then he saw it.

A bloodied soldier being treated by a medic.

Ian was visibly shaken. I read the caption below the picture: "simulation exercise for Reserve medics. " The blood was not real, but it sure looked real.

I was angry at this publication. Online the military materials very clearly said DON'T have your children see the news or other things that can scare them, and here, the Army Reserves went ahead and sent exactly that sort of thing directly to our house. When I mentioned this to Colin in our next communication, he replied that I gave the Army too much credit for thinking they could put two and two together:

My husband is NOT home. Maybe you should send his mail to him in Afghanistan?

My son does NOT want to see bloodied soldiers – even if it is fake blood. Thank you very much.

Colin told me to have no expectations, but I could not help myself.

I was so sorry for Ian's innocence, chipped away each day. I knew it would happen at some point, but I did not plan for it to happen this way and this young. Oh, I forgot, I was not in control of this plan. Yet I lacked the needed PhD in the science of flexibility.

*** My flagpole broke today. The flag had not only twisted, but the tension from the wind actually snapped the pole in half. So I bought another one.

Pulling out the three-step ladder again, I secured the leg into the groove, where the weeds peeked up between the cement of the garage and the tar driveway, and climbed up. Reaching up as high as I could, I balanced on that top step to unscrew the bottom three inches of the old pole. Oh, how those screws held tight. Sweat started beading again. My fingers swiftly rehooked the flag to the new pole with a built-in de-twister plastic ring, and I started screwing it into place. That is when I noticed the one-quarter inch gap between the pole and the holder. It wiggled, which meant inevitably there would be another snap or break. The holder was for a one-inch wide pole, but unable to find one I had settled on the three-quarter inch one. So as a backup, I found a small rectangular shim of wood to fill the gap for now. By the time I stepped down the ladder, the flag had already completed a full rotation around the new pole, and it had not furled. Success.

Until the next morning when I walked outside and saw the flag sadly furled on itself again. This time I just grabbed my son's lacrosse stick, waved it above my head and used it to shove the flag back over itself. The motion was not just one of flipping the fabric of the flag back the right way, but rather it required a simultaneous flip and twist. After a few awkward heaves with the stick while I jumped into the air, I succeeded in righting the flag. Until the next time. Which meant, pretty much, day after day. It was hard to be patriotic.

As I started paying more attention to my flag, I began noticing American flags everywhere. In fact, I had passed them hundreds of times but had never before really seen them. There were flags on three consecutive mailboxes by the playground. And an enormous flag hung above the 7-11 beside a sign about our pride of the Marines. Only much later did I learn that the storeowner had four sons at one point or another over in Afghanistan. Four.

I noticed the flag at the Newport bank waved high on a 30-foot flagpole. A flag in front of town hall flew every day, often at half mast. A flag on a neighbor's house caught my eye. And another.

I found it strange that I had never noticed those flags before. They had been staring at me, but I had always stared right through them. It was like I had lived a parallel life with all these people who served our country, but our lives had never previously intersected.

***

While I had found some traction with Pamela and Operation Military Kids, I still felt isolated since I did not know anyone who *currently* had a deployed spouse.

Then through happenstance, I met Cara, another working mother just like me, whose Reservist husband was also now serving in Kabul. And she lived just on the other side of the bridge. I was thrilled. Her husband was stationed on a different base than Colin. He was Navy. Colin was Army. But Cara and I were one. Instantly, we shared a connection and understanding; we were no longer alone. We could share our daily bouts of tears, gripping fear, and feelings of isolation.

Cara told me a wonderful story about her own experience with the kindness of strangers. When a cashier at Trader Joe's made a comment about all the granola bars and bags of nuts that filled her shopping cart, Cara explained that they were going to her husband in Afghanistan. After a few minutes of chatter and paying the total, Cara turned to push her cart and saw a bouquet of flowers in it.

"Oh, m'am, here, someone mistakenly put these into my cart," Cara said.

"No," the cashier explained, "they are for you from us. Thank you. "

***

Whenever I thought of Colin, my hand would slowly rise to my throat to find the round topaz stone set in a silver knot that dangled from a simple silver chain. Colin gave me the necklace the previous summer, for my 40th birthday. When I first heard about his deployment, I started wearing it, like a rabbit's foot, and quickly it

Beth Jackson

became the only necklace I wore. As I stroked it, flipping it around the chain casually, almost subconsciously, it gave me a little comfort. Maybe I was being overly superstitious, but every day that passed and Colin was OK, I secretly hoped that if I wore the same necklace again the next day, he would be safe one more day. So I decided to wear that necklace every single day until Colin returned safely home.

As humans, all of us need touch. To me, touch was the most powerful way to communicate love and affection. That necklace gave me the power of touch. Every morning when I walked Thais into school, she held my hand. Alone in her bedroom, she hugged those plastic photographs. Every night when I tucked in each of the children, my hand reached out to gently hug them or touch the top of their heads as well.

Both boys wore dog tags that Dad had sent them to school. I didn't know if they fingered them the way I did my necklace, but I hoped the touch near their chest gave them a feeling of connection.

The front of the tags read:

Warrior Ethos
- *I will always place the mission first*
- *I will never accept defeat*
- *I will never quit*
- *I will never leave a fallen comrade*

And the back read:

Army Values
- *Loyalty*
- *Duty*
- *Respect*
- *Selfless-Service*

- *Honor*
- *Integrity*
- *Personal Courage*

After a week or so, though, I started to notice that Karl only wore his dog tags at home, not at school. "The other boys are too nosy," he explained. He wanted to feel the dog tags, but he did not want other's hands touching them. I did not know what to say. I did not have any experience or wisdom to share. So I just nodded when he explained how he put them next to his bed for safe-keeping.

Chapter 8 – Bold Self Care

Late May 2011

We had just finished a lazy Saturday pancake breakfast, when we heard the happy chirp of a Skype call from Colin. As each of the children got five minutes of one-on-one face time with him, I listened in. On the weekends when Colin was able to call, I never really spoke with him. There was not enough time. He never had more than ten or fifteen minutes to chat, and often the line cut off mid-sentence. So for the children's sake, I put my needs aside. At least I could hear his voice.

But that day, I overheard Colin say something that immediately bothered me. When Ian asked if he was going to travel to other cities around Afghanistan soon, Colin replied, "Not in the next two days. "

What the hell did that mean? I kept the thought to myself. That was a very specific response. In three days he would be traveling? In three days, he would be flying around in helicopters, wearing his body armor, and becoming a free target to any of the insurgents there? Great, just what I needed to know. Or not.

We were running out of time. The connection was likely going to drop, and we were already going to be late to Thais's soccer game.

Colin said he would call again tomorrow. We all said goodbye. Every night since Colin and I had been married, one of us would make three kiss sounds out loud, and the other person would echo three back as our final "I love you" before falling asleep. But on Skype, we no longer said the words or even attempted to make the sounds because the audio reception usually jumbled them anyway.

Beth Jackson

So I made the silent hand motion of blowing three kisses, a visual cue we did every time we closed on Skype. He motioned the same back. Something felt wrong, though, and I could not figure out what.

***

In my attempt to create an enormous distraction from reality for my children, I invented "Plan Fun" to keep ourselves busy. So, the following day we attended the Barnum & Bailey circus.

The children broadcasted their enjoyment of the circus with wide-open jaws and uproarious laughter. The $12 cotton candy was tasty, too. Afterwards, we went to McDonald's for lunch before continuing onto Ian's soccer game. We brought along his uniform and cleats, plus my laptop and wireless card, hoping that Colin would indeed call us. All afternoon, my eyes kept glancing at my cell phone and laptop to see if there was an incoming call. But they remained utterly quiet.

We then stopped at Trader Joe's to pick up some snacks for Thais's school class and for goodies to send in another package to Colin. Still no call.

We arrived at the soccer field early and were pleased to find a playground nearby. The children and I swung on swings and went down slides. For that half hour, I actually felt like a kid again, but my mind was elsewhere. Still no call. There had been many other times when Colin had indicated he would try to call but then could not. But it was his comment to Ian the day before that bothered me.

I did not share my disappointment or worry with my children, but on our way home from the game, Ian read my mind, "Is Daddy going to call?"

"He was really busy today," I made up. "I don't think he had a chance at all. "

Little did I know what was transpiring. The next morning, I quickly glanced at my phone as I was helping the children get ready for school. The first thing I saw was a text from a friend.

Hi! Are you following the news? Is Colin ok?

Shit.

What happened? Another attack in Kabul?

Was someone coming to my door today?

My heart started racing. Again. I glanced out the front window. No car was pulling up my driveway. *What happened?* I wanted to know, but not know, at the same time.

Was this what Colin was referring to in his cryptic comment the other day?

Panic.

I quickly clicked over to view my e-mail messages, until I saw one from Colin titled, *Osama Bin Laden is Dead.*

My chest felt like a balloon popping. I felt both huge relief that Colin was OK and a huge sadness as the memories of 9/11 came flooding back into my mind. I remembered those planes. Those towers. Tumbling down. The ash. My building in Houston was then evacuated, and I quickly drove my car to get baby Karl from his daycare. Holding on tight. Not sure what the world was coming to. Melancholy filled my eyes as I thought of my college friend, who lived next door to me my freshman year and was killed in the attacks.

Beth Jackson

My mind snapped back to the e-mail as I regained control of my emotions. I instantly knew such news would be discussed at school, so I felt I had to share it with the children right then and there. As the boys gathered their shoes and backpacks and Thais finished getting dressed, I told them, "Dad e-mailed. Let me read it to you. "

Which I did. Ian's first reply was, "So does Dad get to come home now?"

"No. "

Though the knot in my stomach was still there, it gave me some comfort to know that an evil terrorist could no longer do harm. But what about retaliation? Were Colin and his fellow servicemen now in even greater danger? Would they specifically be targeted?

***

It was nearly Mother's Day, my first on my own. I knew I had to make the day special for myself. At first I thought the children would want to make me breakfast in bed, but I squelched that idea when I thought about having to get up and go downstairs to turn on the stove and do most of the clean-up. It did not sound relaxing.

Somehow, I came up with the idea of "playing *Eloise*" on Mother's Day, and another Plan Fun idea was born. I had thousands of Marriott points from my years of business travel, so I called the Newport Marriott and booked a free room for the Saturday night before Mother's Day. My children were just as excited about my plan to play *Eloise* as I was.

We left for the hotel with plans for a high school babysitter to sleep over at our house to take care of Charlotte. And oh, how we had a splendid time. Our favorite activity was scampering around the hotel, just like in the *Eloise* book. The only rule was "walk" if we saw another guest or hotel staff, but we had fun riding the elevators and running up and down the emergency exit staircases. We also made our way to the pool and video game room. Three movies filled our evening, along with room service. And we all slept well that night. It was the perfect sleepover. I actually felt relaxed. I might even have taken a few breaths. We then ordered room service yet again, this time for eight waffles as each of us wanted two. Our time was truly filled with countless giggles and fun.

When we arrived home late Sunday morning, there was a box from FTD.

I slowly peeled back the cardboard lid and discovered a bouquet of a dozen pink-colored roses.

> *To the world's best mother.*
> *You carry the world on your shoulders without seeming to try.*
> *I love you and miss you terribly. Colin*

If only he knew. I cried again. My emotions were ripe, one hundred times even more intense than when I was pregnant. They were just below the surface like hot lava ready to erupt at any moment. The littlest happy or sad thing just triggered me.

The next time we Skyped, I told Colin that playing *Eloise* might become an annual event. And I thanked him profusely for whatever effort he had gone through to send me the flowers, and the note. I saw his smile on the screen, and I blew him more kisses.

Throughout the day on Sunday, several friends unexpectedly called and sent texts to tell me they were thinking of me. They included Colin's best friend, Will, who lived in D. C. but had been checking in on me at least once a month, letting me know I was not alone. One friend, Molly, even invited us over to her house for dinner.

Beth Jackson

On her annual day to be taken care of, she was taking care of me instead.

***

Back to our daily routines, that package from Daisy had still not arrived, so I sent a follow-up note.

> *Daisy,*
> *Hi. I am following up to see when you will be sending that packet and when I can at least get the chain of command information from the Reserve unit?*
> *Thank you,*
> *Beth*

This is what I got back...

> *Classification: UNCLASSIFIED*
> *Caveats: FOUO*
>
> *Hey Beth,*
> *I apologize. I will send it out tomorrow or Thursday. I just got really swamped plus I haven't felt too good lately. Thank you for emailing me.*
>
> *Daisy*
> *Family Readiness Support Assistant*

She has been busy? Really? Last thing I heard, her husband was not deployed for a year. This was her job.

A week went by. Colin had not been paid in over two weeks. And no two paychecks had been the same, so I still had no idea how to budget.

> *Daisy,*
> *Hi. I am checking to see when I can expect the packet.*

Also, Colin was not paid on Friday, May 27. He has not been paid since the last paycheck, May 13. Can you please advise with whom to follow-up on this?

Thank you,
Beth

She replied back the same day, in an e-mail riddled with poor grammar and errors, not to mention misspelling Colin's name...

Hi Beth,
I haven't forgotten about sending out the info to you. Collin gets paid on the 15th and the 1st of every month. So from what your telling me he is getting paid his last check was for 15 May and now you will see a deposit hit the bank on 1 June. I think your thinking it's every 2 weeks it's not.

I will be stopping in my office on Wednesday, I will put a packet together and get it out then, because I leave for FT Dix on Friday for a week I have 260 soldiers coming back from Iraq and I need to be there to assist the demobilization process. It's been a long year for me the soldiers and their families. It's nice to see it come to a final end...

I was shocked. How was my family any different than the 260 families that have been deployed? Yes, it has been a long year. FOR ME and MY CHILDREN, TOO. And I still had no formal briefing or the information I needed to know how to be a good Mom to my children while their Dad was gone.

Frankly, I didn't feel there was much needed at this point. I had found Pamela. And through trial and error, I was figuring out the single parenting with Dad at war. All I really wanted was some acknowledgement from my husband's Reserve unit that we actually existed.

***

Beth Jackson

No one reached out to us on Memorial Day. I was surprised at myself that I was so disappointed.

On the other hand, Colin sure heard something. From me. I e-mailed to say how proud we were of him and how much we loved him. The meaning of the holiday did not slip past me this year, as it often had in the past. I wondered, *was I forcing it?* Was it really fair to expect average citizens to think about Memorial Day and that it meant something more than just a long holiday weekend? I knew my whole life was centered on our family's unique situation at this special time, but I was also feeling a sense of shame that I had spent over four decades of my life not really paying tribute to those who served before us.

The day after the long weekend, I was scheduled to fly out of Providence for another business trip.

It was the second time I had flown since Colin left. This time my layover to North Carolina was in Atlanta. As I walked up to the gate in Providence, I realized this was the exact gate where we had said goodbye to Colin. He, too, had been on his way to Atlanta to begin his journey. That whole scene came back to me in a wave. I took a short breath and sat in a chair away from the windows. I did not want to sit where the children and I had held up our flags.

My trip was fast. By 6 the next evening, I started my journey back home, again via Atlanta. As I navigated my way through the terminal to my connecting flight, I saw a very moving scene.

As hundreds of travelers hustled by, an older man stopped a young woman who was dressed in her Army uniform. He shook her hand, and I could hear his words, "Thank you, ma'am, for your service. "

"I really appreciate that," she responded.

A stranger just saying thanks. Of course, once again, my throat tightened, and tears formed in my eyes. Instinctually, my hand rose up to my neck and found its place of comfort on that chip of topaz surrounded by the silver knot.

***

One night after dinner, the energy from the table quickly flowed outside onto the deck where the sunshine of this beautiful late spring day beamed down on us. Ian picked up the hula loop. Karl watered the tomato, blueberry, and raspberry plants that he insisted he would plant in the garden this weekend. He had planned to take over this responsibility, something Colin always did each year. And Thais just ran around in delight over finally being outside after a week of solid rain. I even recall hearing the birds singing to each other.

Suddenly the happiness halted. Thais yelled out, "My foot is bleeding!"

I looked down and saw a gaping ½ inch long cut covered with bright red blood. Quickly I scooped her up and brought her to bathroom just off the kitchen. I placed her on the counter and ran the water to warm up. She dropped her foot into the sink and soaked it while I washed the wound with soap. Once the blood was removed, it was clear that it was not a gaping hole but rather a very long splinter.

Leaving Thais on the bathroom counter, I ran upstairs to get tweezers. Scared of any word she did not know, she started crying for me not to use the "tweezers. "

I paused and started showing Thais how I plucked my eyebrows with the tweezers. There goes one. And other. Pluck. Pluck. Pluck. My distraction worked, and slowly she started giggling. But she still did not want me to touch her boo-boo with the foreign silver tool. So I gently touched a different toe with the tip, so she could feel it and know it did not hurt. But she squealed anyway, so I put the tweezers down. I finally used my fingernail to scrape at the end hoping that it would come out easily. Thais continued to squirm and squeal more from fear than pain. With a few quick swipes with my nail, most of the wooden splinter came out. *Phew!*

As Thais soaked her foot again, I started to clean up after dinner. Ian reluctantly emptied the dishwasher, only after my cajoling him with the reminder that his allowance was just not free money. After taking the garbage out, Karl returned to his homework.

No more than twenty seconds later, there was a loud high pitch crash sound. "Oh!" Ian screamed out.

A glass had slipped from his hand as he was transferring it to the cabinet, and it shattered into a thousand pieces.

I could have yelled like I did other times. I could have wept like I so badly wanted to. I could have just gotten up and walked out the front door, an escape I so badly craved. Instead, my body paused and my voice calmly said, "Don't move. "

I bent down and started the process of picking up the large pieces. When I saw the space behind Ian was clear, I guided him slowly backwards away from the microscopic shards. Methodically, I brushed the entire floor near where the glass had fallen into a dustpan. The clean up took a good thirty minutes. When I was done, air blew out from between my lips. Maybe I actually exhaled. It could have been worse.

Karl finished his work, a skit he had to write for Spanish class, and sent it from the downstairs laptop to print up in my office. Ian then used the computer to finish an autobiographical poem and sent it up to print as well. I went upstairs to get their printouts and read what they each had written. Karl's skit was a cute dialogue about ordering food in a restaurant; Ian's poem caught my breath.

Bio poem by: Ian

Ian
Happy, easy going, athletic
Sibling of Thais and Karl
Lover of the dark, radio, and Dad
Who feels in need of a father
Who needs water
Who gives toys to homeless
Who fears death itself
Who would like to see himself as a paratrooper
IJ

His words broke my heart.

Ian, my introverted love, did not talk much about his feelings, but given this forum, they came flowing out. As I struggled to be a good Mom, what he really needed was Dad.

I, too, was finding solace in words. But when my sister first read some of the journal I was keeping, she commented that it was simply a recording of events that included nothing about how I felt. She asked me, "How are you? How are you *feeling* in all of this?"

I didn't actually know at the time. I didn't allow myself to feel. I didn't have time to think. All I knew was I was depleted. I was scared. I felt alone.

I still had not been acknowledged by anyone in the official ranks of the military. *Was this really what happened?* A husband was plucked up from his home to protect his country's freedom, and no one even called to check in on how his spouse and family were doing?

Beth Jackson

However, whenever I caught myself in self-pity, I forced myself to remember that I was with the children. Dad was the one in Afghanistan, with shared showers, mess hall food, and ever present hypervigilance of needing to be prepared at any moment for a possible insurgent attack. He missed our every day life. And so did so many others.

Nevertheless, I very honestly continued to feel that my job was actually much harder than his. He was doing his job, which he signed up to do. I had mine delivered to me, and I was juggling multiple jobs on top of this new one. And the stress of all of this meant that the urgency of my raw emotions were more intense than any other situation I had personally experienced before. I felt I was moving inexorably toward crisis, and I worried about what I could become.

Chapter 9 – When the Animals Died

Early June 2011

Why is it that something always goes wrong when your husband is gone? I have caught my fair share of dead mice in the attic. And a dead mole in the pool. Each episode absolutely grossed me out, for the record.

So there I was. The third full moon of deployment had come and gone. I was working in my home office in the late afternoon, while the three children played around the house. At the particular moment, I was on a conference call with at least twenty people. While most of my clients knew I worked from home and that I had three children, some did not, and most definitely among them was the extended group that joined this particular call.

Well, with speakerphone on and me mid-sentence, in burst Ian with the loud proclamation, "The frogs are dead! They are all white!"

As quickly as he announced this, my finger dove for the mute button. I turned around and looked at his wild eyes of shock and sadness. I gave him a hug and responded gently that we would give them a proper burial as soon as I finished my call, and that I would be down in just a few minutes. When the mute button was relieved, I explained the drama to the group, and thankfully, all replied with sympathy.

After my call ended, I began the three-hour long process of burying the frogs and cleaning the tank. First, I had to get a utensil that was large enough to scoop them out without squishing them. Tongs? No, too squishy. A spoon? Too small. A soup ladle? Yes, perfect.

Beth Jackson

But as I carried the white plastic ladle downstairs to the basement playroom where the tank was, practical Karl shook his head, "We make pancakes with that one, Mom!"

So I found an acceptable larger spoon instead that would itself eventually meet the garbage can. And I gathered two plastic bags, you know, the kind that cover the newspaper in the morning, along with a small box from Amazon that had once contained a book. I scooped and I dropped. I twisted and I tied. I inserted and I taped. OK, the cardboard coffin was ready.

Next it was time for the burial. Shovel in hand, we proceeded to the far side of the lawn near the big pine trees. Three little children followed me like the Pied Piper. I put the coffin down on the ground and grabbed the shovel with two hands.

Thrust down. Bounce. The shovel simply bounced off the dirt. It had not rained in days, and the ground was very, very dry. *Let's try it again.* I grabbed the shovel with both hands and thrust it down again, this time at a better angle. Bounce.

Oh, crap. This was going to be much, much harder than I had imagined.

So I put the shovel in place and stepped up onto the edges. I had seen others do this before with great success. It just needed my body weight to help cut through the dirt.

I stood on those edges and jumped. Oh, I think I felt something. Maybe an eighth of an inch of movement into the ground? *Oh, let's try again.* So on and on I jumped. Like a pogo stick. Ever so slowly a hole was dug through. I was panting and sweating by the time I finished and sure wished I had chosen a smaller box.

Finally, I called the children over, we said goodbye to their beloved froggies, and we traipsed back inside together.

Once the burial was complete, the task of cleaning out the tank was next. This tank was not that small, by the way.

I was so grossed out by the idea of dead frogs being in this tank, I wore rubber gloves and scooped the water out with a disposable plastic cup and a bucket. Scooping and scooping. Carrying the water bucket outside and dumping it. Over and over again. At least fifty times.

At some point during this process, my cotton skirt rubbed against the edge of a shelf and started falling off my bony hip. Both of my hands were covered in gloves that in turn were covered with dead frog juice. My undies were showing. And I had to walk outside to dump more water again. But I did not want to touch my undies with the gross gloves. So I jimmied the edge of my cotton skirt against my elbow and the wall to slip it just back above my pointy hip bone. It was quite a sight. Organized chaos or dysfunctional insanity? Your call.

A week later on a sunny June day as I drove my car onto the ramp of a highway, a white seagull suddenly flew in front of my car. I still remember how startled I was as it seemingly appeared out of nowhere, just a white blur. I was unable to maneuver the heavy vehicle quickly enough to avoid it, and my bumper hit and instantly killed the bird with a thud.

I caught my breath as the car continued onto the highway, and my heart hurt. I had never killed anything bigger than an ant or fly before, and I felt horrible. Death took on a whole new meaning to me this year, and the fact I killed something undid me.

Then the dying continued, as our beloved fifteen-year-old Vizsla dog, Lilly, who had been living with Gramp ever since we came back East, passed away quietly. And I had to send the news to Kabul.

Beth Jackson

Colin,
Your Dad just called. Lilly died. She had a stroke yesterday late
afternoon, and was put to sleep shortly thereafter. Your Dad is going
to bury her in Annapolis. He says she was truly a wonderful gift.
I love you,
Me

Chapter 10 – Not in a Groove

Mid June 2011

So everyone kept talking about the "groove" to me. "Are you in a groove now?" I don't think so. "New normal" is not a "groove." Maybe our friends were in a groove more than I was. When I sent out e-mail updates to our family and friends, I only heard from five people on any given update. The distribution list had grown to about 90 people, so did that mean only 6% of our loved ones were actually thinking of Colin and us at any given time? I know that was not the case, but at the time it felt that way.

The offers of help randomly would come, but mostly from people I had not seen since Colin left. And they were usually just the vague, "Let me know how I can help." After a while, most offers of help faded away to nothing.

Except from those special few friends who just kept doing. To drive one of the children home from a practice. To hang up in our garage the car luggage rack from last winter's ski trip. To pump the tires on the children's bikes. In times like this it became really clear which friends I could count on.

So, no, I was not in a groove. Unless losing my mind with percolating fear passed for a groove.

One Friday night, Karl had an away lacrosse game in East Greenwich. Rather than juggling yet another evening dinner and multiple sport commitments or paying more for our sitter to stay until 9, I e-mailed Ian's soccer coach excusing him from practice.

Beth Jackson

"We move in a pack," I exclaimed as we began our 50-minute drive to the field. My car pulled into the parking lot exactly on time, and Karl scurried out of the car with his gear and stick to join his team.

A few minutes later, Ian, Thais, and I made our way. As we approached, we noticed the slow procession of fans around the perimeter of the field. The main gate was locked, so we had to walk half way around the fence that surrounded the track and turf field in order to enter by the other gate, and then half way around again to get to the bleachers on the other side of the field. Thais insisted on walking on her own, so we took our leisurely time to walk the quarter mile. Eventually, we climbed up the bleachers and laid out an armful of blankets to sit on.

The irony of the event was Colin's absence. He had been the team's coach each year, but now he was working sixteen hour days, seven days a week, far, far away in a war zone. All he did literally was sleep, eat, and work - without a break, except for the daily work-outs. I knew how much he would have loved to be on that lacrosse field instead.

Thais quickly left our spot on the bleachers in search of something more fun. The name of the school, East Greenwich, was painted in huge capital letters on the ground just at the base of the bleachers. So we started playing a game where I would call out a letter, and she would go stand on it. I would call out another, and she would look around and run to the next one.

A short while later, the lacrosse game started. There I was, sitting on the bleachers ready to watch Karl play. Ian was still with me in the stands, though growing bored.

By this point, Thais had stripped off her shoes and was enjoying running around on the side of the field. Then she called out, "I need new pants. These got wet from the grass. "

Not wanting to miss Karl's game, I asked Ian if he would run back to the car to see if there was an extra pair of sweatpants or a towel there. He was thrilled to have something to do and obligingly took the car keys. My eyes followed him as he made his way around the track, out the gate, and around again to the parking lot. But then I lost him. Our car was hidden several rows back.

The minutes passed by as Thais continued running around on the letters and Karl ran around on the field. And more time passed. I stood up expecting to see Ian's return, but I did not see him. I could barely see the top of our car shielded behind the others. And as my eyes followed the path back from where he went, I still did not see him.

He is ok, just reading in the car. I hoped.

And another minute or two ticked by.

But what if someone just took him? My irrational thoughts started circling the drain that was my brain. *I could not lose Ian. What else could go wrong in our life right now?*

I stood up again. No Ian in sight.

Two more minutes passed. I was restless.

I was suddenly reminded of the time in 2008 when I lost Ian in the shopping mall. Colin and Karl were going into Target. Ian was following me as I carried Thais, then a toddler, into the Apple store. I turned around, and Ian was nowhere to be found. I screamed at the top of my lungs, through my raspy nasal cold of winter that distorted the sounds of my words. I ran out to the hallway and back into the Apple store. Out and in. Again and again. People just stared at me as I frantically called out Ian's name over and over again, unsure of where to go first and how to find my child. Finally

Beth Jackson

I got some sense and yelled, "He is six! Blond hair!" My face was
stricken.

As it turns out, Ian had changed his mind and had run after Colin and
Karl to join them in the Target store, but he had not told me. He had just
slipped away silently. Colin heard my delirious screams from a hundred
yards away, and the three of them found their way to me before I totally
melted down. It was the most frantic moment I had ever had in my whole
life.

Back at the lacrosse stands, there still was no sign of Ian. Finally,
I had to go. I scooped Thais up, put her on my back, and scooted
quickly around the track and out the gate.

Several minutes later arriving by the car, the door started opening.
It was Ian. With a book in his hand. Happy as a clam.

"Honey, please don't stay out here all by yourself," I said with love.
"I was worried about you. This parking lot is too far from the
stands, so I don't want you to linger here. "

As a pack of three, we made our way back, across the parking lot,
around the fence, around the track, and back up the stands again. I
felt more comfortable with all of my children in sight.

***

Without me asking, two of Colin's friends went out of their way to
include the boys in boy activities. One had invited Ian to quarry
rock at the river as part of a Providence Museum outing. Another,
Karl's lacrosse coach, brought Karl along to a college lacrosse
tournament. I was grateful for such manly influences.

When Karl was gone for his full day lacrosse outing, though, Ian's
jealousy reached its peak. Upon his brother's return, all three

children started bickering over everything and nothing. Karl was only half trying not to brag about the fun day he'd had, and he also started pushing back against my request that he empty the dishwasher. Ian was grabbing toys from Thais, and accusing Karl of gloating. And Thais was spent for the day, cranky, overtired, and ready to go to sleep. The banter grew in volume. And energy. And volume.

Finally, I just yelled, "STOP IT." The children looked at me for a second to see if I really meant it. I could feel the heat bubbling inside of me. But rather than letting it explode again, I somehow kept it together enough to say with a firm no-nonsense voice, "SIT DOWN ON THE FLOOR – RIGHT WHERE YOU ARE!"

Slowly. Quietly, they each sat down on the wood floor of the kitchen and watched me. I lowered my voice and said, "I hate to yell. But why is it that yelling is the only thing that gets through to you? All of you are just bugging each other. Just let it go – and please help until we have dinner."

Ian was the first to raise his hand. Yep. His hand rose as he sat on the floor in silence.

I let out a giggle, and he responded in kind.

"Yes?" I asked with a wry smile.

"Can we get up now?" Ian asked coyly.

The ice was broken. Harmony was restored again. At least for a few minutes.

***

Beth Jackson

Plan Fun included family nights when our schedule was free of the children's activities and we nestled at home for an evening of games, a movie, or charades. Often, ice cream sundaes made an appearance those nights, too.

One Friday, the Boston Bruins were playing in Game 7 of the Eastern Division Championship against Tampa Bay. Whoever won this game would play for the Stanley Cup.

The children, Charlotte, and I snuggled on the decade old couch, our eyes glued to the TV. Goalies from both teams moved with exceptional fluidity, saving unbelievable shots. And then the scoreless tie was broken in the final period when the Bruins scored. We were so excited. The sugar kick from our ice cream added to our joyful cheers.

After I got the kids to sleep, I went back downstairs to clean up. My right hand turned on the black plastic knob of the kitchen faucet to rinse the ice cream bowls. As I pulled on the knob back to the left to turn it off, I felt a crack reverberate through my fingers. The water continued to rush out of the faucet at full speed. My eyes zoomed in on the knob and could not miss the tiny fissure that had appeared. Water was erupting everywhere, like a spraying geyser.

Panic. How could I turn the water off? Sweating and mumbling under my breath - okay, maybe swearing under my breath, too - I wiggled the lever back and forth to see if I could get the broken piece to catch on the inner valve that had to move to stop the flow. It felt like minutes with all that rushing water soaking my arm and face, but it was probably only seconds before the lever somehow caught the edge of the valve, and the water stopped. *Phew!*

The clock read 11:32 p. m. After wiping down the mess, I went straight to bed, but it took a while for my heart to slow to a normal pace.

In the morning, I called the handyman who had helped with the flag holder, and over the phone he told me where to find the turn-off knobs under the sink in case the water went off again. After I pulled out all plastic grocery bags stuffed into every nook and cranny under the sink, I finally found the knobs. Who would have thought there were water valves under the sink? I didn't. Colin always handled the home improvement details. I felt like an idiot.

The handyman also suggested a local plumbing supply store nearby to buy a new faucet and indicated that he would come by Tuesday to replace it.

So for the next few days, we used paper plates, and we washed what we had to - pots and pans - with bowls of water that I carried from the bathroom sink. It was a very manual process. But like all the other little things that had gone wrong - from the flagpole to the animals - I was grateful that things were not worse.

***

Every year, we hosted an end of school year pool party. Early summer in Rhode Island was not always guaranteed to be terribly warm, but with our pool heater in full gear, the children happily swam all afternoon long.

In years past, I hosted two parties. One for Karl's class, one for Ian's. Often they were consecutive afternoons. This year, with Thais now in nursery school as well, in fairness to her, I hosted three parties.

In my typical ease of party planning, I asked each of the moms to bring salad, dessert, or beverages, and I provided paper goods and ordered five pies from the local pizzeria. I hired a college girl to be the lifeguard, and Dana focused one-on-one on Thais, who could not yet swim.

Beth Jackson

For three afternoons in a row, all fortunately with sun and warm temperatures, over 40 children ran around our yard, swung on our wooden swing and ladder tied to a maple tree, and splashed in the pool. The moms watched and occasionally handed out a dry towel. Clean-up was a simple process of collecting any uneaten food and paper plates and dumping them into a big plastic garbage bag. Lickity split.

The contrast of our poolside life to Colin's life in Kabul was stark. One of my friends and family e-mail updates included tidbits Colin had recently shared with me.

Afghanistan is an underdeveloped barren country of mountains. The settlements follow the rivers, as irrigation is very limited in scale. A key goal of the NATO work there is to build a road that would connect different settlements, so goods and services could flow more easily. The electricity is not always consistent, and garbage removal is done by donkey cart.

Colin says that the NATO base where he is stationed has a lot of character. Most people working there speak fluent English, but not all. The Euro is the main currency for the two "convenience stores"

- one run by Brits and the other by Germans, so all personal care products that Colin buys are from either of those two countries.

The various nationalities have "houses" where they occasionally host BBQs on a Sunday night. As Colin described, these "houses" are more like tree houses with shipping containers stacked on top of each other in an asymmetrical fashion. During any of these events, all nationalities (except those with religious reasons) are allowed to drink alcohol, except the Americans.

Hygiene has different interpretations by country. Colin and his roommate are in a room next to two officers from a country that doesn't believe in showers (or none that he has witnessed or olfactory proof of such).

The air quality there is really an issue. Colin exercises inside to try to avoid sucking in the pollution when running, but he did mention that Australians who serve there for six months or more are given disability for life because of long-term lung issues.

***

Looking back now, I see that I was overcompensating and overdoing. My objective: this year was going to be a year of fun, damn it. And wanting so badly to achieve that, I kept up my extracurricular focus around Plan Fun. Next stop: Disney. With a 40% discount for Active military families, this was an affordable luxury I knew would delight the children.

When packing for the trip, this time I double-checked our suitcases to make sure each of us had undies and PJs. I wanted to bring a favorite summer cover-up as well, but for some reason I just could not find it. I spent nearly an hour walking around the house, searching through my closet, Colin's closet, the children's closets, the suitcases from our March trip, and in the laundry room. Everywhere. But I could not find it. Then on my third pass through my closet, I found it on the top of a pile in plain sight. I started to think my mind was messing with me.

Beth Jackson

The day we were to leave for Orlando, Florida, all was ready, but the logistics had made my head swim. Part of the planning involved what to do with Charlotte. With our five-day trip to Disney, an upcoming ten-day visit to Michigan to be with my family over the Fourth of July, and a possible two-week mid-deployment R&R with Colin (still unconfirmed), I worried about putting our elderly thirteen-year-old dog into the kennel for what would amount to over a month. Then Gramp stepped forward with an offer to take Charlotte for the summer - something that would also help fill the void over his recent loss of Lilly. "Camp Gramp" was a win for everyone.

To get Charlotte to Gramp, she was scheduled to fly out of the cargo terminal of Boston Logan to Dulles in Washington, D. C. several hours before our flight to Florida. Everything was organized: crate, bottle of water, leash. Then the airline deemed her crate too small, so she could not fly. A rush trip to the pet store followed and luckily we were able to rebook her on the next flight. After checking her in at the cargo terminal, we proceeded to the main terminal.

After parking, we began our trek of mom, three children, four roller suitcases, and four carry-on bags. Thais had fallen asleep in the car and wanted to be carried, which normally was fine, except when I was already pulling and carrying four bags on my weakening frame. Now with a child hanging off me, those 30 yards to the terminal entrance felt like a mile. I momentarily wondered if all this effort for Plan Fun was really worth it.

The line to security was gratefully short. As experienced fliers, the children each started the process of removing shoes, putting their bags on the conveyor, and pulling out coins from their pockets. Even little Thais insisted on doing it all herself, including putting her shoes in her own grey plastic bin. The boys walked through the x-ray machine first and began the process of collecting their things. I encouraged Thais to go next, but she wanted me to go first, so I obliged and immediately turned around to face her to call her towards me.

"Is Dad coming, too?" the security man asked, unsure if any of the other men in the line behind us belonged to us.

"No, he is in Afghanistan," I replied mildly.

Shocked by my answer, he did not say anything. But I noticed all of the security people around us instantly seemed even more helpful than they had been just a few seconds later. Nothing else was said, but I thought about how their job and my husband's were all focused on the same goal. I thanked them, as we continued on our way to the gate.

When we arrived in Florida, there was a voicemail from Gramp. Expecting to hear that he had Charlotte, I instead heard his worried voice, "Beth, do you know where Charlotte is? The flight seems to be delayed several hours. " My phone was on its last legs, and the battery was dying even as I charged it. The stress was unimaginable until I was able locate Charlotte and get confirmation from my father-in-law that she finally had arrived safely.

These past months had been as long as they had been fun. But the distractions I had created for the children, and myself, worked only so far. My worry over Charlotte and always, that fear-inducing obsession with Google alerts, still followed me to Florida. *Was I trying too hard? Doing too much?* Yes, but I had no perspective then.

***

After we returned from Disney and the fourth full moon was shining bright against the pitch-black sky, I had a truly delusional moment. Colin had told me that his General had asked him to attend a meeting with the locals, dressed as Dr. Jackson, the professor, rather than as an Army officer. I had no idea the subject of such a meeting, or who would be in attendance, and I just assumed it regarded some basic daily coordination or ongoing goodwill outreach. Since all Colin had was BDUs (battle dress uniforms), he went into Kabul to have a tailored suit made. And then he met with the locals, I presumed without his weapons.

And that thought warped my brain. While replaying the phone call in my mind, something snapped, and I started surfing the Internet, looking for a specific statistic. Click. Click. I found it.

A website that listed the fatalities of U. S. military servicemen in Afghanistan. Colin had been there since the end of March.
- In April, 46 died
- In May, 35 died
- In June, 47 died

That was three fatalities every two days. There were even more if you included contractors and foreign servicemen, if you really wanted to add it all up.

I knew I should not have been looking up these things, either - Meghan had warned me not to - but it was always on my mind. And technology made it so easy to know more than I should, frankly. But for some reason I wanted to know, to prepare myself. To lessen the eventual shock. Was it my way of coping?

Well-meaning friends told me, "He is just as likely to get killed in a car crash over here. " Or "The odds are not that bad. " I found such comparisons ridiculous, and in truth they made me feel worse. Several days had passed since I last heard from my husband when I thought I would. No phone call. No e-mail. Nothing. My cell phone rested in my sweaty palm at all times, and every hour or so, my eyes kept peeking out the front window in fear that that black car would pull up with two strange men, one a chaplain. Every single day.

The reality was that a war zone was not the same as a random streak of lightening or car accident. It was not the same as living on the wrong side of town somewhere here in the U. S. There was a reason Colin's life insurance premiums increased quite significantly when he deployed to Afghanistan. The insurance companies have done the math about the likelihood of an adult male dying in a war.

Chapter 11 – The Crash

Late June 2011

My Google alert came predictably into my inbox just after 11 p.
m. The four words of one headline were brutal, "Attack on Hotel
Intercontinental. "

My finger immediately clicked on the link, and I proceeded to read
about how a number of suicide attackers (later confirmed to be nine)
broke through the security at the hotel. One suicide bomber exploded
himself at the back guard while the others slipped into the kitchen and
stormed the hotel. It took one thousand Afghan troops over four hours
to secure the building. Eventually a NATO helicopter and Special
Forces team were brought in to help bring the episode to a close.

I had no reason to think Colin would be at the hotel, but I never
knew. He had been out into the city and met with Afghans
regularly. Nevertheless, my mind raced to places where it should
not have gone.

The children and I were at my parents' house in Michigan for ten
days before the long Fourth of July weekend. The children were fast
asleep, but I walked into my parents' room and asked if they knew
about the hotel. They told me yes, that they had been debating
whether or not to tell me. My actions recently did not make that
answer easy for them.

Just two nights prior, Carrie, who also came in town, and I had been
talking with my parents over dinner while the children played in the
yard.

Beth Jackson

"How is Colin?" my mom began. I had talked with him earlier that day, and she sincerely wanted to know how he was.

"Fine. Tired. "

"How is his work affected by the announcement of the surge troop withdrawal?" she continued.

"I don't know. We don't really talk about the details of his job. "

"Has the new General taken over there yet?" She would not give up.

"I don't know. Soon I think, but I don't follow the specifics. Our conversations are quite limited, so I don't have many details to share. "

This peppering of questions about things I didn't know was irritating me. I was not the expert on these things. Colin was. When I spoke with him, all I really cared about was hearing his voice, asking what he may need us to send him, and other basics of just staying connected. I didn't ask about policy and strategy or the particulars of his job. I didn't know anything more about the bigger issues surrounding Afghanistan than what anyone else heard on the news. And honestly, I did not want to talk about it.

My sister sensed my fatigue and shifted slightly in her chair. She always has a good instinct for people, and I could tell she was thinking of ways to turn the conversation. But before she could, my mom sighed and asked, "When will the killing season end?"

I was speechless. My mom had no idea that this question, the kind you might hear at a cocktail party when discussing politics, was absolutely the wrong thing to ask a woman with a husband in that war zone.

"Do you want to change subject?" my sister quickly interjected.

"YES," I blurted out. And then I faced my mom, "Please don't ask me about the killing season. Think about that question. I really don't want to think about things like that. "

Conversation killer.

So when the news of the hotel attack surfaced, my parents were reluctant to tread on any sensitive ground, so they stayed quiet. "Walking on eggshells" around me, my mom called it. She wanted so badly to help me, but she became scared to say or do anything wrong around me.

I told them it was good they had not told me. I didn't need more information about things that might be scary to me, at times when I was not ready for it. I had my trusted Google to do that in a more objective, predictable way.

For the record, it was another two days before I heard an e-mail reply back from Colin. Since we were in Michigan during this period of silence, I thought about how those two men in a black car were going to track me down to tell me of horrible news if I were not home in Rhode Island. Would they have knocked on neighbor's doors asking about my whereabouts? Would they go to the next family in line to inform them first before me? Would they contact Colin's parents? I did send his parents a note to see if they had heard anything, and they called to reassure me everything was probably fine.

Probably.

When I heard directly from Colin, I breathed in a fresh gulp of air.

That night, I had to fly out to New Jersey for a one-day meeting with a client.

Beth Jackson

The client knew I was on vacation, but their fiscal quarter ended June 30, and they needed to use up their marketing budget before the end of the month. I agreed to meet with them for a handsome fee and their full knowledge that my billable travel costs would be higher than normal since I would be flying in from Detroit.

Leaving Wednesday night, I was scheduled to be gone for two nights. My parents were ready to hold down the fort and care for my three children. The boys were in a Robotics camp across town for most of the day, and Thais was in a little day camp in the mornings just down the road from their house. My mom had also arranged for a high school babysitter to come in the afternoon, so she had the help of a younger set of hands around. My parents were almost 70, and their energy was not quite what it had been. I knew they were doing me a big favor.

Everything was fine on Wednesday night. I spoke briefly with Thais before she and my mom went to a friend's house for dinner. My dad had taken the boys to attend a Detroit Tiger's baseball game.

On Thursday morning, I called to touch base before my work started. All three children were happily off to camp. That afternoon, during a work break, I checked my e-mails. Nothing from Colin and nothing significant from my other clients. I turned off the phone and slid it into my black bag for the rest of the session.

Oblivious, I had no idea that the protective fortress around my children had collapsed at 4:10 p. m. I did not learn of this for two hours, when I was in a taxi on the way to the Philadelphia airport.

Relaxing my shoulders from the long-working day, I sat back into the seat and pulled out my phone.

Three missed calls from my dad. I clicked on voicemail and struggled to hear the low recording of his message. Later I learned he had been whispering in the hospital corridor.

"Ian... accident.... He is.... At hospital.... Call my cell. "

I quickly replayed the message again to better hear the missing words, but to no avail.

All hairs on my body were on instant alert. My heart started racing and my fingers were shaking as I quickly dialed my Dad.

"Is Ian OK?" I asked breathlessly. "What happened?"

"He was hit by a car. "

Time stopped. I was in a silent chamber of this taxi. I heard nothing. No sounds of the tires on the road. No engine. No radio. Not even the breathing of the taxi driver. And of course no sound from me, as I held my breath.

Hit by a car. Hit by a car. The four words repeated themselves in my head.

"They have been doing Cat-scans and examinations of his body. He is OK. "

I barely heard the rest of what my Dad told me. Something around the doctors being very cautious, so they had not yet removed the neck brace until all the tests come back...

Neck brace. Neck brace.

And that he had pain in his right leg, so they were doing scans and x-rays of his leg as well... that he had cuts on his face and chin...

"Can I talk to him?" I pleaded with my Dad.

Beth Jackson

He paused. "He is getting a Cat-Scan right now. And the cell phones don't work very well in his room. I am out in the hallway right now," he explained.

"Is there a landline in his room?" I asked, not giving up.

"Yes, but Ian is a little woozy. They gave him some morphine for the pain. And the neck brace and oxygen tubes make it hard to reach his face. "

Oxygen tubes. Oxygen tubes.

HOW CAN I GET TO MY SON? I wanted to scream.

My dad e-mailed me this picture, unaware of the power of an image, with Ian in traction and worry spread across the faces of Karl and Thais.

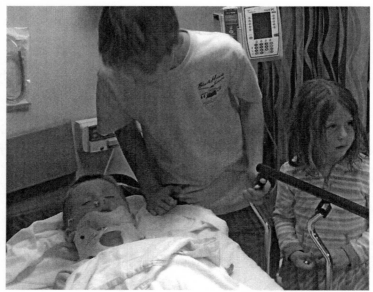

Ian in traction at the hospital with Karl & Thais

My mind reeled.

I felt helpless.

Nauseous.

Alone.

The sound of a thump beat in my right ear.

As my technology-impaired dad figured out how to send a picture from his phone for the very first time, he also typed the e-mail addresses of my three siblings and Colin. When I received this e-mail and saw that Colin had been copied, I was livid. Besides being unable to protect Ian, I had also suddenly failed in protecting Colin from unnecessary distress. Months later, my dad apologized.

***

As I have heard the story from Ian, Karl, my mom, my dad, and the driver of the car, here is how the accident happened.

Ian and Karl had been dropped off at my parent's house after camp and were playing on the computer when my mom called. Karl answered.

"You guys have a tennis lesson right now, so run up to the country club. Thais and I are here. I have your tennis whites. "

"Okey-dokey," Karl said in his typical upbeat fashion.

The club was less than a block away. The boys opened the front door and started running. Karl and Ian liked to race, so Ian darted out in front.

It was 4:10 p. m. To the left of Ian was a large red landscaping truck parked on the street. There were no sidewalks. Ian, shielded completely by the truck's enormous height, ran in a full sprint straight into the street. Karl was fifteen feet behind and saw everything.

The driver of the car was on his way home from work as a bartender at the country club. He had worked at several parties for my parents, and my mother described him as "one of the nicest guys in the world."

The car was parallel with the landscaping truck when the driver heard something hit the side of his car hard. As he described this to me, I knew exactly what he meant by the thump sound. Startled, he looked to his right and saw Ian spinning away from the car. The rear view mirror had actually clipped Ian on the left side of his face, and the impact folded and shattered the mirror back towards the car. As Ian's right foot was planted in the sprint, the force of the mirror stopped his body and spun him clockwise, away from the car. By the grace of a mere second and something greater than I will ever understand, Ian missed being hit full throttle.

I still don't know who called 911, but several adults attended to Ian as Karl ran the remaining quarter mile down the road to the country club to get my mom. As she pulled up to the scene, four police cars were already there. She saw the truck and car and heard the siren of the ambulance. My mom ran over to Ian, who was surrounded by the policeman keeping him still and talking to him.

A fifth police car and the ambulance arrived within seconds. The EMTs immediately put a brace on his neck to immobilize him before they lifted him onto the stretcher.

As the EMTs worked on Ian, several of the policemen interviewed the driver, Karl, and other bystanders about what had happened.

Before my mom climbed into the back of the ambulance, she walked up to the driver, clearly beside himself with shock, remorse, and fear, and gave him an enormous hug. There was nothing he could have done to prevent what had happened. All of the policemen watched this touching moment with their jaws dropped open.

A policeman drove Karl and Thais to the hospital, following behind the ambulance. Thais told me all about the sounds on his walkie talkie.

When Ian and my mom arrived at the hospital, eight doctors and nurses from the Trauma team pounced around Ian. My dad arrived at the hospital shortly thereafter. Around 5:45 p. m. , he made his first call to my unresponsive cell phone.

***

Now that my dad had reached me, I went into action mode. I tried to find any flight out that night (negative), but also spoke with Ian's doctor (mostly positive). He told me that all of Ian's test had come back fine except for his leg. He had two breaks in his right leg – the tibia and fibula. Buckle breaks, he called them.

"What are buckle breaks?" I asked for clarification as I was still processing the idea that Ian was hit by a moving vehicle and was being treated by a trauma team.

"Buckle breaks. Like the buckle of a belt. "

"The tibia is quite a strong bone," the doctor continued, "but when there is significant enough force, the bone can buckle on itself. That is what happened to his leg. There is significant swelling in the area, so we may hold off casting it for a few days. But I would like to have a pediatric orthopedic trauma surgeon look at it for a second opinion, so we are going to transfer Ian to Beaumont Royal Oak Hospital where those experts are. "

I was processing all the information. I was not able to see Ian's face or see the swelling or see the films, so I was just listening as intently as I could to every word the doctor said. He had said *"the tests were fine."* Right? He said *"fine,"* didn't he?

"And there are no pediatric orthopedic trauma surgeons where you are?" I asked.

"No," he replied. "I am the ER orthopedic doctor, but I want a pediatric specialist to look at it. "

With a child, there were extra worries about a break that was close to the growth plate. I felt helpless. Of course I was going to go with the doctor's recommendation.

"OK," I said cautiously.

My dad then got on the phone and told me, "We have called our friend, Dr. Lee, the best of the best of pediatric ortho surgeons. He does not typically operate in this hospital, but he is a family friend and we are going to ask him to come by for an opinion before we transfer Ian. The ambulance is waiting, but we have asked it to wait 45 minutes. "

What could I say? I had to let go and trust that the doctors and my parents would make the best decisions for Ian.

Phone calls back and forth continued every time my parents had an update.

Unfortunately, it would not be until the next morning before the next flight to Detroit. I tried to focus on how calm the doctor sounded.

I texted my sister.

> *Ian has been hit by a car. He is OK. I will call you as soon as I eat something. XO*

She immediately replied.

I am here.

I did not realize it at the time, but looking back, I see that she was sending me a tiny message of faith. "I am here."

As I sat alone trying to force myself to eat something, waiting and beyond worry, I just wanted to cry. I called Carrie from my table. I was so lonely and scared. And helpless. I needed to talk to her. It was so comforting to hear her voice. My armor was gone. I was bleeding guilt.

I had to do something. I asked Carrie to send me back one of my friends & family e-mail updates. I knew Ian would need a pediatric orthopedic surgeon back in Rhode Island, so I wrote a note to all my Rhode Island friends explaining briefly what happened and asking for referrals.

I spoke to my parents again, just as Ian was going into surgery with Dr. Lee. Then I watched the clock. Minute after minute passed. Watching. Waiting. Willing time to move forward.

Half an hour later, the phone rang and I learned that the surgery went well, but that Ian was still asleep from the "conscious sedation."

I had already tried to reach Colin to tell him what happened. I sent an e-mail to both his personal and military e-mail addresses, but with the 9 ½ hour time difference, I knew he was probably asleep, and I had no idea when he would have access to check his e-mail.

Without any chain of command contact information, I did not know how else to contact Colin. Every communication we had had in the last four months was on his time and at his initiative. I did not have the phone number of anyone in the Army, anywhere. At

Beth Jackson

the suggestion of a retired military friend on my e-mail list, I called
The Red Cross.

As I learned at that time, The Red Cross was the only way for
military families to communicate emergency information to a
serviceperson. If, for any reason, there were a life or death situation,
only a message from The Red Cross would allow the service person
to fly home for emergency leave. As we already knew Ian was
going to be OK, there was no need for Colin to come home, but
I desperately wanted him to know what had happened as soon as
possible. Frankly, I needed him, his calm, and his voice.

I had never called The Red Cross for any purpose before, but I
looked online and dialed the number listed. Somehow, I had all
the information they needed. Colin's social security number,
APO address, rank, Ian's location, name and phone number of the
hospital.

I told the woman at The Red Cross what had happened. My request
was specific: just to pass along a message. I was not asking for
emergency leave.

The Red Cross had a process to verify the emergency. They
called the hospital, and, contrary to what the hospital staff had
previously told me, The Red Cross was told that Ian was going to be
discharged later that night. Ten minutes later The Red Cross called
me back. The good news was that they did not deem Ian's accident
a current state of emergency anymore; the bad news was that they
would therefore not pass along any information to anyone.

I felt like I had truly failed as a Mom, unable to protect my child.
I was unable to be with Ian when he needed me. I was filled with
guilt and loneliness. I finally turned the light out in my hotel room
in an attempt to shut off my brain, for just a short while. But I
kept replaying the awful scene of what had happened in my mind.
My phone chimed just before midnight with a text from my mom

that they were discharged. What the hell was the hospital doing releasing my nine-year-old boy at that late hour when he had just been hit by a car, was still in pain, groggy from medication, and could not even stand to pee? *Were they mad?* I sure was.

A faceless dark weight seeped throughout my body, pushing out silent tears. Sleep finally overwhelmed me, for a few scant hours, until the sound of the alarm at 4:20 a. m. woke me. It was time to catch my flight home.

Back at my parent's house by 8:50 a. m. , I gently squeezed a sleeping Ian's hand as I studied his injuries. His face was beaten up and chin was all red, where it had been bleeding the day before. Hints of a black eye were appearing.

He lay perfectly still on the couch with his leg carefully elevated on two pillows. The only visible movement was his chest gliding up and down with each breath. Ian was such a strong boy, but at this moment his body looked so small, and fragile. The sight was wrenching for me. I gently kissed his cheek and rubbed my thumb on his hand. His body responded to my touch, as he mumbled, "I am OK. " He was still on codeine and very sleepy.

Minutes later, Colin opened the e-mails from the night before. It was afternoon his time. He called my cell phone in a panic. Thankfully, I was able to reassure him. We both felt immeasurably better knowing I was now at Ian's side.

Mid-morning, my dad drove Karl to his Robotics camp for his last day, while my mom, Thais, and I took Ian to Dr. Lee's office. Getting there was a feat in itself. First, I helped Ian hobble to the car, get in, and arrange his body sideways so he could keep his leg up and flat across the seat, while still being able to use a seatbelt.

At the doctor's office, I went inside to get a wheelchair and brought it back out to Ian. It took minutes and several different tries for him to inch his way out of the car, turn, and then sit back into the wheelchair, without touching his leg in any way that caused pain. My mom carried the crutches in, and Thais helped me push the wheelchair.

The rest of the day was a test of patience. Another x-ray. New cast. Monitoring the swelling. A cast could cause a clot, so this was an important precaution, especially since we would be flying back home. Oh, and the cast could not get wet. We needed a plastic sleeve, and a nurse gave us instructions on how to shower. No baths. Couldn't risk the leg dropping into water. Ian would need a seat for stability, something solid that could fit in the shower.

Last night the hospital had discharged Ian with crutches that did not fit him. The handles were too high, the height too low. It was impossible to move with them, so my mom had had to virtually carry him to the bathroom in the middle of the night last night when he had to go. And the doctor indicated that Ian had to keep this leg immobilized anyway. He needed to be in a wheelchair. The crutches, which the nurse now helped to adjust properly, were only for those occasional couple feet in a non-handicap accessible bathroom.

Finally, with a prescription in hand, we drove to the medical rental facility a few miles away. Signed in. Waited again. Talked with a woman. Waited. Waited some more. Patience. After two hours, we finally had our wheelchair.

***

Our return to Rhode Island was still a couple days away, but I began to think about the enormity of movement it would require to get back home. Ian still could not move any part of his body without pain, and I thought this was going to be like having a newborn all over again, but one weighing 70-something pounds!

That night I helped Ian take a shower.

First step was to bring my parent's plastic lawn chair inside the house and through several rooms down the hallway to the first floor shower. I gathered three towels. The cast HAD to stay dry. My hands carefully opened the plastic sleeve that we had purchased at the doctor's office.

I helped Ian undress as he sat on the daybed just outside the bathroom. Gave him a hand towel to cover his privates. Together, we then pulled the plastic sleeve over his cast. The trick was not to jiggle his leg in any direction that would be painful for him. Every step was slow and careful. It was actually more meticulous than bathing a newborn for the first time.

Once we got him into the shower, he shampooed and soaped up enough to call it clean. My arm reached in to turn the shower off, while turning my head so he felt he had privacy. I accidently doused my sweater arm. I handed him a dry towel and offered my other arm as he hobbled over the lip of the shower.

Only a gallon or two of water was on the floor outside of the shower when we were done. Hopefully the caulking around the tiles was good to avoid any flooding. Clearly we would have to perfect our technique, but Ian was warm and clean and felt much better. I did, too, as I was finally able to be his Mom.

***

On Monday, we returned home after a relatively uneventful flight. We had given ourselves an extra hour at the airport and needed it. I had not realized how much I took for granted having a free hand. Balancing the carry-on bags on my shoulders, I pushed Ian's wheelchair, as Karl and Thais trailed behind.

Beth Jackson

Back home, I reconfigured all of Ian's summer plans. Sailing. Tennis. Ice hockey. Lacrosse. All cancelled. And maneuvering the local sandy beaches was going to be a challenge, so we would have to avoid those most of the summer. I tried to think how I could keep Ian busy, and I found a week-long photography camp at the Newport Art Museum in August. I e-mailed the camp to confirm the wheelchair would not be an impediment to the course's explorations of the Newport mansions. The reply was a genuine relief. Yes, Ian could join.

Friends had referred me to a fine pediatric orthopedist in Providence whom we now saw regularly. The handicap valet became our new friend. After seeing me struggle with the heavy wheelchair for a few seconds, he helped me pull it out from the back of my car. I realized I was going to have to figure out a more graceful way to heave this 40-pound awkward frame of metal to and fro.

I scurried around to the side door to help Ian out. It took a minute to guide him gently down off the car's ledge onto the pavement with the good leg, as the other leg stayed straight, and then around again until he could lower himself into the wheelchair. We did this several times until we had success.

Our first appointment confirmed the leg did not have to be reset. *Phew.* Then a week later, we repeated the same three-hour visit for another x-ray and another new cast. The good news was the bones were already starting to heal. And this new cast was waterproof, so showering would be easier. And, best of all, Ian could at least enjoy a bit more of the summer as he could now swim in our backyard pool.

The array of physical therapy and orthopedic surgeon appointments became yet another new part-time job. My work was squeezed in between these times, as Ian and I began to spend hours and hours of time together during his slow recovery.

One friend invited Ian on a weekly playdate with her son. The playdate, ironically, was to watch her son play ice hockey. If Ian's leg had been healthy, he would have joined on the ice, too. But Ian was thrilled just to have his boredom relieved. Any change of scenery, even to an ice cold rink with him in a wheelchair, was welcome. I welcomed it, too; it was also was one less child for me to entertain and feed one night a week.

What I really needed was to have a night off. No driving. No dinner clean up. No bedtime routine. No Google addiction. Nothing. After four months of this 365 day deployment, I was really, really tired. Just like my husband, I had not had a day off, or even a few hours since this began. I guess I could have called a babysitter and asked some girlfriends to join me for a night out, but I felt I already spent so much money on babysitting while I worked. And maybe I just wanted to go watch a movie by myself. In the dark. With no one with whom I had to converse. Just to be alone. In a different, calm, world for a few hours. I wanted to escape.

No responsibilities.
No fear. About Colin. Or the well-being of my children.
No bedtime stories when the eyelids were fighting gravity.
No mediating between the children about a toy.
No house or pee-drenched sheets to clean up.
No weeds to pull.
No fear.
No child to bathe.
No job.
No bills to pay.
No fear.

Just escape.

I was immediately pulled back to reality from this dream out of my deep love for our children. But this had been a hard year for them, and they were more emotionally needy than they had ever been.

Beth Jackson

So I felt stuck.

        Here.

                Exhausted.

    Guilty.

                        Overwhelmed.

This marathon was not even half way over, and I had not yet realized that I needed to change my pace.

Chapter 12 – Kindness of Strangers

July 2011

Once we got into the flow of our world with a one-footed Ian, things calmed down a little. My work was busy again, and the long days at my desk, spending time with Ian during his various appointments, and taking the children to their summer activities were frankly good distractions from thinking about my husband at war every second of every hour.

Then the children and I experienced a gift we would always remember – our little escape to the Operation Military Kids Family Camp at the University of Rhode Island. We arrived around 5:15 p. m. Friday night and were immediately greeted by three college-aged girls wearing bright red Operation Military Kids t-shirts. They had big smiles while waving red, white, and blue pom-poms and guiding to Weldin Hall. There we met our energetic team leader and several more young volunteers, who helped me unpack the car and carry our gear around the corner to the dormitory.

Ian wheeled himself with sure delight down the slight hill, while Karl, Thais, and I followed. We approached four tables staffed with more volunteers who registered us, gave us room keys and meal passes, and helped the children make decorative pins with fun military stickers.

I saw a woman in a bright purple Operation Military Kids t-shirt who wore the nametag Pamela Martin. I had not yet actually met her in person, so I approached her and just gave her a kiss on the cheek and said thank you. She had been our lifeline. She, of course, was the one that told me about the camp, and that was why we were there. Pamela helped give me the strength to do what I needed to do for my children this year. More than just information, she also made me feel like I was someone. I counted. And so did my children. Standing next to her, I could not say anything more as my throat was rock hard.

After we got settled in our rooms, the children dropped their backpacks and ran back out to the action. Ian tried to keep up with his wheelchair. Karl came back a minute later with Thais in tow and markers, streamers, and tape in his hands to decorate the whiteboards on the outside of our dorm room doors.

They ran back upstairs to make more pins, and I just sat down in our dorm room for a minute to compose myself. I was so touched by the incredible outpouring of love and support for us from these strangers that I found myself just needing a moment to soak it all in. As the puddles continued to stream down both sides of my face, I texted my sister about this incredible kindness of strangers that just enveloped us. These strangers who then became our friends.

I could go on about how Pamela's husband took care of Ian with special golf cart rides, so his handicap would not keep him from any of the amazing activities. Or how the EMS driver friend drove Ian around at night because the golf cart did not have lights. Or how another Dad, who was recently home from Afghanistan, even offered to carry Ian "evacuation style" (i. e. fireman style), up a dirt path back to the dorm. And how Thais willingly went along in all of these rides, so I could peacefully walk back up the campus hill to our room without a heavy koala bear on my hip.

Of course the activities were all incredible, too. All three children LOVED each and every one of them, from kickball to photography to crafts. The staff gave instructions, hot-glued, passed around materials, propelled their creations, helped take pictures, and colored with each of them. I did not have to prepare anything; I could just participate as well. I had no responsibilities, only freedom.

During one moment as the boys were making space art with spray paint and safety goggles, Thais and I sat on the quad lawn. The sun was out, but there were enough clouds that the heat was not too strong. Another little girl came over to play with us. I asked her if she knew how to do a cartwheel, and then Thais, this little girl, and I started doing cartwheels and summersaults and handstands out on that lawn. Two young boys came and joined us as well.

Our next activity was yoga. At first my boys were skeptical, but when we entered the darkened room and sat down on our mats, the energy level quickly faded. Within just a minute of the stretching exercises, Thais came over to my mat. I asked if she wanted to lie on me, which she did. She rested her head just below my shoulder and locked her arms in mine. After a few minutes, she rolled off me onto the floor but continued holding me. Her breath slowed, and I knew she had fallen asleep.

My ears could hear the teacher's instructions, but my mind was not listening. Instead I focused on Thais's breathing and my own. My head turned to a more comfortable position. I could hear the boys' breathing as well, but they were in more of a controlled yoga pose, holding inhale and exhale releases.

As my breaths deepened, I, too, fell asleep right next to my little girl. Forty minutes later, the lights came on and Karl leaned over me, "Wake up, Mom!" Thais continued to nap, even as I scooped her up in my arms. The rest of the weekend continued in such incredible peace and acceptance.

We so enjoyed meeting the other families and children. We all exchanged e-mails and made plans to meet again soon. I personally now knew four other wives with husbands currently in Afghanistan. Before this weekend, I only knew one, Cara. And when the four of us joked about how each of us cried on Friday night when we first arrived, or how we communicated with our husbands on e-mail, or how we juggled work and caring for the children, there was a connection stronger than anything I had experienced before in my life.

***

Not long after our exhilarating family camp weekend, a friend mentioned to me an article in the *New York Times* about the challenges of reintegrating when soldiers come back from Afghanistan. When I had seen the paper that morning, my hands quickly hid it from my children's sight. Later that night, without a witness, I read the entire article. I could not help myself. The article described the experiences of three soldiers returning home. One was facing a divorce. Another was feeling like a stranger to his toddler son. And still another, who after a year's deployment was still just twenty, was returning to prospects of fatherhood with his pregnant fiancée. The article described the soldiers' fatigue and their difficult transition from a war zone, including the inability to relax after such prolonged hypervigilance. It also highlighted the frequency and issues with PTSD, something one in five returning soldiers would have.

I wondered what had been the paper's objective in placing that article on the front page? Were they telling anecdotal stories in order to sell more newspapers because pity sells well? Or were they trying to make a political statement about the impact this war was having on so many soldiers? There was no mention at all about the support systems and services that were available to veterans that may need them, or for the families and communities around them. There was no discussion about what friends and family members like me could do to help a loved one readjust. Instead, the story was just about how miserable it was.

Before he had left, Colin had heard that the reintegration could take as long as the deployment. If one were deployed for a year then it would take at least a year for the returning veteran to get back to normal on all fronts: personally, as a couple, as a family. Having that information was very helpful in alerting me about how to manage our expectations, but Colin's return seemed so far away, the idea of yet another worry drained my emotional energy. More than anything, I just wanted Colin back the same Colin *inside* as the husband and father we had seen off to war. According to the *New York Times*, that might simply be too much to ask.

The fifth full moon had vanished without me even noticing. Dana worked 65 hours one week. Without school for eight hours of the day and Colin's flexible summer hours, I needed full-time child care to cover my long work hours and Ian's orthopedic appointments and twice weekly physical therapy sessions. Without being aware, my body was still shrinking in size as sleep and self-care continued to evade me.

Chapter 13 – Quest for Faith

Late July 2011

The couch in our family room with shrunken cushions was really starting to bother me. Colin and I bought that couch - a French country pattern of yellow with blue swirls - when we lived in Houston over a decade ago. A subtle but elegant style that would lighten up our family room.

The first day that couch arrived was the last I got to enjoy that beautiful fabric. It was raining out, and our dogs Charlotte and Lilly leaped and bounded in from the outside, delighted to be out of the rain. Before I could grab them, they pounced onto the couch, leaving behind footprints of mud. Yikes! Our next purchase was a slipcover. Then after years of wear and tear from the children, the cushions were worn and the frame no longer comfortable. So in the spirit of continuing to control what I could, the couch joined my hit list.

***

As Camp Gramp continued for the summer and without Charlotte around the house now, I started to get scared as the sun would set. Usually I was not one that was scared of the dark, but now my body seemed to pause an extra second before I entered an empty dark room. And my bed suddenly felt even more empty with just me.

For the first time, I started to worry if an intruder could watch me at night without me knowing. The front of our house had a huge bay window, and our neighborhood had no streetlights, so any interior light was like a beacon to the outside. With both Colin and Charlotte gone, my desire for protection grew.

This was more than a dismissible, irrational fear, and my friend Karen agreed. She immediately offered up her husband to come hang curtains for me and help with any other honey-do jobs I had on my list. The next week, he came by the house, hung up the new curtains I had purchased, set up the wireless router to work on our flat screen TV, and fixed a broken kitchen drawer.

I gave him a bottle of wine as an insufficient thank you, and I promised him a debt that Colin, who was equally handy and excellent with wood and all things home improvement, would repay upon his return.

That night, I slept a little more soundly and worried a little less that I was being watched in the dark.

***

One Saturday, a good family friend took the boys for the afternoon. It was the first time since Colin had left that I had one-on-one time with any of my children, without having to pay for a sitter. This friend was a father of Karl's classmate as well as Colin's friendly rival lacrosse coach from the next town. It was such a creative plan - the boys were going to make two lacrosse sticks for their father. Our friend had already prepared the activity for hours beforehand, so the boys could just enjoy the fun of dying the head of the stick in red, white, and blue colors. After the boys left, he spent another hour tying the strings. Then he packed up the sticks, included a note, and mailed the box to Colin. It was an incredibly thoughtful and patriotic gift that focused on, and came from, the boys.

That afternoon, I was able to savor the rare alone time with Thais, whose dark eyes seemed a little lighter and happier for those few precious hours.

***

When we learned that Colin would get his two week R&R in August, I began planning a dream vacation. Our wise military friends advised me that Colin should not come home for his R&R, as that usually resulted in honey-do lists, too many people to see, and more pain of having to say goodbye from home all over again. So we needed to select a place to meet, away from everyone, family and friends included, and somewhere ideally halfway between the 9 ½ hour time zone difference in order to minimize everyone's jet lag.

So we chose my favorite country, France, a place where Colin and I already had wonderful memories. We also thought it would be a real treat for the boys, who were fascinated with WWII, to visit Normandy. I did pause, however, to seriously consider whether the gravity of the lives lost during WWII was an appropriate setting for our trip at a time when Colin was deployed to war. But those worries were put aside because the children were genuinely excited when they heard the news, and I also felt this could actually help put their Dad's service into a bigger context.

So at a time when what I really needed was just more sleep, my nights after the children went to bed became filled with research and planning to create this dream. Dreaming was more fun than worrying, and it was actually a most enjoyable diversion. It was a master puzzle to figure out how to use the 800,000 American Express points that I had accumulated over two decades of business travel to pay for our flights and hotels. It took some doing to track down and lock in everything. I was ecstatic I made it all work. Never mind the sleep.

Beth Jackson

Colin and I decided, after days of e-mails, that we would bring Dana with us, so he and I could have some alone time together. I also decided that to help pay for the food expenses, I would try to rent out our house in Rhode Island for the two weeks while we were gone. I just needed to find a responsible renter, and hope the days matched up perfectly. Travel planning had become yet another part-time job.

***

I was excited for Colin to see the children for so many reasons. They had all grown taller in the months since he had left, and the boys were filling out. But I was also eager for him to see how much all three had matured. OK, so I had been paying them an allowance as an incentive to do some additional chores around the house. Empty the dishwasher. Take out the recycling. Feed the dog. Typical stuff. But nonetheless, they were super helpful.

The children had also become more independent. I had started leaving Karl or Ian alone with Thais, so I could do a half hour run around the neighborhood. They were thrilled for the sliver of time to sneak in a few cartoons. And for safety precautions, there were strict rules that included neither toaster nor microwave use. And no answering the door or phone. Except my cell.

At first, I would call to check in half way through my run. Over time, I left my cell phone home. The children knew how to call 911. They knew where the neighbors were. They were growing up, and this gave me tiny moments of freedom that I so badly needed.

***

Like every night, I tucked in the children and told them I loved them. I touched their head and back or welcomed a hug. I then
150

ducked into my office to dive back into my world of work. I had
a deliverable due to one client the next morning, and another
due at the end of the following day. With back-to-back meetings
schedules, I had a late night ahead.

A few minutes into my work, Ian called for me.

Silent, so as to not wake the other children, I walked down the
hallway to his room and entered the darkness. "Hi, love," I said in a
quiet voice. "What do you need?"

"Can you get my blankets for me?" he asked. "They are downstairs
on the couch. "

"Of course," I replied. I slipped quietly down the stairs and
gathered up his three blankets - a blue fleece one from last
Christmas, the blue and red flannel patchwork one that in years
before had doubled as his cape and was now frayed from years
of love, and a cotton one with a large sailboat handmade by my
mother-in-law.

I returned to his room and laid them gently on top of him. "Thank
you," he yawned.

"You're welcome. I love you," I replied, hoping for a reply.

Silence.

I left the room.

The next night as the children were falling into slumber and I sat
in front of my computer, my mind registered the sound of a chime.
The doors in the house chimed when they were opened or closed, a
safety feature we had installed when we first moved here to monitor
access to the back yard, near the pool.

Beth Jackson

In response to this unexpected chime, I grabbed the scissors on my desk with one hand and the portable phone in the other. Suddenly, I wished that Charlotte were here. I walked nervously to the top of the stairs, peering ahead as I started descending with small steps.

I stopped and listened. Nothing.

Nothing was there. But the door was slightly ajar. I looked around. Nothing. I closed the door and locked it. I turned off all the other lights and locked the back door as well.

As I walked back upstairs, I heard Ian's small voice. "Mom, did you hear the door chime?"

"Yes, honey, I did. "

I hid my own fear as I comforted him. Trying to convince myself at the same time, I said, "It was just the wind that blew it open, since it had not been closed all the way. "

"Oh. Okay," he replied.

"Good night, my love," I whispered.

I longed for an echo, but again there was no reply. And I slipped out of his room.

***

After a month hiatus, I decided to take the children to church again. This time, I was greeted by a new female interim priest. The interim priest from the last few months had left for his normal summer position at a different church. Tears replaced my words as I attempted to introduce myself to this third priest since Colin had left, explaining that it was my husband who was listed in the prayers of the people.

During the service, I read the pamphlet that outlined the service hymns and prayers and noticed a headline, "Do you know someone who might need a little extra help?" If so, please contact the office with the person's information, and a group of women who cooked and froze meals will deliver one. I wanted to contact them. *Yes, I needed a little help.* But I still hoped people could read my mind, and instead I did nothing.

I questioned what I was getting from these visits to church. I had been looking for a personal connection or some sense of spiritual comfort here. I still remember attending a service back in Houston on the Friday after 9/11. The church was filled to overflow capacity as we held hands with strangers on my right and on my left and cried together. We all shared the pain we felt when our innocence as a nation was shattered. Church then gave me comfort both as a community, and as an institution. I think that was what I was looking for now.

After a service last month, an elderly woman with snowy white hair and a face defined by years of laugh lines squeezed my hand with the tender warmth of love when we met. I don't know if she knew anything of my circumstances, but I sure appreciated her kindness. Her touch had brought tears to my eyes, as I hoped that a connection was beginning.

But this time, that white-haired woman was nowhere to be seen. And a week later when we entered the stone walls of church again, the new female priest did not approach us. I only knew a few regular churchgoers there, none of them very well, so words were barely exchanged. I was alone again and did not feel part of any community there. It was neither relaxing nor peaceful, as I had hoped. There was no church school for the older boys, and Thais was too shy to go to the one for the children her age, so all three of them joined me in the service each time. I was trying to coach the children to be good churchgoers, but I wondered if it was really worth it.

***

Our summer ambled on, our routines filling the time until the day of our departure for France. Not much drama or excitement - until I was on my way to meet a client when a text from Dana popped on the screen of my phone.

> *There is a swarm of bees that went into the house. Your neighbor says not to worry. She knows a bee guy. Call her.*

I was in shock. I quickly dialed my neighbor, who also happened to be a beekeeper. As she described it, the black swarm outside the window was two stories high and spun like the sound of a freight train. It was loud and scary and growing in energy. Faster and faster. Thankfully, the kids were all at camp.

My friend told me not to worry and gave me the number of a bee guy, who indicated he could come the next afternoon. Evidently, the swarm of bees decided a pocket of wood next to the chimney was going to be their new home. As soon as the queen bee found her way into this little pocket, all the other ones instantly followed behind. And the freight train transformed into an almost silent humming sound from behind the wall.

All night that night, there was no sound inside the house, but knowing there were bees in the wall completely ratcheted up my already nightly terrors.

The next afternoon, donned with thick gloves and a white cloth helmet with mesh on the front, the bee guy began his work. It took him a couple of hours of slow, methodical work using a long-tubed vacuum that resembled a shop vac.

"Six pounds," he told me after he had vacuumed them out and placed the bees securely in a container, so he could relocate the hive.

"How many bees is that?" I inquired.

"Twenty-four thousand bees," he replied nonchalantly.

Some say bees are a sign of life and hope. They represent tireless work and social order. They often appeared in historical religious symbolism, such as in Egypt where they were the gift of life and resurrection. In Africa, they were believed to carry supernatural powers. Just as I was pulling back away from the church and faith in God, maybe the bees were a sign that some greater being was bringing me nourishment and hope. Well, at least this was something I could use, and I didn't even have to pray for it.

Chapter 14 – Out of Balance

Early August 2011

Control. I wanted control of everything around me, but instead something had taken control of me and I could not stop it. Sometimes, whatever this something was transformed me into someone I neither recognized nor much liked.

One day in between business calls and e-mails, I popped downstairs to play with each of the children as Dana ran some errands to the grocery store and dry cleaners. It was a glorious summer afternoon - the humidity was low and the sun was high. Thais joined me outside in the garden to water the plants, and then Karl and Ian used the hose for a water fight. The spontaneity of the unexpected break soothed me, and the warmth and fun of being together calmed my soul.

Later, after my afternoon work calls, I walked into my bathroom, where our sweet cleaning lady greeted me with a bright smile and announced, "I cleaned out your medicine cabinet!"

She pointed to a huge stack of medicine bottles and pills on the floor of our bathroom, "Those are all expired. Can I throw them out?"

At that moment, my mind snapped. The dark force inside me escaped, as I was suddenly overwhelmed by the idea of not having some medicine the children or I might need at a moment's notice. We might have needed Cortizone for a bee sting. Or Tylenol for a fever. Or Nightquil for a stuffy nose. And on and on. I did not care that the medicines were expired and therefore useless. There were at least twenty half empty bottles strewn on the floor. I didn't want to have a tantrum but, damnit, I did not want another task to add to my to-do list. I didn't want to buy new medicines. I had no excess capacity.

I tried to smile to be nice as I scooped up each of the bottles and threw them back into the plastic bin where they had peacefully lived on the little shelf behind the white cabinet door.

"I don't want to replace these medicines in my medicine box. I might need one of them and might not remember to get more," I tried to explain my irrationality.

I picked up one translucent bottle of Motrin, and my eyes found the expiration date: 1997. The pink liquid was almost fifteen years past its expiration date. I paused for a second, but I could not deal. I threw it back into the cabinet with everything else.

"I'm so sorry," I apologized to our cleaning lady, who was just trying to take the initiative and help me. "I just cannot handle change," I explained as a pain tightened on both my chest and the center of my forehead.

I felt guilty for hours afterwards, but my mind simply would not allow me to let go of control of any piece of my life I could grasp and grip so tight.

***

My life was a ying and yang of stress and calm. Calm and stress. I had started my own business seven years before, a risky adventure with no guaranteed revenue stream. I had to pitch for every job, and I got paid by the hour. When I worked, I got paid. When I didn't work, I didn't. The hours I spent doing paperwork, accounting, and contracts for my business were unpaid.

The years had been filled with ups & downs. Just the summer before, I lost a big retainer client of three years with only thirty days notice. I went from a very regular income stream to nothing. And there were no unemployment checks to collect. In contrast, this summer had become the summer of all summers. There was more work - good work - than I ever expected. Then, my largest client made me an offer to become their full-time Chief Marketing Officer.

Now, let me be clear. I left the corporate world (kind of, since all my clients were still in it) to get a little more balance in my life. Although I was still at the beck and call of my clients and worked 24/7, I could take as much vacation as I wanted or leave the office at 3 p. m. whenever I wanted to watch one of the children's games. I could volunteer at school to serve hot lunch simply by scheduling out two hours on any given day and telling my clients I was not available at that time.

But Chief Marketing Officer (CMO) of a large company was another story. That is THE top job that every marketer dreams of. Admittedly, I was thrilled to be asked. It validated all of my experiences over the years, and I really enjoyed the work.

Ego versus reality. Ego versus reality.

Why *this* year?

I was not sure if I could commit to this top role without Colin being here. The company even said it would be incredibly flexible with me, but I worried I could not even keep up a four-day a week, two-hour per day commute for very long. I needed to be able to turn off work with a split second notice, which I didn't think I could do if I were an employee.

Beth Jackson

Oh, how I wished Colin were home, so I could talk this through with him. He was always such a balanced sounding board, giving me perspective on things I would not have even thought about.

I knew my work was way out of balance, but I LIKED work in general, liked it a lot actually. It was intellectually stimulating and kept me engaged. And work allowed me to temporarily forget where Colin was and what he was doing. It took me away from worry and anxiousness. So I asked my client if I could have some time to think about the offer.

Looking back at this summer, it is clear that I did not have enough "just be" time. My work hours had simply grown too much. Two weeks in a row, Dana worked more than 60 hours again, plus three overnights. I was working, travelling for work, and away from the children for that many hours. I would not admit, nor did I even see, this was not sustainable, and that I was headed for a crash.

***

As a working mom, I had long given up the need to be perfect in every aspect of my life. My house was never quite tidy. My clothes were rarely ironed. Thais's hair might not have been brushed on a given day, or week. The first line of Colin's reply to a picture I had recently sent him read, "Karl needs a haircut!" I had noticed but not cared that they needed a cut, as I had let this thing go, too.

But the boys laughed at Dad's e-mail and said they wanted cuts. So I took them to Willie's, a good old-fashioned barbershop where I had never been before. Colin had always taken the boys. Karl told me the way.

"Are you the Mom?" the young barber asked me.

"Yes," I replied. "My husband is in Afghanistan. He usually brings them."

"I know," the barber replied very matter of factly.

Karl liked having long bangs, so the negotiation with him was that the bangs were to be cut above the eyebrow. The barber complied and began to cut away.

Thais sat on my lap as I read her the story of the *Jungle Book*. Then it was Ian's turn.

"A number one," Ian pronounced.

Now, I had no idea what he was talking about.

"How about a one-and-three-quarter," the barber countered.

Ian held firm. "A one."

The barber looked at me for consent.

"I am fine with whatever," I stated, practicing letting go.

And the sheers came out. The bzzzzzzz sound was louder than I expected, and in the end, Ian smiled at his bald head shaved down to the stub.

I grabbed my phone and snapped a picture to e-mail to Colin.

Beth Jackson

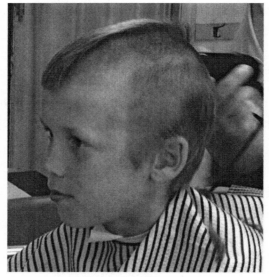

Ian getting a buzz cut

Everyone was happy. It was just hair anyway.

***

Bedtime again. Brushed teeth. Read books.

Ian played Legos. Karl read. I sang Thais songs.

After Karl and Thais were tucked into bed, I walked into Ian's room and said, "Goodnight. I love you. "

"Night," his voice echoed back. Nothing more.

"When are you going to tell me you love me?" I asked with a smile.

"When I am twenty-two," he replied with an even more sly one.

***

On Sunday morning, Karl woke up early to make the batter for "skinny pancakes," a fourth generation butter-laden rum-splashed breakfast from the Swedes on Colin's side of the family.

After indulging ourselves into the deliciousness of breakfast, I stood at the kitchen sink doing the dishes. As I looked down, the stains on the wood floor from the burst faucet the night of the Bruins victory peeked out from under my feet. My eyes quickly jumped out to the windows. Beyond the wooden fence of the deck, I noticed the pool looked a tad green. Algae.

As the children ran outdoors into the sun of this summer day, I walked with a large coffee mug in hand to unlock the gate around the pool and take a closer look. Weeds sprouted everywhere up through the rocks bordering the concrete patio. Algae grew on the edges of the pool.

I put my cup down and began to weed. It was a bit like yoga. It gave me great satisfaction to grab at the root and pull an entire weed out with one tug. Victory felt so good each time the challenge was greater and required two hands and several tugs. After a while of addressing the most blatant weeds, I went searching for the metal wire brush. For the next hour I reached deep down into the water and scrubbed at the yellow and green areas that had grown into irregular shapes along the pool's edge.

Thais came outside for a little while and rode her bike around the deck as I worked. We talked about how she would soon learn to ride the bike without her training wheels. Her favorite thing to do was to ring the bell as she biked around and around in circles. Eventually, she returned back inside.

After a while, my right arm was aching. I looked now at the pool to survey some progress, but the green was still there. I spent a few more minutes scrubbing at the most egregious spots on the last section and then finally gave up.

Beth Jackson

Like taking the boys for haircuts, the pool was Colin's job. With him gone, this task fell on my lap. Just enough was going to have to be good enough.

***

I was in Connecticut working for a client on my birthday.

I received this photo via text from Dana. It showed beautiful long-stemmed roses next to the pictures of Colin.

Roses in front of the pictures of Colin on the window

Yep, a lovely gesture from my husband in a war zone, and I was not there to receive it. Two weeks earlier, both Colin and I had forgotten about our eighteenth wedding anniversary. There was really nothing special we could have done to celebrate, as we were on polar ends of the world. But we could have at least sent e-mails of love. Instead we both forgot. *What had my life, and our marriage, become?*

During that intense work blitz, we were fortunate to spend time with my sister and then Colin's friend Will.

Carrie flew in from San Francisco for a week and helped to maintain the semblance of sanity at home during two overnight trips I had to make. She transformed herself into super aunt, taking over the night and morning responsibilities when Dana went home. Carrie took the children for ice cream and to the beach for wave jumping. Even Ian hobbled out with his crutches to join. She was a delight, and the children couldn't get enough of her.

One afternoon when I was working from home and on a conference call, Thais tiptoed into my office. I waved to her and put my fingers to my lips, indicating I was on a call. Thais wanted to tell me something, but the phone was beckoning me as a dozen other people on the line were waiting for my reply, so I shook my head no.

Dana had followed Thais upstairs and quickly whisked her away, closing the door quietly behind them. Ten minutes later, when my call had ended, I opened my door and called out down the long hallway, "Thazy-lazy, come tell me!"

Silence greeted me.

I called again, "Thais, come show me what you wanted to show me!"

Still silence. Dana had taken the children out to go to the beach, and my voice just bounced off the plaster walls and hardwood floors of my empty house.

The emptiness spilled inside me as well. *How many more times could I fail?*

Sensing my raw, ragged state, Carrie lovingly wrote me about what she saw, and how this deployment experience had changed me.

> *Your heart is more available since Colin got deployed. Not only are you more vulnerable than I have ever seen you and giving yourself permission to say no to things you usually would have overachieved*

*on, but you still care deeply, and in a way even more so, about my
goals and dreams.*

Dear Carrie was the only one I had truly allowed all the way into
my vulnerable heart and anguish; everyone else interfaced with my
hardened shell and painted smile.

Carrie left on the same day Will came to town to take Karl and
his friend on a day-long kayaking trip, another outing offered by
the Operation Military Kids program. I felt sorry that Ian, still in
a cast, had to stay behind. It made me smile, though, when Karl
later related the day's adventures that afterwards also included a
modified version of a P90X workout, a guy thing that both boys
absorbed liked a sponge. I was more grateful than words could fully
express by how so many men in my boys' lives quietly stepped up to
try to fill the void of Dad.

***

And then we were sucker-punched back into reality. Will had taken
the three children to the playground before he left for the airport,
while I went to a nearby beach for a run. On the drive home, my
radio blared the news that 30 Americans had been killed, including
22 SEALS, when Afghan insurgents shot down a helicopter. It was a
CH-47 Chinook.

Rationally, I knew Colin was not in that part of Afghanistan, but
my heart immediately sank and my mind cracked for the families
uncertain if there would be a knock on their door. Anxious that
I would spiral further down, I tuned out the news for the rest of
the day. It was the only way I had found to protect myself from
generating even more fear and worry.

Later that night, though, after the children were tucked in bed, I
clicked on the Google alert.

A flurry of e-mails had arrived asking if Colin was OK. I wondered why they hadn't asked about him on other days; two soldiers died just the day before. At least one soldier a day has died since Colin had been there. But after seeing all the attention that followed from that crash, I realized with shock that those living their normal lives *forgot* what was going on in Afghanistan. It took a major fatality fed by the media to remind everyone that people were dying over there. When the news covered the war, people remembered that Colin was there and shared their concern. The rest of the time, they went about their normal busy lives and forgot altogether. What my friends and family didn't know was that I thought about such things for hours on end every single day.

I closed down my computer more quickly than most nights. My eyelids actually fell closed before midnight, trying to shut out any noise and be in complete blackness. I rolled my body up into a ball, like the fetal position. I was living in fear. Numbness was my only defense.

Chapter 15 – The Surreal Vacation

Mid August 2011

Before we left for France, I sent Colin a note asking him what he needed most from us when we would be together. Did he want alone time? One-on-one time with each child? Or just total family time, all the time? He did not answer that question in any correspondence that followed.

I also reached out to Anne to ask her what I should expect from him during those two weeks of R&R. Could I expect him to parent? Would he be too exhausted to do anything? Maybe even too tired for sex? I knew better on that one. Would he be jittery?

Anne wisely told me, "He may not even know what he will need. But no, don't assume he will do any parenting. "

Good perspective. I felt exhausted and wanted a break from being the sole parent, but I knew he was the one that was in the war zone, so my needs would be overshadowed again.

My needs in fact kept getting pushed back behind something else. Behind my children's needs. My client's needs. My husband's needs. When my clothes, already a size smaller, hooked at the waist, there was yet again a little extra slack. My ribs had recently been sticking out from beneath my bra, and my legs no longer touched at the thigh.

But I was not the one in the war zone. I kept telling myself that, like I was trying to convince myself that my current state was OK.

***

Beth Jackson

We stopped at Ian's orthopedist the day before we left for France. Our hopeful expectations were crushed when we learned that although Ian's cast was now replaced with a walking boot, he was still was not allowed to put any weight on it for the two-week vacation. The orthopedist gave Ian the boot only so there would be no clotting issues with a cast on the long plane ride.

Crutches. Hmmm...

I knew Paris was a walking town. And there would be lots of it. But I could also see, as Ian hobbled on his crutches back to the car, that he was not very comfortable using them for more than a block. I had just returned the wheelchair he had been using the day before... so on our way from the orthopedist, we stopped to pick it back up again. It, too, would be going to Paris!

***

Never since summers in college had I taken a two-week vacation. Ever. In almost two decades. Never more than a week.

Excitement kept me going, but there was a lot of preparation to do to be able to carve out this time. Work deliverables, including active engagements with four different clients, had to be completed. One colleague was going to check my voicemail every day and e-mail me if there was something urgent. Two colleagues were leading research and ideation projects that I had subcontracted to them since I was not available. But they were sending me updates and overviews that I had to review and send to the client. Late nights of work were repeated night after night.

Preparations to get the house ready to rent also took time. When I had this great idea to rent out our house, all I had was an abstract notion that doing so would help make our budget work. I did not think through all the logistics that would be required, including that I had to "declutter" the house. I filled ten boxes with the contents from counters and bedside tables to store away. Fortunately, the renters agreed we did not need to empty the clothes from any of the dressers, a huge relief. I also arranged for a high school neighbor to be our house sitter - to check the mail, water the plants, and put the garbage bins back into the garage after the garbage truck came.

The renters were parents of friends of ours, also a relief because I knew our belongings would be respected. I hoped nothing would be unintentionally damaged, though. And I assumed that kitchen items would end up in the wrong drawers and cabinets - that was to be expected, but still I fretted. Our house was the one thing I was trying desperately to control, and now I was letting strangers live in it for two weeks. It was totally counter to my needs, but my second-guessing was too late. They were coming to rent the house. And that was going to allow us to afford an incredible vacation with Colin.

On the Friday before our departure, I still had a mile-long to-do list. There were bills to pay and loose ends on work projects. We had packed our bags the previous weekend, but I double-checked we had not forgotten underwear and PJs. I had packed a bag for Colin as well, since all he had was military uniforms.

When the day finally arrived, our cleaning lady came to do a thorough clean and change all the sheets. Simultaneously, Dana took the children out for a movie, so they would not pull out toys to play with as we were leaving out the door. I surveyed each room to be sure nothing was out of order and did last minute touch-ups. I emptied the dishwasher of all the clean dishes, ran two last loads in the washing machine, switched clean clothes to the dryer, and put them in a basket. With no time to spare, I moved the whole basket of clean unfolded clothes into my office, locked the office door, and hid the key. My body simply moved without pause around the house, packing up the last things like toothbrushes, snacks, and the children's special blankets.

The house had never been so clean. Wow. I had not comprehended what effort or stress it was to rent our house, and I continued second guessing myself. After a quick take-out dinner on disposable paper plates, we put one last bag of garbage out to the corner and waited for the airport van that was to take us to Boston Logan.

As the children and I looked up the road to catch the first glimpse of the van turning the corner, I saw the front of a white car start down the hill. And the car kept going and going. What was this car? Not a van, that was for sure. It was much longer.

Oh, please no! It was a white stretch limousine. I was so embarrassed.

"The van is in the shop," the driver explained. The limo was their only other vehicle big enough to hold all five of us, the luggage, and the wheelchair. The children were shouting with sheer delight. "A limo!" Karl exclaimed.

As we rode, the children played with the lights that changed color and found where the water bottles were chilling on some ice. They were having the time of their life being celebrities on their way to see Dad.

I sat back and watched them. But I also looked at my phone. It was well past the end of the workday on a Friday evening, but I still checked for any last e-mails. Nothing. My clients were actually leaving me alone. I had completed everything I had due for work. My to-do list was actually done.

As my eyes watched the children play with the various delights of the limo, my thoughts drifted to the adjustment leaving a war zone and the difficulty in physically relaxing. It was a totally different mindset to move from a hypervigilant state of alert to sitting at a table having a beer. A slammed door or loud noise could cause a physical startle. Was this going to be true for Colin, and would it be true for me? For the next two weeks, I was going to be withdrawing from being that incessant list maker and home-front sergeant barking orders, and from the subconscious need to check in on work. We both clearly were going to need a little relaxation, but I was not good at relaxing. I would have to try.

I looked out the window as we rode and noticed that it was a full moon. The sixth one, just like the night before Colin left.

***

Colin had been able to e-mail me several times since he left Kabul. Each stop took at least one day. Kabul to Baghram. Then Baghram to Kuwait. Two nights in Kuwait. Then Bahrain. His itinerary indicated he would be in Paris on Saturday morning at 7:32 a. m. , just four hours ahead of us. The timing could not have been more perfect. We would meet at the airport, and I imagined the children's excitement, coming out of baggage claim and into their Dad's arms. But I told the children we would meet him at the hotel and kept this small secret to myself.

Our plane arrived a few minutes early, just before 11:00 a. m. local time in Paris. The Charles De Gaulle airport did not have the planes pull up to the terminal; rather, hundreds of shuttle buses transported passengers between the planes and the terminal. Also they had special "medi" buses for those who need extra assistance, like Ian.

It seemed like forever until we arrived at the terminal. With the wheelchair in checked luggage, Ian was proceeding ever so slowly with his crutches. One slow foot forward at a time. The sides of his chest were already aching from the rubbing of the crutches. The airlines had called ahead for a wheelchair escort, but it had not yet arrived. I looked at my watch. It was 12:32 p. m.

I knew Colin had been at the airport for almost six hours by this point. After what seemed like another hour, we asked the airline person again when he thought the wheelchair escort would arrive. Could we just walk with his crutches, if it were close enough? How far was it through immigration and luggage? The man advised we wait since it was quite a distance, and the escort would also allow us to get to the front of the line. *Front of the line? Really?* That would be lovely. And definitely worth the wait. But how much longer would it be? The anticipation was mounting, but I practiced patience along with my exhausted children.

Another twenty minutes later, our escort arrived pushing an empty wheelchair. Ian climbed in, and I took his crutches in one hand. The same hand that was holding on the strap of my bag that hung on my shoulder. Thais held my other hand, and we proceeded. Karl and Dana followed right behind.

Indeed, we did go straight to the front of the line. I had never been through immigration so quickly. We were through it in two minutes, with all of our passports stamped.

Around the corner, we found the elevator to take us downstairs to the luggage claim area. We waited just a few minutes and then saw our first bag. One. Two. Three. Four. Five. Six.

Oh, and Ian's wheelchair. Where was that? We looked over to the oversized luggage area, and there we saw it with the pink tag hanging off the wheel.

Karl helped pull out a luggage pushcart and loaded up the bags with me. Dana opened up the wheelchair and helped Ian get into it. I held the crutches, and Thais tagged along, holding onto to the bottom of my shirt.

Karl exited the doors of baggage claim first and immediately saw
Colin. Karl sped up as he pushed the cart his way and ran into
his father's arms. Ian, Thais, and I followed suit. Hugs. Smiles.
Embraces. As people in the terminal looked on, they had no idea
about the intensity of this incredible reunion. Dana tried to snap
some pictures to capture the moment, but it all happened so fast.

Greeting Dad at Charles De Gaulle airport

Sheer happiness. It felt like a dream. I had escaped from our life
of war, fear, work, responsibilities, and awkward silences, and our
family was reunited again, at least temporarily. Almost instantly,
my breathing felt easier. Still, I had some worries.

Where did one even begin when reuniting with your spouse? Or
your Dad? Or your son? Or daughter? We had been living two
totally different lives.

After my quick embrace with Colin, I stepped back and let the
children take center stage with him. Thais got the best seat in the
house on his shoulders. Karl told him about his ice hockey camp

of this past week. Ian started planning what they would see in Normandy. I knew we had two whole weeks. My turn would come, so I hoped.

After checking into our hotel, we ventured out to the streets of Paris. Over a late lunch, the language of our reunion continued in full fluency without any lull in the conversation. We all had so much catching up to do.

Following lunch, Colin shared some special gifts from Afghanistan with each of us. He gave each boy an antique coin. He handed Thais and me each a precious stone of topaz. I could make a ring out of it to match my necklace. He had no idea that I wore that necklace every day or why; I did not share my superstitions with him.

That night when we went to bed, Dana slept with the children in the room across the hallway from Colin and me. I helped the children get ready for bed. Dana read Thais a book, and I kissed each of them goodnight.

Returning to our room, I found Colin about to doze off. I asked him to go kiss the children goodnight. Colin had forgotten that he usually did that at home. After he returned to our room, his fatigue quickly disappeared, and the intimacy we had both missed for so many moons came back as naturally and lovingly as it had been before he left. I had forgotten how much I had missed the full human touch.

The next morning, the Louvre was first on our plan. Our hotel was right beside the Jardin de Tuilleries, so we walked through the perfectly manicured gardens with colorful flowers under overcast skies. It was a little challenging pushing Ian over the wide dirt and pebbled paths, but we slowly and bumpily made our way towards the museum.

When we entered the main cobblestone courtyard of this enormous stone building, we saw the admission line snaked around the glass pyramid entrance to the archway behind it. Slowly, we walked and pushed the wheelchair on its way, in itself a workout. The imperfect cobblestone made the wheelchair an off-road experience. With each push, the chair bumped side to side, making moaning metal sounds. Sometimes, I had to give great force to the handles or lift the wheel to get over one of the larger stones. As we reached the arch, our eyes followed the line that continued beyond sight, snaking into the next courtyard as well. And the next. We walked and we walked, pushed and pushed, trying to find the back of the line.

Thais rode on Colin's shoulders. Karl carried Ian's crutches. Dana carried the bag with the guidebook and snacks.

More than once, Colin said, "The line is too long. Let's just skip it. "

I was too stubborn and did not want to admit defeat that quickly, yet my hopes were quickly dissipating as well. I approached a guard and asked in my broken French if there was a handicap entrance. Pushing Ian on the cobblestones had just become too impossible.

"Oui," he explained with minimal enthusiasm. He pointed back through the multiple arches that we had just come through towards the main entrance. So we turned around and began to back track. Shortly thereafter the skies opened! We were still fifty yards away, but my eye caught a sign that had a handicap wheelchair image on it. I approached another guard and asked where we could enter. He immediately ushered us in, out of the rain, to the front of the line. Again, the kindness of strangers.

We enjoyed the audio contraptions that we rented for our tour of the Louvre as we tackled the mummies and Egyptian art section of the enormous museum. Crowds encircled us, so it took a while to maneuver Ian's wheelchair through. After two hours, our minds were saturated with a sufficient amount of art culture, so we went back outside where the rain had stopped.

We found a restaurant nearby with a covered outdoor patio. It was a rather nice restaurant, as is typical in France, and the service was paced to encourage a relaxed long meal. But our young children grew understandably fidgety, and as they did, Colin became uncharacteristically unsettled. He was not used to having meals with children and forgot that there was constant movement. At one point, Thais said she had to go to the bathroom. The sign indicated it was upstairs. I got up from my seat and lifted Thais out of hers. I walked to the side wall to get Ian's crutches, as he said he had to go, too, and there was no elevator. Karl popped up out of his seat to join us as well. I could tell by the look on Colin's face that he was actually going to enjoy the few minutes of quiet as we left him at the table. He needed time to adjust.

Later that night, we planned to have to dinner at an Italian restaurant. The concierge had told us it was very close to the metro stop, so we chose to only take crutches instead of the wheelchair. But something got missed in translation, and we ended up walking eight very long city blocks down the busy Champs Ellysee.

Poor Ian was hobbling along through throngs of people. His face conveyed the sheer discomfort he felt as he moved, but he did not say a word. Several times Colin and I each offered to carry him or give him a shoulder, but he obstinately refused. The crutches continued to rub against the side of his ribs, causing a large red rash, but he still insisted on being independent.

We finally made our way to Pino Pizza. Basically a glorified Pizza Hut. We had been hoping for something a little more authentic, but tired and hungry, we were happy to find a seat as soon as we did. Our waiter, however, was a bit of a curmudgeon. He barely spoke and never smiled. Service was slow, not in the wonderful Parisian way, but because he kept forgetting to put in our order.

At one point, the children had devoured two baskets of bread as they waited for their meals. Then, when Colin was in the middle of a sentence, a loud sound shattered behind him, causing a massive startled jerk of his body. A simple wine glass had fallen to the floor, but Colin reacted reflexively, just as his friends had predicted. The moment passed as quickly as it started.

On our way back from the restaurant, we took the closer subway. Thais rode on Colin's shoulders for a while. She then clamored down and grabbed his left hand with her right one. And my right hand with her left one. She just wanted to touch us both at the same time.

"Mommy," she looked up at me with her beautiful eyes as we rested on a sidewalk bench for a minute. "I hope we can all die at the same time, so we don't have to worry about each other. You, Dad, me, Karl, and Ian. " Her confession stole my breath. Deep down, I think I agreed with her.

Back at the hotel, Colin immediately went to the bathroom. I could hear through the door that his stomach was violently upset. This situation repeated itself for four days. Every meal. Immediate reaction. His system was experiencing a total shock and reacting quite severely. Still, Colin just adapted and did not complain. He was grateful to be eating good food and cold beer.

***

The kindness of the French continued throughout the week, as Ian's handicap brought us to the front of the line at the Eiffel Tour, where the wait was over two hours. At the Musee D'Orsay, we joined the relatively short line at the back, but a guard sought us out and brought us to the front. Everywhere we went.

Beth Jackson

Jackson clan traversing the Seine in Paris

One night, Dana watched the children, so Colin and I could go out on a date. He wore a pinstriped shirt, blue jacket, and tie. I wore a pretty summer dress with heels. The blue necklace hung towards my modest cleavage.

It was strange to be alone with my husband after so long. To others, we must have just looked like a normal couple enjoying a regular night out. The passage of time and the vast array of unshared experiences, however, made conversation topics a bit awkward. There was so much to cover but clearly insufficient time for it, so we floated on the surface and mostly caught up on the trivial topics of the last six months. It felt very empty.

***

In preparation for the second week of our trip to explore Normandy, we rented a car. On the way to the rental place, I made a quick detour to the Pharmacie. After six months of no sex, and then some, my body gave me the gift of a raving itchy yeast infection. *Who would have known?* I didn't. So there I stood asking in broken French for something like Monistat, wishing there had been deployment materials warning me with some practical tips.

We got our car. And, well, imagine Chevy Chase with the Von Trapp clan and Dana crammed into a small station wagon. Avis claimed our station wagon seated seven people, but that was without luggage and a wheelchair. We were packed to the gills, but ready for our next adventure.

Chapter 16 – The Fight

Late August 2011

Let me tell you a little more about the reality of our two weeks.
While we loved our time together, Colin and I did have a major
argument in the middle of it. So nothing was Utopia. Regular life
was not. And R&R was no exception.

Our first stop out of Paris was with my cousin, with whom we spent
two nights while visiting Versailles and just relaxing in the French
countryside with her family. Next, we headed for Normandy,
although an hour into our journey, my cousin called to tell me that
we had left Ian's crutches behind. We had no choice but to turn
around.

Late afternoon, we arrived in the quaint flowered city of Honfleur.
Over lunch - French fries again for the children, although Karl
also ordered steak, and Ian at least said he would try some fish - I
glanced at my cell phone and saw a text. My girlfriend Karen, who
kindly offered to serve as a contact for the renters of our house,
wrote to tell me the dryer was not working and the renters wanted
to call a repairman or buy a new one. Visions of an expensive
service call or even costlier new dryer cluttered my mind, when
I remembered that only one cycle of the dryer ever worked,
something I had mentioned to the renters. They must have
forgotten. I quickly typed back to have them try the other cycle,
but before I could complete the message, my battery died and phone
cycled off. And I had no way to recharge it; I had left the charger at
the hotel days before.

After the late lunch, a short stroll by the waterfront, and a ride on
the town's antique carousel, we returned to our car and drove for

several more hours. The Normandy countryside was beautiful with its flat meadows and farmlands. But at 7 p. m. , we were still on the road and clearly going to be very late for Colin's birthday reservation in St. Malo. With my phone dead, we could not call the restaurant. Nor did I have the directions to the hotel or the restaurant. Just addresses.

The sun was just beginning to set around 9 p. m. when we finally arrived in St. Malo. I knew our hotel was along the waterfront, and I searched for street signs. Nothing. We drove past private homes, a bakery, and a butcher shop, but no hotel. Colin drove down another block or two against my suggestion that we turn around. He continued on, clearly frustrated with me, as we all had eyes searching. A few streetlights started popping on.

Colin maneuvered our car across a small causeway to what looked like a museum or fort. I noticed huge parking lots on our right as we then passed some sort of walled city on our left. Thousands of people were milling about the sidewalks. A carousal. Music. Policemen directing traffic, as they had blocked off one entrance to the city.

My eyes kept scanning for a sign or anything that would suggest a hotel. At one point, I did see a sign that said "Hotele," but our car was long past it by the time I called out, "Slow down!" I was not sure if it was for our hotel, but I was hopeful.

With the deep traffic, the road had no clear place to pull over, and my suggestions of where to turn were always a second too late to be safe. Colin scowled back at me each time, continuing to the end of this peninsula before finally finding a place to turn around. Tensions were starting to rise.

I asked him to drive slowly, so I could read the signs this time. Colin defiantly explained that he had to drive with the flow of traffic and could not just stop in the middle of the long skinny road.

We continued back, approaching the walled city again, this time on our right with the parking lot on our left.

Approaching a policeman directing traffic, I suggested to Colin that we ask for help. But with no place to pull the car over, Colin countered angrily with a simple, "No. "

"You are so stubborn," I pointed out to him.

"You should have gotten directions," he snapped back.

My temper started to boil. Did he have any idea how many hours of late nights I had put into planning this trip? After working long days and doing everything for our children and household while he was gone. This was the only detail of a perfectly planned trip that I had not attended to, and he was criticizing me for it. I bit my tongue.

And then my eyes noticed a sign on a building just behind the blocked entrance that read "Hotel Chateaubriand. "

"Chateaubriand!" I called out. "I think I saw it!"

Colin was already determined to return to the first entrance of the walled city where I had seen the first hotel sign, so he ignored me. We continued another minute or two with cars in front and in back of us as we moved along the road.

The sun was close to the horizon now, and light was vanishing.

Colin turned the car into the entrance of the walled city. Immediately after we entered, there was another sign "Hotele" with an arrow pointing up a narrow cobblestone street. So we followed the sign up the street.

Beth Jackson

At the top of the small hill, there was no sign but there was a fork in the road. We turned right. A few blocks later, having traveled down several steep narrow one-way streets that were lined with parked cars, we ended up where we had started.

So we tried again. Up the narrow cobblestone street. Trying to avoid hitting the other cars that were just inches away. This time we turned left. Oh! We saw another sign for "Hotele" with an arrow pointing at the next turn. So we followed it. A few more blocks, but then we did not see anymore signs again.

This continued for a while. The tension was thick – our gas tank was sliding toward the empty mark. "Only 5 kilometers of gas left!" Colin declared as he read the dashboard out loud. Once again we ended up where we had started. There was no place to park, and we were lost in a rat's maze.

Finally I was able to convince Colin to stop to ask directions. "Je ne sais pas!" a kind man replied to my question. He did not know the Hotel Chateaubriand, but he simply suggested we continue to drive up the hill toward the southern part of the walled city. Besides a few hand gestures pointing up, we did not have much direction on where to go. So, back to our zig zag up and around tiny streets.

"This is terrible," Colin shouted at one point. "How could you not know where the fucking hotel is?!?!"

Every time I tried to give a suggestion of where to turn or where to park, Colin cut me off. Soon he was yelling and cursing at me. I yelled back. And Dana and the children sat silently, just a foot behind us, confined in our compact car, listening to Mom and Dad fight.

I was so upset. How could Colin treat me like this? Why was he so angry?

186

At one point, Karl tried to help. "Please don't fight," he implored.

Colin and I paused for a few seconds before we continued arguing about where to try next and what to do.

At some point, we were at the top of a hill. We had progressed southward, but not as far as we both knew we needed to go, but we could not find any roads leading back down the other side of the hill.

"Ian needs to be brought close to the hotel!" Colin exclaimed, for the first time revealing out loud the real reason behind his stubbornness of trying to penetrate the endless maze inside the walled city. But it was too late. We were both just so angry and upset with one another. He was probably right that we were very close to the hotel, but unfortunately the car could not get through.

"Then stop!" I yelled with bitterness in my voice. "Let Ian and me out here, and we will find our way. You go park back outside the walled city, and we will meet you at the hotel. "

Doors opened, and my body spilled out of the overstuffed front seat, while my hands grabbed two of the bags that had shared my foot space. Dana opened her door to let Ian out. I reached behind her to take his crutches and grab another shoulder bag.

We slammed the doors shut, and Colin drove off.

Ian and I stood at the top of the hill in the middle of the street. Three bags and crutches. I could hear music and festivities in the background. I remembered that in one of our circles, we had seen a police precinct a block or two away. So Ian and I slowly hobbled down the road to ask for help.

Beth Jackson

I approached two policemen who were standing just outside the front entrance and asked if they had a map and told them the name of our hotel. "Nous sommes perdus," I confided. We were lost.

Within a minute or two, they had located the hotel on their wall map, and one of the officers emerged to point us in the direction.

We had to amble very carefully down an extremely steep staircase of twenty or more steps. Ian had refused my offer to help him maneuver, but I stayed just ahead of him to be a buffer in case he slipped. The bottom of the staircase greeted us with an alley that turned with the road to the left. And there it was. The sign of Hotel Chateaubriand hung directly above our heads. I sighed.

We approached the hotel, Ian on his crutches, me schlepping three bags on my shoulders, sifting through all of the people and activity and music in the plaza in front of us. Later we learned that it was summer festival, the busiest day of the year in St. Malo. Little had we known.

Ian and I checked in and asked the front desk if they could implore on our behalf to get us a table at the restaurant where we had missed our reservation. Over three hours late. The tables were all full, so no. Sorry.

I had gifts and cards for Colin's birthday, but frankly, I just wanted to cancel any sort of party. Instead I wanted to say, "So sorry, I hate you right now, and I don't want to celebrate with you. "

It took a lot of mental fortitude to put my anger aside, for the children, if anyone. I pulled out the first card and asked Ian to sign it.

It was almost an hour later before Colin, Karl, Thais, and Dana arrived at the hotel, burdened and panting under the weight of the suitcases and their journey. The wheelchair and a few remaining bags stayed behind in the car.

Our mutual exhaustion eased the earlier tension. A lively restaurant just a few doors down from the hotel was graciously willing to seat us at 11 p. m. It was Colin's birthday after all. And we were voracious.

As Colin and I spooned in bed at the hotel later that night, I could hear the festivities and music continuing below our open bedroom window. I felt safe in his embrace, but I was still upset by the unacceptable way he had spoken to me in the car.

"Don't come home if you are going to do that again," I chastised. The room fell silent. I felt guilty at the forcefulness of my word choice, but I was very hurt.

That night neither of us made our three kiss sounds, a poignant contrast to our entire marriage and every night of the vacation thus far. We continued to spoon in silence, but after a few minutes, when sleep started to fall on us and our muscles started to twitch, we both just rolled apart.

The next day, Colin explained how his back had been cramping up the last two hours of the drive that culminated in our fight. When we were lost in the maze of the walled city and he had to shift gears every ten seconds to negotiate the steep, winding streets, it made him all the more uncomfortable. I had not considered that after almost six months of not driving, his body was in no state to be at the wheel for over eight hours of stressful, stick-shift maneuvering. If only we had communicated better, we would not have yelled at each other or scared the children as badly as we did. But I was still pissed.

I wondered why the military did not give us any materials about R&R. I had heard that they supposedly debriefed and counseled soldiers for a full week before they went home at the end of a deployment, but they did nothing for R&R. They didn't give us any tips about what to expect or prepare for. Just have at it.

Beth Jackson

So we awkwardly navigated on our way. By the next day, Colin apologized. I understood the circumstances and accepted his apology.

***

The rest of the vacation resumed back to blissful family togetherness. The next day, at Mont St. Michel, I had not realized how steep this monastery was or had even thought about how Ian was going to get up to the top. But Ian was an example of calm patience, and he slowly crutched his way up. At one point, Colin simply carried him. He was so incredibly buff from working out every day that he flipped Ian over his shoulder with one arm like he was carrying a light jacket.

Dad carrying Ian up Mont St. Michel

Ian relished the attention and special time with Dad. We all laughed. We enjoyed each other's company. We took it all in. We remembered once again what we loved about each other.

After our visit to Mont St Michel, we drove onto Tuilly sur Suelles, on the quest to find the small country house we had rented. I had a map of this town, so directions were not an issue. Our car proceeded through farmlands, past old barns, cows, and fields of wheat sprinkled with bright summer flowers, and down the country road to our destination.

Eventually we found the number carved into the stone wall. There was a grand black metal gate between two tall stone posts. I got out of the car and pushed the call button by the gate's hinge.

As I climbed back into my seat and could hear the gears working, the gate started to slowly swing open. In front of us was a six-acre preserve of deer, enclosed by a simple wire fence. The road to the house surrounded this preserve in a large oval.

The car proceeded to the right, and through the trees and green grass, a grand chateau peered out into our view. Oh, my! Ahead of us stood a mansion. It was even nicer than it looked online. We entered a fairytale.

Historic chateau in Tuilly sur Suelles

Beth Jackson

The family that owned this home was so gracious. The owners were
a Parisian family with four young children. The woman who met us
explained how they had bought and renovated the house a few years
ago. She was an artist and pointed to some modern paintings on the
wall that she had created. We talked about the details of the house,
got the keys, and said goodbye. As we started unpacking our car,
the six of us just stopped and looked all around. We walked to the
edge of the wire fence and stared.

Woods.   Deer.

A chateau.

Just us.

Quiet.   Peace.

A family back in balance.

***

The rest of that week was the best part of the vacation. We
continued to do some sightseeing around Normandy and its famous
WWII sites. When confronted by the enormity of the endless rows
of white crosses at the American Cemetery, Colin's and my fight
from two days before lost all of its significance. The French showed
their gratitude for the Liberators who freed them half a century ago,
as they maintained the cemetery like the greens of a golf course and
thanked any American they saw.

American Cemetery in Normandy

Visiting this historic place helped give me perspective on my feelings over this year. I was not alone; there had been many millions more before me. And so many never had their loved ones come home. The backdrop made us focus simply on the blessing of having each other; that we should cherish what we had.

The next day, we visited the war museum in Caen, where I had a personal connection, as my German grandparents were among the first donors to help build the museum. After we toured the exhibits, I found the library. When I asked the librarian about the "red leather books of donors" she left the room and returned with one oversized book at a time until I found my grandfather's signature on the top of one page of one of them. Ronald Reagan had also signed that same book. There were dozens of these books, listing all the donors. This tiny personal connection to the war, and to this memorial, excited me. History was part of me.

Through the remainder of that wonderful week together as a family, we just enjoyed the simple things the countryside provided. Colin brought at least one child with him to the local bakery each morning to get armfuls of croissants and bread. I cooked delicious meals with locally grown French food. We played card games as a family while listening to a CD of Frank Sinatra that we found at the house. We slept. We read. We drank wine.

Beth Jackson

Thais pulling Karl in tractor

And each of the children had special time with Daddy. For Karl and
Ian, the D-Day beaches and museums topped everything else. They
enjoyed a special boys' day when they studied bridges, bomb craters,
and views from the cliffs above the beach. Thais enjoyed riding the
carousal in each city we visited. Her favorite activity, though, was
swinging between Colin and me. As she held one hand in each of
ours, she yelled, "Again," and together we would thrust our arms
forward to fly her into the air. Looking back, I recall that Colin and
I never held hands those two weeks, but I guess we did through the
connection of our daughter.

What struck me most about this time was how the children played
like children again, care-free and happy. We all smiled and laughed
more than we had for months. Being there all together, my worries
faded away, and my body and mind were both actually able to relax.
Besides the obvious gift of having Colin with us, the second best
part of the vacation was the actual escape from all responsibilities.
After the withdrawal of not needing to check my phone all the time,
and even better once my battery died, I actually was able to turn off
work completely and enjoy the vacation.

Chapter 17 – Destruction

End August 2011

It took a hurricane to pop my bubble of mental rest. We learned that Hurricane Irene was bearing down on us at home. The stress I had so happily abandoned was suddenly back as we discussed whether or not we should proactively change our return flight. The predictions of landfall varied quite a bit, but after hours of discussion, the choice was made for us; Delta cancelled our flight.

Our house rental week over, we drove back to Paris. Back at the hotel, when I got my phone charger and was finally able to get e-mails again, we learned that our Sunday flight was now automatically rescheduled for Wednesday. Oh, and rather than being a direct six-hour flight from Paris to Boston, we were now being routed through Cincinnati, a fifteen-hour odyssey.

Wednesday was the first day of school for the children. I was due back at work for my client on Tuesday. I needed to do something to change our flight.

The six of us quickly ventured out into the Parisian streets again to grab dinner. And then after we put the children to bed, instead of savoring our last moments together, Colin and I became snippy with each other over my stubbornness as I insisted on calling Delta. Three hours and a $325 phone bill later, we were rebooked for Monday on a direct flight back to Boston.

Once the return plans were confirmed, I was sort of able to relax again. We had not known that Colin's two-week R&R was counted in full days, so the days of his arrival and departure did not count against his fourteen days. We had booked our original departure flights far in advance of knowing his itinerary. As it turned out, we were now both flying out on Monday. The hurricane had given us an extra gift of time.

On our last day together, I felt an intense longing to stop time as we sat in the shade under a tree-lined walk at Fontainebleau and watched the children play with sticks in the dirt. I wished that we all could be immortal, as I desperately hoped that Colin would come safely back to us at the end of his deployment. That Sunday we were all together and so carefree, but twenty-four hours later, this dream simply disappeared in a haze of rushed goodbyes.

Our rescheduled flight on Monday ended up leaving just ten minutes after Colin's, from a different terminal. Our goodbyes lasted only seconds, as we stood on the pavement outside the drop-off entrance at the airport. Colin helped unload the bags and wheelchair before circling around to return the rental car by himself, so after quick hugs while cars behind us honked, he was gone. The brevity and location of the separation actually made it a little easier than a prolonged, sad exchange.

***

A pool of destruction that Hurricane Irene left behind welcomed us back home. Thankfully, I learned that my girlfriend had helped secure our house before the hurricane hit. She took the flagpole down, moved the patio furniture to under the deck, and secured the wooden porch swing.

Two different neighbors greeted us with milk and flashlights within an hour of our arrival home, as the power was still out. Our kitchen floor had become a puddle of ice cream soup from the freezer defrosting. So there I was on the floor scrubbing and cleaning, using more than five rolls of paper towels to get up the sticky mess. Then I moved on to the refrigerator. Everything inside had to go. I have to admit, it actually felt good, even cleansing, to start over with the fridge and freezer. There were some items tucked and hidden in the back that should have been tossed long ago.

Power came back on the next morning and interrupted the silence that had permeated the house. The phone rang for the first time the next afternoon, and I realized how much noise the humming of the refrigerator and air conditioning made but had always gone unnoticed. Leaves and tree branches still covered the ground outside, our pool looked like a massive squirrel's nest, and significant century-old trees lay turned on their side on nearly every street in the neighborhood. The most interesting discovery from the storm was the layer of thick salt that now coated our windows from all the seawater. The usual glass transparency was masked by cloudiness.

If the storm clean-up hadn't, our schedules quickly brought us back to reality. School and work once again filled our days. Ian had another physical therapy appointment and was told he could start putting partial weight on his leg. The walking boot could finally be used for walking. That was cause for celebration, although now he had to slow down on his crutches, put weight on the heel first, and then roll forward to the toe, a necessary but uncomfortable motion required for his body to learn how to walk again.

Colin e-mailed that he was already back in Kuwait, ready to make his first hop into Afghanistan. I knew he was already back in country by the time I was reading it, and the muscles in my shoulders instantly tensed up. Unconsciously, I was pulled back into the routine of surviving my day-to-day anxiety.

***

Saturday was an exciting day, at least for me; I took the children to the furniture store to purchase a new couch. Finally! I had been

Beth Jackson

saving money over the past several months for this, and now it was time for action. But after we had pulled into a parking spot I instinctively checked my phone for messages.

There was an e-mail from Dana. The subject line read: September.

> *Hi Beth,*
> *I want to let you know that I have accepted a job and I will be starting full time on September 26th. I will be working part time with the company until then. I've put together a schedule that I'll be able to work for you.*
>
> *September 6th 3-6*
> *7th 3-6*
> *8th 3-6*
> *9th 3-6*
>
> *September 12th 3 - overnight*
> *13th - drop kids at school - pick up at 2:45 Ian PT*
> *14th 3- ?*
> *15th 3- ?*
> *16th 3- ?*
>
> *September. 19th 3-?*
> *20th 3-?*
> *21st 3- overnight*
> *22nd drop kids at school, then overnight*
> *23rd drop kids at school, pick up at 3pm, overnight*
> *24th AM- overnight*
> *25th AM - late night - Last Day*
>
> *See you on Tuesday*
> *- Dana*

I started shaking. I had to reread it to be sure. Dana had just quit. She was deserting the children and me.

I had two business trips planned in September. With the children now back in school, I only needed childcare help for a few hours after school each day but also overnight for my trips. In particular, one of them called for four overnights over five days at the end of the month, so I could attend an annual trade show for my largest client. Months earlier, I had reached out to both my parents and Colin's to ask if either could come for those few days to stay overnight with their grandchildren. Unfortunately, none of them were able to come. So Dana had agreed to sleep over for the four nights, and now those would be her last days with the children, before she started her new job full-time.

Then it hit me that she had quit so impersonally. By e-mail. There was no apology in her note. We had made it very clear when we first learned of the deployment that we wanted her to stay at least the whole year. The one thing I wanted was consistency for the children. They adored Dana and were comfortable with her. And, frankly, I needed her. She was a calming influence on me.

Then my mind shifted to anger. *Who quit via e-mail?* Was I so old to think that was inappropriate? And what about the beautiful French vacation we had just treated her to? Had she been looking for a job before we left? Was she quitting because of Colin's and my fight?

What was supposed to be a fun outing to find a new couch suddenly became one more chore, just like finding a new afterschool sitter was about to become - one more thing I had to do to keep my single working mom life functioning.

***

Our life was spinning out of control again. The rain was pouring as I dropped the children at school a few days later.

Karl carried his backpack, lunchbox, trumpet case, and a small duffle with his soccer gear, and briskly ran full steam out of the rain into school. The big deal this year now that he was in middle school was that he got a locker, which he equipped with shelves and a white board. He was also thrilled he now got to play trumpet in the band. The trumpet was Colin's from his childhood.

Under the rain, Ian shuttled into school with his crutches, with his heavy backpack and lunchbox secured to his back. He no longer used the wheelchair. He had been slipping a lot recently, though, as he tried to move too quickly on the crutches and the bottom rubber had worn down. The rain did not help, so I called after him to slow down and be careful. I planned to pick him up early from school for his PT appointment, where he was slowly working to regain flexibility in his ankle, which had become very stiff and weak.

Thais wore her new French dress and pigtail braids this morning, and I held her hand as we navigated the parking lot and shielded our faces from the raindrops with our other hands. I always walked her into her classroom and watched as she wrote her name on the white board, tracing letters the teacher had written. The night before, Thais had told me she cried at school every day because she missed me, so as we said goodbye for the day, I kissed her hand so I would always be with her. It had become our special signal.

***

Ian's emotional and physical recovery continued slowly, sometimes in sync and sometimes at different paces.

One Saturday morning, I left Karl to watch Thais while I took Ian to physical therapy. As Ian rode in the backseat, he started re-strapping the walking boot, which he still needed because he could not yet bend his ankle. There was a lot of work still to do.

"God fucking, damn it," he yelled from behind me. The words startled me. The cotton liner was not fitting quite right. The

Velcro was rubbing painfully on his leg. He undid it and redid it. Again. And again.

Ian had a similar outburst two days before when getting ready for school. I offered help, but he yelled at me to stay away. He cried out, releasing all his pain and frustration with his leg, as he adjusted the liner yet again. I asked if he wanted any help, and he yelled, "No!" I felt helpless as a Mom unable to comfort him, but I gave him his space. That was what he needed. I was practicing patience.

In the car, his rants and raves in the back seat continued. I just drove silently, listening to the soft pop music on the radio, but when I heard a pause, I gently asked, "Can I help you?"

He responded in kind, saying "No," with less anger than a few seconds ago.

Oh, how I wanted to tell him how much I loved him in that moment, but I also knew it was not the right time.

Ian's trainer was an engaging man, who made the recovery work somewhat fun. I was so grateful for this strong male presence. Squats. Bicycle. Punching a bag, as an exercise to shift weight and strengthen the ankle. Lunges. Leg lifts. Pushing a scooter. Side steps in his hockey skates. Catching a ball. The physical therapy continued. Slow. Steady.

After physical therapy, Ian and Karl had an appointment with Pat, a counselor that the boys had been seeing for a few months. In another attempt at doing everything I could for the children, I had signed them up for counseling a few months prior just so they felt they had another adult they could confide in about their feelings. The military insurance deemed Thais too young to benefit from counseling, a perspective with which I disagreed, so she and I played at the playground instead during these appointments. *What was the downside?* I remember thinking. Nothing. Maybe it would do good.

Frankly, I probably was the one that needed Pat, but my boys were my surrogates. I kept my feelings bottled up inside, sharing only some of my worry and exhaustion with my sister. I knew I needed to be strong, so I stayed physically and emotionally closed, so no one could see how I was crumbling away inside. I simply participated vicariously through the boys' debriefs of their sessions.

The boys would tell me how they played the board game Sorry! with "Miss Pat," and on each Sorry! space, they had to say something they were sorry about. I think they drew pictures as well. And just talked. They went every other week, and seemed to be enjoying it. But on this particular morning, Ian told me he was done. He did not want to go to his appointment, which was within the hour. I digested this and slowly asked him, "Is Miss Pat helping you with your feelings about Dad being gone or your broken leg?"

"No," he replied.

I was not surprised. Ian seemed to have matured tremendously in those past months, and he still resisted fully opening up to others. Despite the occasional outbursts, Ian actually had seemed more at peace with himself, even as he still could not walk.

"Okay, then. You don't have to go again if you don't want to. "

Karl went to this one last appointment by himself. Afterwards he was completely indifferent about going back. Maybe it was not as much fun without Ian.

One less thing to do, so our trips to Miss Pat were over.

***

Today was a long work day, capped by a Board of Directors meeting and dinner. As I dropped the children at school, two different friends commented how nice I looked in my black dress, heals, and double strand of pearls. The perfect professional outfit - if only they knew.

The last time I wore those shoes, my feet started squeaking in the middle of the day. When there was just enough sweat on my feet, they rubbed against the leather and made a loud squeak sound, like a bike horn. The September weather was still warm enough to avoid the need for pantyhose, so that day, I cleverly brought a small shaker of baby powder to re-dry my feet every few hours. However, after dumping some powder into my shoes and being totally unaware, puffs of powder bloomed out of my feet with the weight of each step I took down the hall at work. Walk, puff, walk, puff. I did not notice the growing cloud of white left in my trail until a male colleague commented that he thought my feet looked like they were on fire, smoldering. So embarrassing.

After the business dinner, arriving back home under the warm darkness of the evening sky, Dana left and I found Karl and Thais already fast asleep, Thais occupying my bed. Ian was awake still.

"I have been having nightmares," he confided. When I asked what the nightmares were about, he described a time machine that turned into a wicked clown face.

I told Ian how I used to have nightmares when I was a girl as well. I told him about a silly one of sleeping bags moving everywhere to the sound of rice spilling. "That's weird," he said. "Not scary."

"I know," I told him. "That is the point. That scary clown face is not real. It is fake. Just remind yourself of that anytime you wake up from a nightmare." I lay next to him and rubbed his back as we spoke.

Beth Jackson

"But then I wake up to dark shadows and things in my room, and I cannot go back to sleep," Ian continued.

"If you ever wake up in the middle of the night," I responded, "you can come just sleep in my bed with me. As you know, there is someone missing in there, and you are welcome to sleep in his spot. "

"I am not a baby," he replied.

"I know you are not. But I miss having someone with me as well. "

Ian thought about this and then quickly sat up on top of the assortment of pillows and blankets surrounding his body. "Can I sleep with you tonight?" he asked.

"Yes, of course," I replied. "Thais is in there, too, but there is room for all three of us. "

I helped Ian carry his three blankets as he used his crutches to hobble down the hallway and climb into the far side of my king-sized bed.

My body climbed over a sleeping Thais, and as we lay under the white down comforter, Ian started telling me more about school and how it was getting harder.

"We are learning long division now. But I don't really understand it. "

"Would you like me to show you a few math tricks in the morning to explain it?"

"Yes. "

"It is not easy," he continued.

"Remember last year when you always told me you were bored at school?"

I could hear him nodding in the darkness. "Well, maybe this year will be a little harder but also more interesting. "

A silent pause rested between us. Thais's heavy breathing was the only sound in the room.

"Can I have a hug?" I asked and rolled towards him. He reached out for me, and we held a strong embrace for a few moments.

There I lay next to Ian in my bed, eventually releasing my arms from around his small frame. I felt at peace beside him, but only looking back do I realize that he was actually breathing life into me that night, too.

After a few minutes, Ian settled in comfortably and fell peacefully asleep for the night, surrounded by a few extra pillows.

In the morning, he told me, "I didn't have any nightmares last night. "

I didn't either.

***

A week later, I was still intently searching for a new nanny. I only needed a few hours of after school coverage, so it should not have been that hard to find someone, but it was. There were local college students, but each could only do two days a week because of class conflicts. The idea of juggling multiple calendars and inconsistency in the supervision of homework was not going to work for me. I needed one person. Also, I needed a sitter who could help the children with math and spelling; I ignored any applicant whose e-mail to me included multiple obvious spelling errors. That excluded at least five women.

Worried that I would not find someone before Dana left, my nights were filled with posting jobs on craigslist, care. com, and at the local colleges, all in between my usual e-mails to Colin and nervous checking for my Google alerts.

When the children learned that Dana was leaving for a new job, the first reply from Karl was "What did we do?"

"Nothing," I reassured them. I explained how she found a job that was more in line with her desired long-term career path. They nodded silently.

Chapter 18 – The Explosion

Mid September 2011

My stomach was really upset today. I wasn't sure if it was due to the emotions of the tenth anniversary of 9/11, my watching replays of what happened that dreadful day, or remembering the loss of my college friend. Or knowing that Colin was in Afghanistan today because of the evil that was inflicted on our country now a full decade ago.

I watched the History Channel with the children, which aired a program using footage from that day when the world changed. At one point, the screen advised viewer discretion. Thais was playing with her stuffed animals in the other room already. Ian chose to leave the room. It was too real. Too scary. Karl watched in awe. He saw me cry for the first time in his life. The boys knew what had happened on that day, but until they saw the actual context and how scared people were, they had not fully understood the feelings felt by those who were old enough to remember it.

Every year around the holidays, going back even before 9/11, the children and I make cookies as a small thank you for the local police and firemen. Years after the Twin Towers fell, some may have once again forgotten about their brave service every day. But I haven't.

Four friends reached out to me on 9/11. Karen and her two boys came over to play with Thais. My brother's wife called to say that she and her family were thinking of Colin. Will sent an e-mail, as did Thais's new pre-K teacher, who said she prayed for us every day.

Once again I was a little disappointed I did not hear from anyone else, but in hindsight, I recognize that I was still expecting too much.

Beth Jackson

Expect nothing, Colin had advised me. As I reviewed my journal to write this book, I saw how supported I was in so many different ways throughout this deployment, but in my anxiety, isolation surrounded me and help from others seemed totally absent. I felt like I was completely on my own in this marathon, physically and emotionally running alone.

That night of the tenth anniversary, after tucking in the children to bed, I had to hustle back to the bathroom. I barely got there in time again before dinner was gone in a second.

***

We were half way through the year's deployment, but it seemed like forever. I suppose I had reached the top of the mountain and could begin the decent, but it didn't quite feel that way.

It was easy to get caught up in the number game. The number of deployments. The length of each. The time in war zones. I don't know what it is like to experience even longer or more difficult hardships that many others routinely do; all I can say is this year was the hardest thing I have ever done in my life.

A friend e-mailed me some perspective.

> *A lot of people think when you are doing something that takes a long time that the hardest part is getting to the halfway point. I happen to believe (as I see you do) that the half way point is the easy part. The harder part is realizing you made it halfway but still have to 'run' the other half...*
>
> *I realized this when we were half way up Mt. Kilimanjaro. The hardest part of the trek was climbing for almost 20 hours and that was NOT at the halfway point.*

*The good news is the rest of the time works pretty much the same as
the first part of your climb - pole, pole. . . slowly, slowly. Each step or
day that you take brings you closer to the end. Sometimes you can take
a bunch of steps and not realize how much time has passed and other
times you feel every step.*

*... whenever you have a doubt, just put one foot in front of the other
and realize you are already that much closer.*

I send you a hug and my best wishes!

In the time since Colin had been gone, the children had changed so
much, as did our small world at home. Karl had grown an inch and
two shoe sizes. A half-mile long bridge nearby had been entirely
repainted blue to cover up the rusted burgundy beams. Thais
had learned to swim and ride a bike. And a plant in the kitchen
grew two new three-foot tall stems. Ian overcame his temporary
handicap and opened up about his fears. Over seven moons had
now gone. Seasons were changing again to Fall, as the air was cooler
and crisp now. And I felt even more alone.

During a run on the Cliff Walk along the coast of the Atlantic
Ocean in Newport, I saw many couples holding hands as they
strolled along the rocks, watching the crashing waves. My panting,
the beats of my Nike running shoes hitting the pavement, and
the crash of the ocean all moved in relative unison as I ran and
ran, trying to escape from everything. But even there, I could not
escape the feelings of jealousy at seeing the couples' tender touch
with each other, as fingers interlaced or an arm gave comfort to the
other's shoulders. Oh, I so wanted to hold hands again with Colin.
My legs picked up pace, as I tried to distance myself from the sights
of those couples.

***

Beth Jackson

An e-mail from Pamela at Operation Military Kids arrived with information about how the Rhode Island National Guard was coordinating snow removal for families with a deployed spouse. The military always tried to say that we were one, regardless of what service we were in. Secretly, I hoped the National Guard could adopt my family as theirs, since my husband's Reserve unit was still missing in action. No package or chain of command information from Daisy ever arrived.

It was not snow season yet, but I took the bold step of asking for help. I sent an e-mail to the Rhode Island National Guard contact listed, requesting that we be added to the snow removal list. Please.

***

In the middle of September, I left for an overnight business trip, which was unexpectedly interrupted by my worst fears. It would change me forever.

The objective of this trip was to lead an eight-hour marketing innovation training session for 95 people. I was in my professional element in the middle of this session in a large high-ceiling ballroom at the historic Nassau Inn when, during a short break, I glanced at my phone.

We had just sent all 95 attendees on an excursion into town to visit various retailers as part of a task to come up with inspiration for new product ideas. The ballroom was almost empty. As my finger slid across the screen, my eyes locked on an e-mail from a dear friend.

> *We just saw some news blurbs about some attacks on the US embassy and wanted to know if you'd heard from Colin. We just stopped to pray for him and everyone over there - for their safety AND for your peace and comfort.*

What situation? No, I had not heard from Colin. The wave of numbness started in my toes and fingers and flowed quickly inwards to overtake my body. I immediately started trembling as I started to click on Google. The Internet signal was particularly slow in this grand room, and the page did not instantly open.

Somehow my body walked the few feet over to my colleague Sarah, and I whispered, "Something happened near Colin's base. I don't know what. "

I must have looked like I was going to be sick. She immediately stepped into action as she saw me desperately willing the screen to give me information, "Do you want me go online and figure out what is going on?"

I shook my head and instead kept trying to do it myself. My trembling fingers gripped my phone and moved it out in front of me and above my head as my feet paced around the room to find better Wi-Fi reception.

Finally, I caught bits of what was happening. There had been attacks on both the Embassy, where Colin visited several times a day, AND attacks on Colin's NATO base. Four suicide bombers. Some of the attackers were still loose.

I went from trembling to actually shaking. My nightmares of faceless bodies running after Colin swept through my mind. I clutched my phone, not knowing whether to stand or sit.

Minutes passed. I was paralyzed.

When the Internet slowed to a stop, I clicked back out to my e-mails before trying to go back into Google, and a new e-mail appeared.

From Colin.

Beth Jackson

> *Beth,*
> *If you see the TV, there's nothing to worry about. The situation*
> *is under control, and I am safe inside a secure facility. Please let*
> *everyone know there's nothing to worry about.*
> *Love,*
> *C*

Secure facility. Secure facility. What did that mean? A bunker?

Situation under control. Under control? Really? Or was he trying to
protect me from worrying? I did not believe him. The Internet said
the attackers were still at large.

I wanted to scream. I wanted to go home. I wanted to go back to the
security of my own insulated bubble, to wrap the children and me under
my big white comforter and go to sleep until this deployment was over.

But I was stuck.

I did not have an e-mail group list on my phone, so I had to think
quickly about who could get the word out to our family and friends.
My sister lived in California, where it was still early, and I did not
want to wake her. My brothers and parents were not always online.
I had just seen an e-mail from Karen, who as a lawyer always had
her phone on her and could simply "reply all" to one of my previous
e-mails. So, I forwarded Colin's note to her and asked her to send it
out, which she immediately did.

The client had invested enormously for this training session I was
leading, and I knew I could not leave. And there was nothing I could
do to help Colin. Except pray. We had 30 minutes before the attendees
would be returning from their assignment in town. Sarah suggested we
take a walk outside. Great idea. I contacted the children's new teachers
as they were not yet on the original e-mail list. I asked them to please
keep the news away from the children. My desire to shelter them was
particularly strong.

I stopped again and texted Dana to tell her the same thing, so she knew what was happening and not to say anything when she picked up the children from school.

Sarah and I walked and walked. The only sounds were the shuffling of our feet along the sidewalk and traffic of the cars passing by.

My stomach still felt like knots, but the sunshine and fresh air had helped, at least temporarily. Time was getting close, and we had to return to the conference room.

The clients returned a short while later, too, and the session continued for the day. Somehow I made it through, wearing a mask to hide my invisible pain.

When the meeting ended, I gathered my bags and quickly said goodbye to the client. I gave Sarah a hug and thanked her. I jumped into a taxi and, as tears began to coat my cheeks, I texted Carrie.

> *Some days I just want to cry. I have held it in all day and now am en route to the train station.*

She replied immediately.

> *Go ahead and let yourself cry. Slow deep inhales and exhales might provide relief as well.*

I was heaving, unable to breathe. I had already started typing more, through my blurred vision and exaggerated chest movements.

> *I don't want to talk right now but may call you later.*

I could not talk. I knew only sobs would come out. She replied back.

Beth Jackson

Love love love. You are not alone with this. God loves you, I love you, and so do many other people....

I scanned my e-mails and saw another note from Karen, just checking in. The tears were simply streaming by this point.

I needed help.

When I arrived at the Trenton train station, somehow my eyes focused long enough to scan the overhead screen to find the track of my Amtrak train that would return me to Rhode Island later that night. I wanted to go home.

As I waited on the cold metal bench for Northeast Regional #137, I had visions of Colin sitting in an underground bunker with his body armor as his only protection. Pulled taut, my body and mind could not take more strain. The months of stress and gripping fear had slowly been chipping away at my sanity, and I felt like I was hanging on a precipice.

Suddenly an Acela train zoomed by at extreme speed, and the extraordinary sound of the powerful engine, metal grinding, and forceful winds blew my head and torso backward several inches. I grabbed onto the edges of the bench, and my eyes looked at the thick black metal tracks again. Suddenly, something snapped and that fear, grounded in the deepest foundation of love for my husband and children, was completely gone. My heart was vacant of any feeling, as a chill enveloped my bones and my breathing stopped. For a split second, the faceless dark weight crept out of my body and began its siege on my mind.

I could easily jump in front of the next 200-ton train zipping by. All this anguish would just be gone. It would be instant.

And then I snapped back. *Oh God! Did I really just have that thought?* I immediately slammed this cracked door shut, and I knew I would never act on such an idea. But never before in my life had I felt so lost and futile, and I realized this might be how people felt when they got to the point where they could not go on. And I did wonder how many people killed themselves by jumping in front of a train.

The fact I even had this thought, while fleeting, fundamentally scared me. *Who was I anymore?* I pushed these doubts out of my mind and tried to pull myself together. I stood and found myself standing in front of a different open door.

My train had arrived. In four hours, I would get out at North Kingstown and then drive the 40 minutes home. So I settled into the cushioned seat in Business Class and checked my e-mails again. There was a newsletter from the church. We had only attended service once in the past six weeks, but I opened the e-mail anyway. I read that we were to have yet another interim priest, the fourth one since Colin had left. In desperation, I sent him an e-mail to introduce myself and ask for help. It began so clearly:

I need help.

But God was nowhere to be found. Literally, this priest did not respond to my e-mail for days.

Pulling into my driveway under the cool overcast darkness of the sky later that night, I saw that my flagpole looked how I felt: broken and hanging like a limp rag. I would need to get another new one.

Beth Jackson

Broken flagpole

When I saw a friend at school drop-off that next morning, she asked how I was doing. My face betrayed nothing but a stoic calm as I mumbled, "I'm fine." But I was not fine. Pain pulsed through my body. I wanted so much to just be held and to cry in someone's safe arms. But she saw no clues to know that I was cracking.

In the Pre-K classroom, my daughter's teacher pulled me aside and handed me a prayer shawl knitted by her friends. When she handed me this gift, all I could say was a soft "thank you." I did not reach out to give her a hug because I knew that close touch would unleash all my feelings. Rather, my throat hardened as I tried to hold back the tears. The thoughtfulness and timing of her gift were more meaningful to me than she would ever know.

Out in the parking lot as I was heading home, a new friend, who was new to the school and whose husband was shortly deploying to Afghanistan as well, handed me a loaf of bread she had baked. "Thinking of you," the note read.

And that night, a neighbor who had moved in just two months before, knocked at my door with a "deployment dinner" that she had baked. That was the one meal brought to us during Colin's entire deployment, yet somehow the timing of her kindness was perfect. She had no idea how much I really needed it.

I also reached out to Cara. Her reply helped to steady me.

> *Oh – I definitely have those days. I am quite sure I cry every day at some point. I was really low after the attack on Nick's base in April and I am sure that's probably what got you. It's too much stress to think about someone you care about getting shot at. I don't know what kind of person can help – no one here is going to make him safe or make you less worried. This is what PTSD is all about – it's traumatizing to be worried so much...*

Molly also sent an e-mail, asking how she could help. There was nothing, really, she or anyone could do, but her e-mail gave me comfort. No one here could protect Colin from being shot. And no one could help me not worry.

My children never knew what had happened in Kabul that day. Protecting them was my mission. And while my friends and family never knew the full depth of my desolation, looking back, I now see that the small gestures of love from them and from others, unexpected angels who were virtually strangers, gave me strength and saved me from falling.

Three days after the attack, Colin called. The "unknown" number that appeared on my phone instantly revealed the caller. I quickly stood up and stepped out of a client meeting to take the call. I only learned much later that they had indeed been in their body armor and were in that bunker for 48 hours. Colin played down the significance of the event and quickly changed the subject as he sought quick stories that would bring him into the daily lives of the children. But my mind had already made the attack into something much bigger and scarier for him than reality was.

When I returned to my meeting, my client asked about Colin.

"He is alive," was all I could say in return.

We then spoke about it for a few more minutes, and I felt better. It was very genuine and kind that we pulled away from work for a short pause to talk about life. That was the only important thing that mattered to me anymore.

***

One day, Thais proclaimed, "Mom, wouldn't it be great if you and Dad had 33 kids, and 21 dogs, and 13 cats, and 15 rabbits? Then you would be so busy, you wouldn't be able to go on business trips. And I could help take care of all the animals. "

I did not want to work anymore. I did not want to be away from the house anymore. Frankly, I just wanted to curl up and sleep until Colin came home. Like Sleeping Beauty, I wanted to wake up to a new life. My old life.

The decision was already clear that I was going to have to stop traveling for work, but I still had that one last five-day trip booked.

That week, in Louisville, Kentucky, my working mom guilt reached its pinnacle. Besides the longer-than-ever business trip, the children's school was saluting its military families by having a picture taken of all of them together. The few military families at the school were typically there for just a year while a parent attended the Navy's professional graduate school; none had a deployed parent.

I had received an e-mail from the school with the date and time of the photo - Friday, September 23 at 8:30 a. m. Within twenty minutes of receiving the e-mail, I wrote back to ask if there was any way it could be moved to another date since I would be out of town on business. Panic overcame me as I thought about my three children appearing to be parentless in the photo.

"We can just put an inset picture of you and Colin," the school suggested, trying to be helpful. *Oh, my gosh, NO!* I could imagine an inset of Colin with the clear understanding he was in Afghanistan, but then I imagined a head shot of me with the caption "working mom is out of town – again. " *Why didn't we just shout from the rooftops that I was a horrible mother?*

I worried that Thais would be a mess if she had to take a picture without either of us there. Yet, despite my protestations, the school stayed firm that the date would not move, as others had "already moved their work around to make this day and time. "

On the night before this photo, I lay in bed in the Crowne Plaza in Louisville after a long working dinner with my client's biggest customer. I sent Thais's teacher a quick e-mail asking her to help Thais with the transition from her classroom. Thais was no longer crying at school each day, but I worried this could start up again.

I also texted Dana a quick reminder to tell the children about the picture in the morning. I sent one more short text suggesting maybe Ian could help walk Thais from her classroom to where the photo would be taken.

Dana texted me back.

> *Beth, I told them about three times today. They are aware - as am I. Talk to you tomorrow.*

Beth Jackson

I re-read it to make sure my mind was not messing with me. Yes, she really just gave me the finger back in her text. I was already feeling horribly guilty, and now my nanny was giving me lip for what I thought was a helpful reminder for the children.

I thought about what I wanted to text back as the words raged in my head. *This is all about the children, by the way, Dana. I don't care what you feel or may have said. I just want my children to feel included and loved when I cannot be with them. I am just asking that you please help me.*

I texted my anger to Carrie instead. And as always, she gently replied to just let it go. And take deep breaths. And I went to bed. Still pissed, my body somehow fell to sleep.

My alarm went off at 6:15 a. m. , and I prepared myself for another long day filled with a series of meetings with media editors and potential customers. Standing on my feet. Constant interaction. The only two-minute breaks I could expect were to use the bathroom and order lunch.

Standing in the lunch line I quickly scanned my e-mails but stopped in my tracks when I saw Ian's teacher's name.
  Beth,

  I hope wherever you are, you are having nicer weather than we are! It is so humid here today.

  FYI - Ian is falling behind on his homework. I assigned both spelling pages and handwriting on Monday that were due today. Ian did not do either assignment. He also turned in grammar homework that was incomplete and practice book pages that were not complete. Both practice book pages and grammar pages were started in class and had to be finished for homework. I know he is worried about his grades and I hate to see him lose points because of homework.

  Ian is so capable and I want his grade to reflect his abilities. Please call or email me if you want to discuss this.

Thanks,
Ian's 4th grade teacher

My stomach wretched. Hundreds of miles away from home, loneliness surrounded me. I missed my children. I just wanted to hold them. I was worried about my husband. My life was held together with scotch tape.

That night, my calls to American Airlines to see if I could catch an earlier flight home failed. I tried Delta. And United. And Southwest. I could not be away from my children anymore. Every airline I called told me their flights were all oversold due to this conference, and they were not accepting any more names on the waitlist.

Two days later, the conference finally over, I arrived home around midnight. Thankfully, Erin, our new kind-hearted nanny I was so lucky to have found, was there having taken over from Dana for the evening until I returned. Today was also Dana's last day.

Walking in the front door out of the evening darkness, a horrible strong smell overwhelmed my senses. It permeated throughout the entire house. The source, it turned out, was in the garage. Dana had forgotten to take the garbage out for pick-up on Friday morning, even though I had written it down on the schedule I wrote out for her before I had left. My disappointment and defeat were palpable.

Dehydrated from flying, I filled a glass of water and took some sips. I reached for a paper towel, but my hand touched cardboard. The roll was empty. I walked back to the garage to get a new roll. Before heading upstairs, I went to the small bathroom off the kitchen. As I reached for toilet paper, I saw cardboard again. The toilet paper roll was also empty. I opened the bathroom cabinet and put on a new roll. I felt burdened that I had to do everything just to keep the house functional. Being gone meant the house just fell into disrepair.

Passing back through the kitchen, I saw a Nerf gun lying on the counter. The Nerf gun was the one toy in this world that always pushed my buttons. The children, on the other hand, loved it and enjoyed using their friends' whenever possible. But at our house, they were not permitted. They caused chaos and made a noise that drove me insane. Yet Dana had decided to give the children, as her parting gift to our family, Nerf guns. I felt like she was giving me the finger again.

Looking back, I realize my feelings towards Dana were overly harsh. She loved the children dearly and gave them a cool goodbye gift. But I felt betrayed. She wasn't just leaving the children; she was also leaving me. Dana had been the closest thing to family in the state of Rhode Island, and I depended on her. She had taken care of me, without my even noticing or appreciating it. In the grand scheme of life, I now don't blame her for moving on to a new phase of her career and not wanting to miss an opportunity. In the tunnel vision that was my reality at the time, however, her departure made me feel deserted.

Chapter 19 – Saying No

October 2011

Today was parent-teacher conference day. When I asked the boys if there were anything I should talk to their teachers about, Karl said softly, "I don't like that the other kids call me a war geek. "

"Just because my Dad is at war, they don't need to be mean to me," he continued.

Ian seconded the thought. "They call me that, too, Mom. "

My heart sank. Children often didn't know how hurtful their words could be. I told their teachers and hoped they could help.

***

Still, there was still no communication at all from my husband's unit. At this point, all I really wanted was a phone call. *"How are you doing? We are thinking of you. "* Instead, nothing.

It had not yet snowed, but I was still hoping for a reply to my e-mail asking for assistance from the Rhode Island National Guard for snow removal. No reply. Not a word.

***

My mom came in town again for a few days. The children and I enjoyed her company over a typically busy weekend of activities. But looking back, I also see how worried my mom was about me.

Beth Jackson

Friday night the children and I had planned to watch a movie. My mom had already gone to bed in her nook in the laundry room, where she washed and folded clothes without me even realizing. Mediating the children's differing opinions over what we should watch, I decided on a Disney movie about husky dogs lost in an Arctic storm. Ian did not like my choice at all, and after months of holding in most of his frustration from his long months of immobility, he now exploded into a full-fledged temper tantrum. I had learned from previous experience that yelling back did not work. So I calmly but firmly explained that he could join us on the couch, quietly, or resume his yelling up in his room.

His screaming continued with the force of a growing tornado, when suddenly my mom appeared and responded to his yelling in kind. She hollered at Ian to stop it right away. This scene was surreal and quite funny in hindsight, but only now do I see that my mother was frightened that I was too fragile to deal with the situation. Her instinct was to protect me from my own child.

***

The three children and I went to church the next Sunday. I continued to look for God, but he was hiding, and that white-haired woman I liked was not there. No one spoke to me or the children. Not even the priest. No one asked about Colin.

Our bodies simply occupied space within the sanctuary's cold, stone walls, but nothing was reaching into our souls. Even the music seemed flat that morning. Usually I sang along, but on this particular morning, I just stood silently listening for a heartbeat or a soft murmur of a prayer among the notes. There was nothing.

And my boys turned the church programs into paper airplanes.

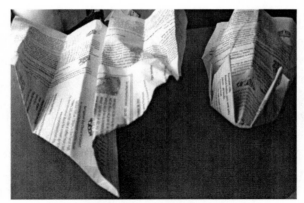

Church programs as paper airplanes

I decided we had had enough church. We did not go back.

***

I don't know why it took me so long to acknowledge that I had long since lost the marathon. My body had been limping along this second half of the deployment, and it was finally time to give up competing. I just needed to make it to the end.

And it struck me that I could not do it anymore if things continued the same way. I realized everything bad happened when I was gone - Ian's accident, the attack on Colin's base, Hurricane Irene - and I needed to be home. For the children. For me. In all my worry and pressure, I had forgotten how to just "be." The discovery of how gaunt and unhappy I had become hit me like a train, so I finally said NO in order to survive.

I had been moving toward this decision even before September when my travel was excessive. I knew I could not put Colin and the children in a literal proactive bubble, but I could at least be there for those impromptu bedtime conversations or snuggles from a nightmare.

Beth Jackson

A client wanted me to attend some new market research in Texas. I was more resolved now, and this time said NO. Another wanted me to lead research sessions in three different cities. NO again. I would not travel until my husband came safely home.

No more five-day work weeks. The pace had become unsustainable.

My biggest client finally asked me to respond to their offer to become an employee as Chief Marketing Officer. There were good reasons to say YES - the regular paycheck, the consistent hours, the professional cachet the title bestowed. But the decision had already become very clear. I could not give up the last bit of my life that I could control. Throwing my long-term goals away, I said NO.

It was the first time that I realized "NO" was a complete sentence; I did not owe anyone an explanation for the decisions I made. I don't know why it had taken me so long to realize it. Every time my sister had texted me to exhale, her words comforted me, but I did not actually breathe any better. I had not actually listened to the content of her words.

But as soon as I said NO, my shoulders felt instantly lighter, and small streams of oxygen rejuvenated the cells in my body.

***

First on my plan to just "be" was to have a Mom Day with each of the children.

While the boys were in school, Thais and I enjoyed her Mom Day by simply being together. The sun-filled day included swinging and climbing on the monkey bars at the playground. We read several long books at the bookstore, and she asked if I would buy her a book "because when Dad took me for Dad Day before he left, he got me the white seal stuffed animal. "

I smiled and said, "Yes. "

I also had plans to take her to a local bakery that made chocolate croissants, so she could enjoy her favorite treat from our French vacation. After a morning of fun, we ran some errands together. The car wash was a novelty, and Thais enjoyed wiping down the doors, while I vacuumed out the sand that still lingered in every crevice from the summer.

Our last stop before home was the bank. Standing by the ATM, Thais stared at a man in an Army uniform. He was the same height and build as Colin.

Thais looked at him and shyly said, "You look like my Dad. "

"But he is in Afghanistan," she continued.

The man bent down to her level with a warm smile on his face, "I have a son who is five years old. How old are you?"

"Four," she replied.

"Would you like a hug?" he offered, so kindly.

Thais shook her head, no, and started crying. This kind, gentle soul was reaching out into her heart, but he was not her Dad. And she knew the difference.

Back home, as I made lunch, Thais disappeared upstairs. She returned holding a single silver star about a centimeter in diameter on her finger. The sticker glittered in the light as her hand moved.

Beth Jackson

"Can I put this on the door to the workshop?" she asked.

"Why?" I inquired.

"It is for Daddy," she responded. And she walked downstairs to the basement where Daddy had all his tools, and she put the tiny sticker on the large white painted door, just for him.

Later in the afternoon, Thais joined me in cleaning out the garage. Sweeping. Moving soccer and lacrosse equipment to the back to make more room for the coming hockey season. We moved the bikes behind the garbage cans, so they were not in the way.

As I put the boogie boards to the side wall and pulled the sleds out to the front, Thais asked one of her favorite questions, "When is Daddy coming home?"

"After Christmas," I replied. Christmas was two months away.

"When will it snow?" Thais wanted to know.

"Probably in another month or two. "

"Can I pull my animals on the sled?" I think she was willing it to snow.

"Sure," I encouraged her. "I can help you. "

With that she smiled happily, as she ran up and down the grassy small hill at the side of our house, dragging the sled full of stuffed animals behind her.

That weekend the annual Harvest Fair at the local Norman Bird Sanctuary, a three-hundred-acre natural preserve, had finally arrived. This fair was a good old-fashioned family event with hayrides, cotton candy, live country music, a ropes course, ring toss games, and various crafts. It also featured a greased pole.

Thais and I wandered around together over the hay-strewn grounds, as the boys, hands full of tickets, darted around with friends to various older kid activities. At one point, Thais and I emerged from a tent that housed pumpkin painting, and out of the corner of my eye, I saw Karl and friends attempting to climb the twenty-foot tall greased metal pole. A $1 prize was being given to anyone who succeeded. It was quite humorous observing the boys, as one propped up another's foot or climbed on another's back, as they tried to help each other up the pole. The grease was a major obstacle, but the boys were determined. Karl's friends tried several times, and after pulling themselves up a few feet, gravity pulled their bodies quickly back down. Ian stood by, unable to participate with his booted leg, but cheering nonetheless.

A few minutes later, Karl's shirt and shoes flew across the hay, and he renewed his attempt up the pole. This time, his half-naked body began making some progress. When he was halfway up, I pulled out my phone to start filming the scene. It would be great footage to e-mail Colin. Minutes passed, as Karl hung from higher heights and his muscles began to shake with fatigue. A crowd gathered, and everyone was cheering for him to make it all the way to the top. Just a few feet shy, I thought he was going to give up, but with one last burst of adrenaline, Karl's feet held tight as they thrust his body up one more foot, then another, and his hand successfully rang the bell on the top. He slid down very quickly, and was so happy to go claim his prize money.

A short while later, after Thais and I made our way over to the pony rides, I saw Karl go up the pole again. Maybe he had wiped all the grease off the pole with his previous attempts, or by now he had mastered his technique and confidence. So up he went again. He called out to me that this was his third time. As he slid down, a little too quickly, he said he wanted to do it one more time.

Beth Jackson

"I can only handle one broken leg at a time. I will pay you $5 NOT to climb the pole again," I offered with a pleading smile.

He agreed.

***

Over four months had passed since the accident, and Ian was finally dismissed from physical therapy. His trainer told him not to return and that he no longer needed to wear the boot. To celebrate this news, Ian and I had his Mom Day on Friday, when he also got to play hooky from school.

Ian scripted the whole day. First, we had breakfast at a local log cabin café known for delicious glazed cinnamon buns. Then we went hiking at Hanging Rock, a large cliff in the middle of the Norman Bird Sanctuary. It was really cold at first, and Ian commented that he should have worn socks. But as soon as he started running along the path, and I joined in, we both warmed up. Up the path. Over the rocks. Hiking. Some climbing. For a boy where movements had been so restricted for so long, this was sheer freedom.

After our hike, Ian and I drove to Providence. On our way, we stopped at the Post Office to mail a package to Dad.

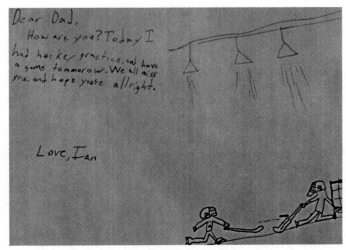

Note from Ian to Colin

We arrived at the Providence Place Mall around 11:00 a. m. and found our way up to the top floor for Dave & Busters. Ian did not know what to expect. He had said he wanted to go to an arcade, and I told him Dave & Busters was ten times bigger, louder, and glitzier than any he'd ever seen. And oh, how it was. Thirty dollars of tokens later, Ian had had his fill of games. He had won 640 tickets on the various games he had played, so he excitedly went to the arcade store to choose his prizes. He started looking around to see what he could buy with the tickets. He paused, did the math in his head, and then chose three rattling toys that dispensed candy. One for him, one for Karl, and one for Thais. With 30 tickets left, he bought three Chinese finger holder toys to share with his siblings, too. His selflessness made me smile.

A week later, it was Karl's Mom Day to enjoy. Not surprisingly, he also wanted to go hiking and to Dave & Busters. We had a wonderful day together as well. In the afternoon, though, Karl shared what he really wanted, "Mom, I just want a Family Day with Dad when he is back. We could all go skiing. Or just stay home and play hearts. "

Beth Jackson

Just be.

***

While we enjoyed our outings, Colin was visiting different places in Afghanistan, too. Not knowing that pictures of him in his body armor or sitting atop an old Soviet tank unsettled me, Colin kept sending me more of them.

Colin at Bala Hissar, an ancient Afghan citadel, on top of a Soviet tank.

And something else seemed wrong, at home. One day, I had left a small white envelope of cash, an extra $170 for my cleaning lady for finally cleaning off the rest of that seawater from Hurricane Irene from the first floor windows. The envelope was on the big family calendar where I left such notes.

I had been working away from the house that day, when Erin was there with the children along with our cleaning lady. Erin claimed she had seen the envelope. Our cleaning lady claimed she did not. I doubted one of them could have thrown it out by mistake. I turned over every single piece of paper around the calendar, piled high with school notices, trying to find that envelope, to no avail. One of them was lying, but I did not know who.

So I paid the cleaning lady a second time. I cringed at the thought of another $170 flying out of our shrinking bank account.

***

In the crisp Fall air, my body readied itself for a run, another typical circular loop around the neighborhood. Down the hill, past the houses on the river, up the other side of the hill, around a loop, through the wooded road, and back around to my house. My feet had pounded this pavement thousands of times; the run was second nature to my body.

But somehow today, as I was rounding the second to last corner before my street, a rusted wire hanger, which was hidden under the crunchy leaves, caught my left shoe and flipped me over mid stride. My body landed hard as my left wrist first hit the pavement, and the air was punched out of my chest. As I pulled myself up to a sitting position on the tree-covered street with an aching left hand, tears drained down my face.

I was exposed and raw on that cool concrete street. Not one car or one person came by. And once the flow of tears slowed to a trickle and were then no more, I pulled myself up off the ground, gently rubbing my wrist, wishing it to feel better, and I starting running again. Once I turned that last corner, the anguish that raged throughout me thrust my body in a full sprint all the way home.

***

Out of the blue and with just a few days notice, my childhood friend, Jen, came up from Washington, D. C. to visit. I had not seen her in over four years, but as my best friend, we could always just pick up exactly where we left off.

Beth Jackson

Even though our busy schedules precluded us from talking regularly, Jen somehow could discern from our most recent communication that I was hurting, and she instantly moved into action. Her husband, Jake, thought she was crazy when she declared her plans to drive with their three children the eight hours up to Rhode Island to visit me for just a long weekend. But it wasn't insanity. She just knew. I needed her.

The time we spent together was so special. Our children ran joyfully through a nearby farm's corn maze and then continued their fun as they played under the late October sun in our yard. My body actually eased into the teak rocking chairs, the first time that I just sat out on the deck since Colin had left over seven months ago. During that time, my body had just been in constant motion, too busy to rest or reflect. But that day, as we slowly rocked back and forth, my ears actually noticed the sound of the mild breeze and my eyes followed the current of the river moving inland. Jen and I talked and talked about everything and nothing. It was the easy feeling of an old shoe that wraps so comfortably around the foot.

After Jen and her family left for their long drive home, I realized how friendship took on a whole new meaning for me this year. Her impromptu visit also made me see how I had neglected the company of my closest girlfriends in my manic focus on the children, Colin, and work. It was so important to break away and reminisce over funny memories and matters between "girls. " That weekend, I felt a bit more balanced, and my heart felt a little lighter.

***

October was also the start of my women's ice hockey league. Several years ago over wine at a New Year's Eve party, I learned about this league from another mom in Ian's class. Having grown up in Michigan, where my mother flooded our backyard every winter to make an ice rink, I knew how to skate. I even played hockey during my last two years of high school, when it became an official girls' sport. But it had been over two decades since I had last donned the extensive hockey gear and held a stick. Yet in a rare act of doing what I wanted to do, and with Colin's whole-hearted encouragement, I purchased used equipment for a few hundred dollars and committed to Wednesday nights at 6:30 p. m. for one hour of me-time. All winter. Every year.

Now, just to be clear, this women's league was an absolute hoot. Imagine book club, but instead of chatting and drinking wine, we would sweat and laugh. If someone fell, we offered a hand to help her up. It was exhilarating to race across the ice, except maybe those few times when my feet caught a funny edge and my legs flew out from under me. But after the shock of even those falls, cushioned by all the equipment, I just laughed.

For a split second, I debated if it would be right for me to play hockey this year with Colin gone. It meant I would need a sitter to watch the children a little longer on Wednesday nights, paying for yet more childcare. Then somehow the decision became clearer than I had expected. Yes, I finally needed to do something for myself.

This season in particular, I looked forward to those Wednesday nights more than anything. After that first night of play, besides my sore butt and thigh muscles that had not been used since last season, I also realized I had laughed more that hour than I had in a long time. Loud, unfiltered, chortling laughs from deep in my belly. And it felt really, really good.

***

The calm before the storm. The news from Afghanistan had been quiet for a week or so. My chest had untightened, and my body felt a little looser.

Beth Jackson

Then I got an e-mail from Colin about bad news in Kabul. I had
not yet seen the news myself, so it came as a shock. Insurgents had
attacked a military convoy, a series of armored vehicles transporting
soldiers across the city of Kabul, with a car bomb filled with
explosives. The news reported that thirteen U. S. soldiers were
dead, plus four from other NATO countries.

Colin did not yet know if he knew any of those killed. He had been
in a similar military convoy, going to visit the ancient Afghan ruins
where he sat on that Soviet tank, just a few weeks before. Later I
learned that Colin's unit held weekly memorial services for those
comrades who died during those preceding seven days. Week after
week. It was war after all.

Sarah, the colleague and friend who had been with me when
Colin's base was attacked, e-mailed me after I sent out a note to my
distribution list that Colin was OK.

> *Praying for the men and women who serve, and for you, too.*
> *Be well my friend,*
> *Sarah*

My friend was praying for me, as she had witnessed what this sort of
fear was like firsthand. Her words made me feel so loved. Another
friend reached out to get together this week, too. I definitely
needed the company.

***

Our household was never lacking for excitement. It was Halloween
afternoon, and I was planning to leave a client meeting within the
hour to drive home for an early dinner and get the children ready for
trick-or-treating. But in the middle of the meeting, my phone rang.
It was my mother-in-law, who had come in town for a few days. I
ignored it, thinking she was calling about dinner. This was not a

time when I could answer a personal phone call, and I planned to call her back in ten minutes after my meeting was over.

But then a minute later, I received a text from Erin.

Karl cut finger w/knife. We r going to ER.

I stepped out of my meeting and immediately called her back.

After school, Karl was messing around in Colin's workshop cutting excess glue off an airplane model when his Swiss Army knife slipped. Erin didn't think it looked too serious, but stitches would probably be required.

I called the hospital to give permission to treat Karl. One of the forms we had processed before Colin left gave authority to our parents and to Dana to direct medical treatment for the children, in case of emergency. Since Dana left, I had not remembered that I needed to get one for Erin. I would add that to my to-do list.

When I met them in the ER, the nurses had already treated Karl's thumb, where only half of his nail remained. It, too, would heal, but secretly, I wished they had made him wait longer. Maybe miss some trick or treating. Just something for a lesson about knife safety to stick.

Later that night, Karl told me how my mother-in-law had become hysterical when this incident first transpired, stating that she had never seen such chaos in one household before and that everything would be better when Colin came home. When I heard these critiques, I was very hurt and offended. I wanted to say something to her, but I kept my feelings inside.

I also felt a little vindicated when Colin mentioned in an e-mail back that he still bore the childhood scar from when he was splitting logs with an axe, unsupervised by any adult, and a piece flew up to hit his forehead with the force of a baseball bat. And for the record, it was Colin who had gotten the boys their pocketknives.

Nevertheless, on my own volition, I gathered up all the knives and saws - six in total - and anything else sharp that I saw in Colin's workshop. I told the boys the basement was off limits for the rest of the month. I just wanted a little quiet. No blood. Just rest. And calm.

It was not until a year later that I met a woman named Margaret, who gave me a much needed different perspective on my self-centered view of the world during Colin's deployment. Margaret's twenty-two-year-old son was a Marine stationed in Afghanistan, and I saw the strain and worry in her eyes the moment I met her. I had of course had had that same fear, but then it struck me that I had completely dismissed the anxiety that my mother-in-law must have felt about having a son at war. I remember actually thinking that my mother-in-law owed me the most help. It was *her* son, after all, who left me behind with three young children and an uncontrollable life. She needed to come help me. Only much later did I see how she had the same feelings as I did about Colin's absence. And I suddenly realized that, as a Mom, it would be utterly gut-wrenching if it were one of my children at war. A loved one is a loved one, no matter the relationship.

***

A few nights later I spent an hour typing Colin a very detailed e-mail about everything going on. It had been a while since I had taken so much time to write. I went to bed at 2 a. m.

The next morning I heard back.

*Thanks so much for sending me such a detailed email. It is my
greatest joy to have a window into your lives at home - my life here is
non-descript and these emails are the ultimate pick me up...*

Recently, I had only been sending a 30-second video of the children
or quick one-line messages. I was just too tired to give him more.
But when I read this, I remembered that he was the one missing us.
The children and I were here together. He was alone.

I told myself I would try to send more long notes, pictures, and
videos. After I got some sleep.

Chapter 20 – The Power of Words

Early November 2011

I knew it was going to be emotional when I started tearing up on my way into school. Thursday the children would celebrate Veteran's Day with a ceremony, since school would be closed on the actual holiday.

I held Thais's hand as we walked into the building together. The boys walked more quickly ahead of us. Thais and I entered her classroom, and I helped her hang up her backpack in her cubby. My eyes watched as she traced her name on the white board. I steadied myself to hold the tears back. I just nodded when people said good morning.

The all-school ceremony began with the Pledge of Allegiance and *Star Spangled Banner*. My hand unconsciously held onto my necklace during the whole song. The gymnasium was filled with hundreds of children, dressed in red, white, and blue. The fifth grade students then read poems in honor of servicemen and women who had once served or currently were serving. There were three rows of metal folding chairs holding young and old honorees who were friends and family of the school children.

My tears began rolling when my new girlfriend, whose husband just deployed the week prior, and I were asked to stand and come sit in our husbands' empty chairs among the other honorees. One of Colin's friends reached out and squeezed my hand as I walked by.

The students started reading the names of the honorees, and then the student related to each honoree brought each a long-stemmed white rose. As a student read Colin's name, Karl, Ian, and Thais approached me and handed me a white long-stemmed rose in his honor. All three of them reached out to me at the same time, and our embrace lingered. I could feel the pull of their arms and the beating of their hearts.

Karl, Ian, Thais hugging me

The last part of the ceremony was a tribute to those who had given their lives for our country. Karl and an eighth grade boy played echo *Taps*. Karl was the "reply" trumpet. The beautiful trumpet sound filled the entire space and silence of the gymnasium as the notes moved up and down and held for seemingly minutes. It felt like everyone held his or her breath until it was over.

That night, the boys asked me why I was crying so much during the ceremony. I told them it was because I missed Dad very, very much, but that I was also so, so proud of him. Those emotions just flowed out of my body.

On the Friday of Veteran's Day, I took the children to the International House of Pancakes for breakfast, where we had also gone the day Colin departed. Waffles and OJ. Perfect.

I showed Karl the e-mail that I had just received from Colin.

> *I loved the video and the pictures of the Veterans' Day ceremony. Karl did a terrific job with Taps. I immediately thought of the 17 guys who died here last week – there is no greater honor than to pay tribute to those men.*
>
> *I hope you have a great day – I will try to Skype later on,*
>
> *Love,*
> *C*

Karl paused and asked me, "I thought Dad was in a non-combat zone. "

Oh, no. I caught my breath. Did I just shatter his world by showing him that e-mail? That was not at all my intent. I was proud of myself that I had sheltered him from the realities of Afghanistan, and I did not want him to worry.

"He was referring to the country," I said quickly.

I left it at that. I remembered how a counselor at the Operation Military Kids Family Camp this summer had reminded us that we moms tended to overtalk.

Karl seemed satisfied with my answer, and we quickly moved into playing tic-tac-toe on the paper placemat that served as the kids' menu.

Beth Jackson

As we enjoyed our delicious breakfast, I noticed the Heinz ketchup bottle on the table. The front label read "Our Turn to Serve." It made me smile.

I told the children we would come back to IHOP when Dad returned. As we sat in a booth, we discussed whether we five could fit in a booth, or if we would need two tables put together.

"In the booth, Mommy," Thais explained. "I will sit on Daddy's lap."

***

Just another busy week in our non-stop life. Up at 7, to school at 8, off to work at 8:15 a. m. Erin did the afterschool shuffle of Ian's guitar lesson, Karl's hockey practice, and homework. I arrived home by 7 p. m. , twelve hours after our day had started, and the children and I enjoyed dinner together. After showers and with Thais snuggled in my bed, I went to check on the boys.

As I entered Ian's room, I asked him if he wanted me to arrange a play date for him the next week. He was on the floor playing with his Legos, and his body perked up.

"Yes! Can I have both Jack and Michael over?"

"OK," I replied. "Time for bed now. "

Ian climbed off the floor and into his bed. He wrapped his favorite blankets around him.

"Good night, I love you. " I said as I did every night. I began walking out of his room.

"Good night," Ian replied as he always did.

"Love you, too," he continued as the words crept unsuspectingly out of his mouth.

OH MY!!! HE SAID IT!

"You said it!" I exclaimed and ran back into his room and threw my body on top of him on his bed.

With a big smile across his face, he hid under his blankets as I smothered him with hugs.

"I love you," I said again, my eyes now very wet.

I always knew he did, too. But oh, what power those words had over me.

***

Ian had a field trip to Plymouth Plantation with his fourth grade class that next day. In my haste the night before, I did not search for the small camera but rather gave him Colin's digital camera to use, an anniversary present from last year.

When I returned home after work that night, the camera was missing. It was not clear if it had come back into the house or not. And if so, where it had gone. Ian said he had it in Erin's car, but Erin said she never saw it. As the black carrying case was at least eight inches long, it would not be something easy to miss. I called the bus company and teacher just to check, but they said Ian had been really diligent about carrying it, and that it was not found on the bus. I called the office at Plymouth Plantation; they had not found it either. I spent at least an hour searching our cars, the garage, backpacks, and various baskets by the door for the camera but found nothing.

Beth Jackson

I was disappointed in Ian that he had lost it, but I felt worse that I had used bad judgment in letting Colin's most expensive gadget leave the house in a child's hand. I decided I would buy Colin a new, even better, one for Christmas.

I had recently started purchasing Christmas presents for out of town family members when I came across something appropriate. The children's school had a holiday boutique fundraiser with many wonderful artists and other vendors, and I had purchased a purse with blue and white polka dots I thought it would be perfect for my brother's wife. I even got organized enough to wrap it in a gift box for her. Erin took it to the post office and mailed it for me.

Weeks later when I asked, my sister-in-law said she never received it. I thought perhaps my brother had seen and hidden it until the holiday. I wondered if I should have paid the extra $2 insurance for the mail delivery. I was so frustrated that my efforts to plan early, with everything else I had to do, were for naught.

***

I got a call today for a new project from my New Jersey client. It was just a simple one-day session. But I knew it really meant two nights away, leaving the day before and arriving back at midnight the next day. I just could not do it. *NO is a complete sentence*, I reminded myself.

I sent a note to a colleague asking if she was free to lead the session in my place. I knew my business margins were shrinking yet again, but I didn't care.

The only way to make it to the finish line on my own two feet would be by maintaining control of the things I could control. And staying home. I said NO.

246

Chapter 21 – Embracing Insanity

Late November 2011

I was a crazy lady today. But this time it was sort of a choice.

On Saturday morning, I opened my front door on our way to leave for Ian's hockey game, and a sudden movement on the right caught my eye. A rather large mouse darted from the corner of the front porch down the step into the bushes in front.

I screamed. Okay, I have to admit, this was not actually a mouse; rather it was a rodent that rhymes with cat. I will just refer to it as a mamma mouse, though, for my mental fortitude. I realized that this mamma mouse just come from inside the house - from an unseen secret hole behind the shingles into a wall shared by the garage and the front staircase. I screamed again and started making loud sounds while jumping back and forth, so the mamma mouse would not dart back *inside*. I was totally overwhelmed by this small creature that itself was quivering from fear, but I had to do something.

I called for Karl to come quickly, and then to take my place standing guard, as I scurried inside and down to Colin's workshop to grab several pieces of long thin wood.

Quickly returning, I jimmied the wood into the porch corner, hoping there would be no room left for the mamma mouse to get back in. I was so grossed out by this rodent that had been living in my house that I found myself shaking. I put a few large rocks in front of the wood, so it would be secure. At least for the time being. And then in my continued crazy lady dance, back and forth making monkey-like sounds. I tried to shoo the mamma mouse away from the house until it eventually darted ahead out of my sight.

***

On Friday night following one of Ian's hockey practices, the three children and I met up for dinner with Cara and her girls. She told me the happy news that her husband would be coming home on Friday, just before Thanksgiving. I was so excited for her, but I was also a little sad. I missed Colin, desperately.

I asked Cara what she was planning for Nick's return home. We both choked up a little. We had both been thinking about this event since the day our husbands left.

Cara told me that she assumed what Nick most wanted was to get out of his uniform, take a long hot shower, play a game of pool in the basement, and sleep. A cousin of hers had offered to arrange a "flash mob" to greet him at the Providence airport, but Cara had shrugged off that idea.

I remembered how, several years ago, we were in the Boston airport when a single young man arrived home from Iraq. He was greeted at the gate by his dad, and the entire terminal rose to gave him a standing ovation. It was an incredible scene. I wanted that kind of welcome for Colin.

I read about how National Guard units and Army Regiments returned to gymnasiums full of people. Applause and celebration. Bands and waving flags. But for a Reservist who went as an individual augmentee, like Colin or Nick, there would be no gymnasium or parade or marching band. No formal welcome. Just the children and wife greeting him at the airport.

So I was very intrigued with the notion of a flash mob. I envisioned it either at the airport or on the front lawn. We knew the town chief of police and a local fireman. I had been thinking about how great it would be to have an escort of flashing lights and sirens. That would be another idea to file away when the time came.

Meanwhile, Cara and I agreed that a quick, five minute flash mob would be ideal. I offered to her to arrange this for Nick and to gently let everyone know it was really only to last five minutes. Coming from me, there would be no feelings hurt to ask people to leave and not linger, so the family could have some immediate alone time. I didn't yet know Cara's extended family, or even Nick, but I could explain who I was, and I knew my message would be understood.

When we said goodbye after dinner, Cara said she would think about it and let me know.

***

My baby's dream was so simple and pure.

Thais had awakened once again in my bed. She slowly sat up with a fleece blanket wrapped around her arms, reaching out to me, and I lifted her to my hip. We walked to her bedroom, so she could choose her clothes. After she picked out a summer dress for this brisk November day, I carried her downstairs for breakfast. I did not feel like fighting with her about her clothes. I was choosing very few battles nowadays.

Karl had already eaten and was reading a book. Ian was eating oatmeal. I cut Thais a slice of cranberry orange bread and poured her a small glass of orange juice. I fixed yogurt and granola, and a slice of bread, for myself as well.

It was a school day, and we were running a few minutes later than normal, but we enjoyed a few minutes of eating and talking.

Beth Jackson

I got up to clear the plates and start the dishwasher.

And then Thais shared her dream.

"Mom... So after Christmas, when Charlotte is back. And Dad is back... When we don't have a sitter... Can you, and Dad, and Charlotte, and Ian, and Karl, and me all go to the beach and climb on the rocks?"

I stopped what I was doing and bent down to her height. I knew she missed Colin, and Charlotte, too, who remained with my father-in-law even after our return from France. There had not yet been the opportunity for someone to accompany our dog back to Rhode Island, and we were not going to let her fly alone again. I looked Thais right in the eye with more love than I could ever express and said, "I would love that. I look forward to spending time all together as a family, too. "

She smiled at me and then hurried off to get her backpack and lunchbox as we made our way out the door.

***

One day Colin called, in great spirits. Again, he most wanted to hear details about what the children were doing and about our daily life. Sometimes, though, I felt like I ran out of things to talk about. There were just too many big things I wanted to share with him. But I wanted to protect him from my stress and failures. And the limited time we had, along with occasional technology interruptions, was not conducive to serious conversations. So we tended to just focus on the little things of interest.

At one point, I told him how much I missed him. And I repeated, "A year is a long time. "

He said, "Well, you are separated, but at least you are home. I am separated, but I have to live here. I sleep on top of a septic tank, and last night it smelled like a pile of shit!" And then we both started laughing hysterically.

What else was there to say?

So while I was not sleeping on shit, things still felt out of control. Even though I was not travelling, my work days were still far too long. Between late nights at my desk and combing the Internet for war news, I got less than five hours of sleep a night. My body was starting to move into full shutdown mode.

I was a robot. Completely numb. Simply executing tasks of each day.

Showered.
                    Dressed.

Reminded Ian to put his homework in his backpack.

                              Left $20 for Ian's guitar lesson.
Packed lunches.

                              Filled the car with gas. Again.

Packed for the suitcases for the upcoming hockey tournament.

              Needed more orange juice.

Chicken was defrosted for two days. Needed to eat or toss.

Put garbage on the curb.
                              Running out of toilet paper.
              Worked.

I could tell I was losing steam. My energy waned. I gave into the children's requests more often. "Maybe" became my answer to requests for sweets or a movie, as it invited less confrontation. So Ian had ice cream for dessert most nights. Thais now ate Rice Krispies for every meal, including dinner. She had always been a picky eater, and I preferred that she eat something rather than nothing. And she wore PJs all the time, too, except at school. Some weekends, she wore the same PJs two days in a row. It made her happy, and that was all that I could muster. I felt guilty, but I was just trying to get by one minute at a time. I kept looking but still could not discern the finish line.

Some of my family and friends wondered why I kept such a busy pace with the children during this time. What, for example, was I thinking taking three children to an away travel hockey tournament all by myself? And how could I juggle all of their sports and music activities alone? Well, I thought we HAD cut back. All of Ian's summer sports were cancelled. Neither Karl nor Ian played their usual fall lacrosse. Ian had not been able to play fall soccer, and Thais did not play that season either. Our activity load was far below its norm.

But, looking back at that particular hockey tournament the weekend before Thanksgiving, with 5 a. m. wake-ups, schlepping all three children to each of the boys' games, napping in the parking lot of the rink like a homeless family, and getting a horrible cold with a whopping fever blister on my lip, I see that I was still trying to do it all. Yes. I needed help, but I was too proud to ask.

We returned home Sunday night from the three-day tournament tired and hungry. Luggage and hockey bags were strewn over the front hall. A pile of mail was on the counter. I had to work the next morning. In spite of my total fatigue, I had to get some dinner on the table.

After pizza several nights in a row, I decided to actually cook. I got a chicken and rice dish simmering on the stove, emitting a delicious sweet tomato aroma. But let me be clear – this was pre-cooked chicken and an Indian sauce that came from a jar. I then opened the oven to take out the flat naan bread that was defrosting and warming in the oven. But its usual golden brown hue was blackened. I had burned it.

So I opened the freezer and took out another package. I tore it open, put it on the pan, and put it back in the oven.

Ten minutes later, after the main dish was done and I had poured milk into tall glasses for the boys, I remembered the bread was still in there.

Burned again. And I heard a sizzle as I burned a scar into my right arm, reaching in the oven to pull out the second ruined bread.

I could have sat down and wept. Or I could have screamed like a shrill monster. Instead, I somehow kept myself together, while running cold water on my burned arm, and I simply admitted out loud to the children that I had messed up. Burnt the bread twice in ten minutes.

"Can I help?" Ian offered.

He was usually not the one to offer help, and I readily accepted. "Yes, please. " I was grateful, actually.

Ian set the table. And he took responsibility for watching the clock on the oven. When I said two minutes, he put the timer on for one. I chuckled inside.

As we ate dinner, with the unburned third round of naan, I told the children for the first time that I was thinking about writing a book about this year. I told them the burnt naan would go in it, and we all started laughing and could not stop. We thought we were so funny, which only fueled our laughter. Karl had all these creative ideas about a cover picture, including this one of me cooking and checking my computer while mayhem reined.

Beth Jackson

Cooking with Thais, checking computer, with Ian with a pot in the air

I loved my children. Through laughter, they somehow were keeping me sane.

And I realized I had to start asking for help. My new flagpole finally arrived in the mail. This one was 1 inch in diameter, so it gave me confidence that it would fit more snuggly into the same size flag holder. I also called my girlfriend's husband, who had previously offered to help when he heard me describe my flagpole travails. The next day, he installed it, securely fitting it into the holder. Within five minutes, he completed the job that would have taken me at least thirty minutes of reaching, sweating, and cursing. Asking for help actually worked.

***

Colin's dad Gramp, step mom, middle sister, and her husband, arrived in town on the Tuesday night before Thanksgiving. Thankfully only two of them were staying at our house, although with all the extra responsibilities hosting entailed, even two was still too many.

The best part of their visit, though, was the return of Charlotte. We all gathered around for her big wet licks. Charlotte immediately moved right back into her happy place in our home and hearts. I bought her two new dog beds: one for her area off the kitchen and one for our bedroom. Gramp had retrained Charlotte to sleep in her own bed next to the adult bed - not under the covers like we had always allowed. Upon her return, I successfully continued this regimen, saving room for one of the children in my bed instead. Every night, the dog whined as she tried to snuggle under the covers with me, but after a few moments of redirection, she happily went down to her bed under a blanket and stayed there all night.

I also detected after months of hiatus as my running partner and some grandparent spoiling, Charlotte had gained at least five pounds. And so she and I returned to our joint running routine with gusto.

I loved the company and feeling of safety of having Charlotte back. But it was also really good to have Gramp with us. When I mentioned that I could use help changing some light bulbs, he willingly took on that task, which was larger that I had realized. An hour later, Gramp and Karl had changed fourteen dead light bulbs throughout the house. Without my even noticing it, our home had been gradually getting darker.

We spent Thanksgiving in Salem, Massachusetts with Colin's extended family. An annual tradition. Thirty-some people. Turkey and pie. The four out-of-town visitors stayed overnight there, so I drove the two hours home with three sleeping children, feeling all alone but calm under the light of the ninth moon.

Gramp and the others returned to our house late Friday afternoon, and we ventured out to a local Italian favorite for dinner. It was Colin's and my date night spot. The food and wine were delicious, and conversation rose like a beautifully orchestrated symphony. At the end of the meal, dessert menus were handed out. The boys each wanted lemon sorbet. Thais wanted something chocolate. The only chocolate dessert on the menu was a cake. "For two" it said in parentheses, clearly indicating large portions.

I asked the table if anyone would help share with Thais. She looked at me and started crying. "I just want to share it with Daddy," she wailed.

My eyes looked at her, and I kissed her on the cheek. "We will come here with Daddy when he is back, and you can share it with him."

Colin's sister and her husband offered to help eat some, and Thais put on her happy face. When the enormous chocolate cake arrived, Thais dove in. But after numerous mouthfuls, she had had enough, and the grown-ups gave up as well.

"Mommy, can we send Daddy the rest?" Thais asked.

"Of course we can," I replied.

So we wrapped the cake in a take-out box to bring back with us. At home, we were out of Ziploc bags; I made a mental note to add it to the grocery list. So I wrapped the cake in plastic wrap and tin foil before returning it to the take-out box. I covered the small package with brown packing tape and added Colin's address, and then I put it in the freezer overnight.

The next day, we went to the Post Office, and I mailed the leftover piece of chocolate cake to Colin in Afghanistan. With love from Thais.

***

That weekend, the children and I went shopping for Christmas decorations for Colin. With the long delay in delivery time, we knew we had to plan in advance. I had hoped to get him a small Christmas tree with lights, but we could not find any that were battery powered, so we gave up on that idea. Instead we bought and mailed off green and red advent calendars, door knockers, and bright ornaments. Some holiday cheer.

We also started shopping for his Christmas presents. Those appropriate for Afghanistan - new slippers from Brookstone, a head lamp, more snacks, and a weather thermometer from Eastern Mountain Sports. And one for his return: a new camera.

Thais described how she wanted to buy presents for me, too. "Shiny high heels that you can wear when Daddy comes home," she announced, her little face gleaming.

She loved to talk about Daddy, but sometimes she would break down in tears, crying for him. "I want to move to another family!" she yelled during one such episode. "I want to live in a house with just Daddy and nobody else." Despite the love I poured on her, I could do nothing to replace the void of Dad.

***

Then more things went missing. Karl's Brooks Brothers blue blazer. His new red winter coat. And my favorite holiday DVD with Frosty the Snowman, The Little Drummer Boy, and Rudolf the Red-Nosed Reindeer.

Was my mind playing tricks on me? Was I so distracted that I walked in circles searching around the house for hours for these items? I remembered seeing the blazer on the kitchen counter. But the next day it was gone. I checked the downstairs closet, Karl's closet, Ian's closet, Colin's closet, and my closet. I looked everywhere. Gone. Same with the red winter coat. Karl had just worn it, but now it was missing. Not left in my car. Not in the lost and found at school.

Beth Jackson

Not at the ice hockey rink. And the DVD was not where I last saw it, under the TV with the other movies.

Had Karl or I just simply misplaced these things? *Or was the new nanny or the cleaning lady stealing from me?*

Then more vanished. A Brookstone shower radio that I had ordered for Christmas for Ian and expensive Bliss body lotions I had ordered for my client's administrative assistants never arrived. UPS claimed both packages had been delivered. A week later, a Kindle Fire never arrived. When I looked online at my Amazon account, it indicated the box had already been delivered. Brookstone, Bliss, and Amazon all sent replacements. This time I had to sign for each of the packages when they were delivered.

Something felt wrong, but I did not have the energy to do anything about it. And I was a trusting person; my instincts were to find the good in people. When I mentioned all of this to a friend, however, she told me to fire both the nanny and cleaning lady. It might seem absurd to others, but in my current state, the thought of having no one around to help me was more overwhelming that the thought of theft. In my inertia, I did nothing.

***

A few days later, I was in a meeting when I get an urgent text from Erin about a credit card fraud call. She was at our house waiting for a repair man to come.

> *Visa called about a suspicious $3,100 charge for floor covering. Did you make such a purchase?*

My meeting continued, as I snuck my phone under the big oak conference table to text back.
> *No.*

A minute passed. Then it struck me, and I texted again.
  Maybe Colin bought a rug?

I also sent Colin a quick short e-mail asking him just that.

Any other time, I would have been thrilled at how surprisingly quickly I heard back from him. Several hours later, Colin replied.

> *I bought four rugs for $3100 - you will love them. . . . I hope.*
>
> *It makes sense to make the purchases together as they take the margin down.*
>
> *Love,*
> *C*

He what? Four rugs. For $3,100?

We had once discussed rugs. Colin had even sent me a disk of pictures of rugs to review. But our most recent conversation, months ago, had been that they were too expensive, so maybe he would get one rug, and definitely one under the $1,000 range. I was livid.

After work, I drove directly to Ian's hockey game. At the rink, I texted Karen about how angry I was at Colin. She called me back. "Don't e-mail back. Fights on e-mail are no good. Just e-mail about other things. You can talk it live next time you talk."

Was this what people meant about what I could expect from Colin's post-war readjustment? I had heard stories about returning soldiers buying motorcycles and other expensive toys, since they felt totally invincible from their experience and were not yet grounded in the reality of a family budget again. It was clear to me that if and when Colin came safely home to us, it would take time for him to get back into the norm of our life of joint decision-making and living within our means.

On our ride home from the hockey game, I called to remove the fraud freeze on our Visa card. The $3,180 in charges were valid.

Still mad, I asked Ian if I should pick a fight with Dad or just let it go.

"Let it go," he said. "Take the money from my college savings. I am going to do ROTC anyway. "

My son, who wanted to protect his Dad, was so much more perceptive than me. Ian knew this purchase was important to Dad, who probably felt like he was doing something special for the family.

**

On Sunday, Thais was playing with my neighbor's girls. They were having fun blowing bubbles and jumping on a small trampoline.

"Do you have a snow service lined up yet?" the neighbor asked me.

"No," I replied. Two months had gone by since I sent the e-mail to the National Guard contact. Still no response. "Colin usually does it. "

"Well, don't get one. I will do it. Although I expect your boys to be out there helping me," he said.

"Thank you. Yes. " I needed the help and was grateful for it. "And of course my boys will help, as they always did with their Dad. Thank you. "

Then finally, in the middle of December, nine months into Colin's deployment, his Reserve unit finally called, asking for Colin.

"May I ask who is calling?" I replied, hesitant to say I was alone.

"It is Sergeant Duvall from his unit," the man explained.

"He is in Afghanistan," I stated without any emotion.

"Oh, that explains why he has not responded to any of our calls!" he replied in a very friendly tone. I did wonder, though, how his unit did not have a record of my husband's whereabouts. Sergeant Duvall must have been trying his disconnected cell phone.

"I am the new unit administrator supporting the Reserve unit, your husband, and your family. "

He continued to explain how he was supposed to reach out to check in on our family. He asked if I had the contact information for the unit. I said, no. He gave me the appropriate information, including the central phone number.

He asked if I had the contact information for the commander, Lieutenant Colonel Sandellis. *Sandellis?* I thought Colin's commander was Santos.

I asked if that was a new commander. Yes, he replied and spelled the name Sandellis for me. There was a change of command a few months ago, although I was never informed. Since Colin was still deployed, Sergeant Duvall proceeded to give me Lieutenant Colonel Sandellis's cell phone number. Oh, how nice it would have been to have had that number when Ian was hit by the car.

Sergeant Duvall asked if there was anything I needed. I paused and then simply asked if there was any information about reunification that he could send me. He acknowledged that he was new but could find out if I had an extra minute. As I held on the line, he pulled up an e-mail and read me off Mrs. Morston's phone number. She would be able to send me such information.

He thanked me for asking that and said he would add this to his to-do list for others as well.

"I have fifty-seven soldiers I cannot find," Sergeant Duvall admitted to me.

Fifty-seven other wives like me.

I tried Mrs. Morston's number, twice, and left a message both times. She never called back.

***

Another sort of volcano erupted today. This time, the insurgents were not taking aim at the U. S. military, but rather at innocent Afghan moms, dads, and children. The headline read about an Afghan suicide bomber who killed 60 Shias. And the image of a beautiful Afghan woman with long dark hair and a vibrant green silk dress, screaming as she was covered in the blood of children scattered at her feet, shook me to the core.

My heart was saddened for the women effected - they were more like us than we ever thought. Weren't they just moms wanting to hold *their* families close, too?

***

It was another action-packed Saturday. No sleeping in for our family. Ian had an away hockey game, so I was up at 6:20 a. m. to get him ready for his coach to pick him up by 6:45 a. m. His coach, who lived a block away, had given me so much help this season by driving Ian to most of his early morning practices and games.

I went back to bed for half an hour before waking again to get Thais up and out for her hockey practice, at a different ice rink. I was one of her coaches, so after lacing her skates, I laced mine as well. Karl had come with us and watched until his practice began, right after Thais's.

The rest of the day took a bit more orchestration. Weeks ago, I thought of the idea of organizing simultaneous playdates for my kids, so Santa could do her shopping, and that plan finally had materialized. My pride had slowly dissolved, and I had started asking for help from more friends.

I first asked the mother of a friend of Karl's. She had replied, "Of course, and could he stay for a sleepover, too?"

I then asked Karen to see if Thais could have a play date with Will. Without a pause, she said "Yes, we are going on a boat trip with some out-of-town friends that afternoon, so I will get Thais a ticket. "

Unconditional friendship.

I then asked a mom of Ian's friend and got my first "no. " Her, "well maybe, but I'm not sure" excuse made me feel bad for asking. So I said I would ask around.

That was why I had not previously asked for help. I didn't want to be told no. It made me feel guilty. And, I hated to impose by asking the same friends over and over again. But I already had by asking Karen. And now I felt I was two-thirds there, and so I e-mailed Molly.

Beth Jackson

She replied back the same day, "Yes, of course, and could you come for dinner, too?" I hope one day I can ever repay such kindness.

I had a list of Christmas gifts still to get during these few precious hours of the triple playdates, so I crammed in as much as I could into that afternoon.

A myriad of stocking stuffers.

A huge teddy bear for Thais from Santa.

Books for each of the children and my nieces.

Dunkin' Donuts gift cards for the kids' coaches.

Chunky jewelry for my mom.

Chocolates for the teachers.

I wondered if I should buy myself some me-to-me Santa Christmas presents this year. *Who else would?* So I did.

***

That night was also Nick's welcome home party. The flash mob idea for his arrival never fully transpired. He had already been home for two weeks now. I was so happy for Cara, of course. But it was also painful as it reminded me what I did not have.

Karl was at his sleepover, and I did not want to ask my friends to keep Thais and Ian late into the evening, so I arranged for a babysitter for a few hours. I drove around the block a bit before finding a parking spot a few streets away from Cara's parent's house. Then I walked alone down the sidewalk in the cold, dark winter night, carrying a bottle of wine.

I did not yet know Cara's family or any of her friends. She had been my friend of common sisterhood, just the two of us, this year. I finally met Nick, who was so sincere in asking about Colin. But otherwise I just drifted from conversation to conversation, my loneliness palpable.

A short while later, Cara and Nick each made a toast. When Cara welled up, her dad stepped in and said a few words to the crowd until she composed herself and could continue.

As I listened and saw their happiness, tears trickled down my face. A woman whom I had just met was standing next to me. She could tell I was upset and started rubbing the small of my back where there was no air. It was so loving and thoughtful. A stranger reaching out to me to give me comfort.

I talked to that woman for a while that night. It turns out she and her husband had been struggling to have a baby for almost three years. She and I were able to share our experiences of overwhelming feelings of loss and sadness. How it affected our every waking day, how it was hard for others to understand our pain, and how as the time passed, it got even harder because others forgot. Just by being in the moment and showing unconditional kindness, we gave one another the gift of understanding.

***

The alarm woke me at 5:55 a. m. on Sunday. I dressed and then roused Ian and Thais. Ian had practice at 7, so we had to be out the door by 6:30 a. m. Thais had practice right afterwards, so she had to join us, even though she would have much preferred the extra hour in bed. The night before, Karl asked if he could stay home asleep, which he did.

Ziploc bags of dry cereal waited on the kitchen counter for the children to grab. Coats and shoes and out the door. I had already packed the car with their gear and sticks the night before.

Beth Jackson

When we arrived at the rink, there were only two other cars in the parking lot. That was unusually bare for practice time. We unloaded ourselves and schlepped the bags inside.

I peered up at the board to see what locker room was designated for Ian's team. It was not listed. *What?* Suddenly, I worried that I had the wrong ice rink. The other local rink was twenty minutes away. *Damn!* I grabbed my phone to check the calendar, feeling horrible that Ian would be late for practice. In the world of hockey when you paid for precious ice time, the expectations were clear: you never missed practice.

Slowly, my eyes found my error. His practice was at 7 p. m. , not 7 a. m.

That afternoon, we went to a local farm to buy a Christmas tree. I struggled to carry in the tree, which Colin always did. Karl offered to help, as he had taken over most of Dad's jobs by now.

Karl helping me put up the Christmas tree

Afterwards, he also helped me put up lights on the pine trees around the back of our pool. We got out two ladders, a thousand lights, and several outdoor extension cords. Karl first tried to lasso the lights up high on one of the trees. After several failed attempts on the wobbly ladder, he climbed down, so I could try.

I swung the lights, sure they would land right in place, but my efforts failed just the same. "Mah-velous, Mom!" Karl exclaimed each time in an exaggerated fashion. "Just mah-vehlous!" We laughed.

Finally, just as early evening darkness surrounded us, we got the top strand on, and we wrapped the lights around and around. We snapped them on. It gave me a feeling of peace, and for the first time in a while, I felt the desire to pray.

As the children and I huddled outside beside the covered pool, Ian crumpled up newspaper and stuffed it below some logs that Karl had carried over. Thais was helping open a bag of marshmallows. I did not care that we had not eaten dinner yet.

Karl lit a match and carried it close to the paper. The flames leapt and consumed the wood. Each of us held a stick as we browned our marshmallows. Thais of course had a s'more with Hershey chocolate. Ian just stuck with plain marshmallows. Karl and I ate our marshmallows with graham crackers, but no chocolate.

As we ate our treats, I recited,

> *Starlight, starbright, first star I see tonight.*
> *I wish I may, I wish I might, have the wish I wish tonight.*

It was cold outside in the dark December air, but we felt warm. The fire gave off heat, and each of us made a silent wish, as we looked up to the sky towards the tiny white dots that were stars.

Chapter 22 – Letting Go

Early December 2011

Thais had been changing, in appearance and in maturity. In some ways, she had even toughened up; she no longer asked for or even wanted her daily Daddy kisses. And I suddenly realized that it had been months since her last bed-wetting incident. I started to wonder if Colin would recognize his own daughter, who had grown up so much.

That Sunday was Thais's fifth birthday party, a day filled with mixed emotion as Thais cried at her party because Dad was not there. She was very focused on his absence, as she had not yet been able to speak with him to report that she lost her first tooth the week before. I remembered hoping I would not forget my job as tooth fairy again that time.

The day was filled with cool sunshine and back-to-back activities, though, so our constant motion kept her a tad distracted.

- 6:15 a. m. Woke-up, drove to ice rink
- 7:00 a. m. Thais hockey game, I coached
- 8:30 a. m. Ian hockey practice
- 10:00 a. m. Home, breakfast
- 10:30 a. m. Thais opened family birthday presents
- 12:00 p. m. Lunch, cleaned up
- 12:30 p. m. Made goody bags for the party
- 1:15 p. m. Drove to the swimming club for Thais's birthday
- 2:00 p. m. Party started
- 4:00 p. m. Home, opened birthday presents from friends
- 4:30 p. m. Drove to Karl's middle school hockey game
- 5:00 p. m. Karl's game

Beth Jackson

- • 5:45 p. m. Ordered dinner at local restaurant in advance
- • 6:00 p. m. Out for dinner, food waiting for us
- • 6:45 p. m. Drove back to the rink
- • 7:30 p. m. Karl's PeeWee hockey game
- • 8:45 p. m. Headed home from the rink

Exhaustion had us all ready for bed. On our drive home, though, I suddenly remembered that Thais was responsible for school snack this week. I had written this on the calendar for today, but I had forgotten to look.

Phew! At least I remembered now, while we were near the supermarket. I thought we might as well pick up a few items I would need later in the week as well. There we were at 9 p. m. with a shopping cart. Thais wanted to ride in the basket. Karl and Ian wanted to push. So they took turns.

As we walked up and down the aisles, the cart filled higher and higher. I saw Karl sneak in two boxes of their favorite sugary cereal, but I pretended not to notice. When we got to the freezer section, I remembered I wanted some yogurt, so I doubled back. I was gone only 30 seconds, but when I returned, I saw my three children squealing with delight as they all rode the side of the cart like a bumper car. Karl had jumped onto the right side. Ian was already on the front, and Thais held on with all her might to the handle as she stood on back with her feet clinging to the bottom rail. Surrounded by an occasional mist from an opened freezer door, the cart zipped down the aisle with no pilot.

An attractive 50-something man who was shopping alone stopped momentarily to watch them as well. I cupped my hands around my mouth and stammered out the pretend sound of a loud speaker, "The mom with the three children, come immediately to aisle eight. Please do not leave your children unattended!"

The man started laughing and immediately colluded with me, "Now is your time to just disappear!"

I laughed so hard my belly hurt. It was 9:30 p. m. on a school night, and the children and I were having the best time at the supermarket.

Yes, our standards for Plan Fun sure had lowered.

***

One night I went to play women's hockey straight from my work at a client an hour away. As I pulled up to the ice rink, I realized I still had on my jewelry. I put my earrings, ring, and the special necklace into the cup holder of the front seat. When I got back home that night in the dark, the jewels sat where I had left them.

The next morning, I took my car to the mechanic to check on a wheel alignment issue that the dealer had told me about during a routine oil change. The dealer told me it would cost $200-300 just to diagnose the problem, and more on top to fix it. I felt like they were taking advantage of me, a woman with no knowledge of mechanical issues.

So instead, I drove my car further away to a mechanic Colin always recommended. I asked if I could wait, so they could indeed see if they could fix it. Within five minutes, the mechanic told me he could easily remove the corroded bolts, but they didn't do alignment. He had a friend up the street, however, who did. With a quick phone call, his friend agreed to align my wheels within the day. For less than $50.

I had already arranged with a girlfriend to be on hold if I needed a ride. She came to get me within minutes and drove me home.

In the afternoon, Erin, the children, and I drove together in Erin's car back to the mechanic to pick up my car.

Beth Jackson

Later that night, my hand subconsciously reached for my neck, but nothing was there. *My necklace!* I quickly raced downstairs. My slippers rested by the door, and my feet quickly slid into them. My beating heart led me outside into the dark of the overcast night to my car.

My shaking hand opened the door and pushed on the light. I looked down in the cup holder and saw resting there my earrings, ring, and necklace.

***

Two days later, it started out as a typical morning.

Dressed. Brushed teeth. Fed children. Helped Thais choose an outfit, then watched her change into another one. Coats. Shoes. Gifts to teachers as Christmas break was starting on Friday. Ian's project. Hands full. Loaded up the car.

Oops, at school, we realized we had forgotten lunchboxes and Ian's guitar. The children handed out the Christmas gifts of chocolates to their teachers, and I promised to return with the missing items.

Back home, I placed the lunchboxes and guitar into the front seat of my car to avoid forgetting them again. My errand list included going to the bank to put a stop on a business check to my colleague that was lost in the mail, but the bank's opening hour was still 30 minutes away. So I went up to my office and did some routine e-mails before heading back out.

After dropping the items off at school, I continued onto the bank. As I sat in the chair waiting for the customer service woman to process the check information into her computer, my eyes scanned my phone. Suddenly, a solitary tear began to run down my face. My voice squeaked as I asked the woman for a tissue. When her eyes lifted from the screen to read my face, she kindly asked me if I was OK. Unexpectedly, I burst into sobs. Like spontaneous combustion.

The fear that had been gripping my gaunt body all year finally gave way, and the floodgates poured. Convulsions, actually, just consumed my body. Like an exorcism, I was releasing the terror I had been holding inside for so long, forcing breath deep into my belly. My mouth created sounds instead of words that were purely primal.

The bank woman stood and walked to my side of the desk to give me a hug as I tried to explain.

Minutes later, I was still sobbing when I left the bank. I turned on the engine of my car and slowly pulled out of the parking lot, worried that I was really in no condition to drive.

As my car continued down the busy road, I thought about pulling over. I thought about dialing my sister or my mom, but I knew no words would form. The tears kept coming. When the car finally reached the house, instead of turning into my driveway under the waving flag, I continued on an extra block to my friend's house, seeking comfort. Another human.

Hearing only my own small whimpers, I walked slowly up to the front door and rang the doorbell. When the large red wooden door opened, my friend saw my face and asked, "Colin?" with absolute dread. She panicked, expecting the worst, and slammed the heavy door on her young son's face so he would not witness the assumed tragedy. Her arms wrapped around my shoulders as they kept heaving up and down.

All of this happened within seconds. But my wails continued, until I was finally able to get out a couple of words.

"Yes. Colin… All good. " And she just embraced me hard until the sobbing subsided.

Colin was OK. He was coming home early! The e-mail I had read in the bank had started with, "I am on the move," as he described how his journey home had begun.

I had unintentionally scared my friend for that moment, and she felt the dread I had been feeling all year. As we stood there for another minute, she simply gave me absolute love until I could breathe again. Deep, long breaths. And then we walked inside her house to have coffee.

Oh, how I was going to be a blubbering mess when I would meet Colin at the airport.

Initially, I had grand plans to keep this wonderful news secret from the children until the day before Colin arrived. I wanted to be 100% certain of the date and time he would return.

But after thinking about my emotional flood this morning, I realized I could not do that. I wanted to share the news with them. And so after school I put an envelope in the tree and told the children there was an early Christmas present.

Ian already guessed what it was before he read the words, "Dad is coming home!" He could feel it, and the excitement bounced between all of us.

Caution, however, still lingered. I want to be excited, but honestly I was petrified. Colin still had several helicopter and plane rides ahead of him. It could be a week before he actually landed in the U. S. Then there would be days of mandatory out-processing. But oh my, it was really happening! Wonderful! Yikes!

But I knew things could change. The date could change. Our wedding changed.

Disappointment scared me. I didn't want to let myself truly believe anything until it was real. So I opened my mouth wide and sucked in as much air as I could. I had to hold my breath one last time.

***

Life continued to swirl around us, and I tried to sustain my energy, and excitement. That night Karl had a late hockey practice, right after my women's league. Erin stayed late to put Ian and Thais to bed, so they did not have to stay up late at the ice rink.

When we got home and Erin left, Karl and I each showered. Once Karl was tucked in bed and I checked on each of the children, I went back down to the calendar to study the days. *When would Colin actually arrive home?* Would he get home before New Year's Eve? Before Christmas? Oh, I did not want to even think about that, as it would just lead to disappointment.

We had so many things to do over the next days, but oh, how I could feel Colin coming closer already.

Before I turned out the light above the family calendar, I pulled out the Dunkin' Donuts gift cards for the boys' coaches. I counted four. I had purchased eight. *Where were the other four?* I moved paper around on the counter, lifting each to have a look under and scanning behind the pencil jar to see if they were tucked behind it. No luck. I would have to make another trip to Dunkin Donuts to get more of them before we were at the rink again on Saturday.

***

Beth Jackson

On Friday, I was going to work early, so Erin was scheduled to come help get the children ready and drive them to school. At the appointed hour of 6:45 a. m. , she had not arrived.

I called her cell, but there was no answer. She was always very reliable, so I was not at all worried. Confident that she would be here soon, I was comfortable asking Karl to babysit his siblings for the few minutes. He agreed.

Five minutes later as I drove north, I called the house. Karl answered. Erin was not there yet. I tried her cell again. No answer.

My phone dialed back to the house again, and Karl offered to start getting Thais ready for school.

A few minutes later, I dialed again. Erin was still not there. I told Karl we had to move to Plan B. The children were going to get themselves dressed and fed and walk the 0. 8 miles to school. There were no busy streets. The boys had walked home from school several times before.

"No, mom," Karl pleaded. "That is too much responsibility to get Thais there. "

My shoulders tightened as the situation was becoming clear to me.

"Please come home," Karl continued.

I tried once to convince him otherwise, but he wanted Mom. It was too much to ask. So I turned my car around and started driving back south again.

In the meantime, Karl poured Thais a bowl of cereal and made sure she was dressed. He and Ian pulled lunch boxes from the fridge.

Trying to optimize our turnaround time, I called when I was within two minutes from the house. "Please put Charlotte behind her gate and be outside with coats and backpacks. "

As I drove down the hill, my eyes found my three adorable kiddos, ready, sitting on the wooden bench on the driveway. As they scrambled into my car, I thanked them for being so helpful. I drove the two minutes to school and parked the car. We started to walk in for Early Bird arrival, which started at 7:30 a. m.

I was going to be late for my work meeting, but it did not matter. Erin had called me when I was already on my way back to the house, indicating that she had set her alarm clock for the wrong time by mistake. I understood. We were all human. And I got an unexpected extra two minutes with the children.

Just when this journey seemed like it was reaching the home stretch, this morning was not what I had expected. Enough already, please. *Hello up there? Anyone? Are you listening?* I am ready, now. PLEASE! Send me my husband home from war.

In that moment, it finally came to me that I was not going to cross the finish line of the marathon alone. I needed the children as my teammates and cheerleaders to walk the last mile with me. And so we walked, hand in hand, into school. Ian even skipped ahead without any semblance of a limp.

***

Days before Colin was to return home, I received a large packet from the Sergeant at his Reserve unit.

I burst out laughing when I opened it. It included three daddy dolls and a lot of information on deployment that I can tell you would have been very, very useful at the beginning of this journey. It also included a packet and a book on reunification. I did read some of it, and it did indeed offer helpful perspectives. But now I had no time to read. Colin was coming home so soon.

The uncertainty of Colin's return, however, continued for days.

He arrived back onto U. S. soil and was at Fort Benning on Sunday, December 18. We had no idea if he would be there for a few days or a week. So it was just a lot of hurry up and wait. Just slow systems and processes. Standing in line and waiting his turn.

On my drive home from work on Monday, I dialed Colin's cell phone. I had already called Verizon to restart the service. It felt strange to be able to just call him. He answered on the fifth ring. My heart skipped a beat. My husband was on the other line.

We chatted for a few minutes. He told me about his out-processing. I asked if he knew when he would be home yet. No. Tomorrow were his hearing and dental exams. And more out-processing paperwork. Wednesday was the medical exam. Did he really think he could be released the same day as his medical? Yes, maybe. *So he might come home Wednesday? Or Thursday?*

I, of course, wanted to plan a flash mob. Well, actually, I had let go the control of planning and gave it to Karen, but I wanted to tell everyone when it would be. Yet these last couple of days continued the year's mantra: I was not in control. I didn't know when I would be able to get wrapped into the big warm arms of my best friend. I just had to wait and see.

Chapter 23 – Beauty in Silence

End December 2011

It was Wednesday, December 21. Ever since my eyes opened this morning, I had been anxiously looking at my phone for a text message. Would Colin be coming home tonight? Or tomorrow? The uncertainty continued to taunt me.

And the children. After breakfast, the children each did a fly by every half hour or so asking, "Have you heard from Dad?" The emotional anticipation pumped through all of our bodies.

Late morning, Karl helped me hang Welcome Home signs for Dad. Admiring our craftiness, I tried to ignore the slightly clogged storm drains and made a mental note to add these the growing list of neglected house projects and fix-its. A few hours later, Karl, happy for tasks that channeled his nervous energy, willingly emptied the dishwasher and took the garbage out to the garage.

Ian hung back a bit, quietly processing everything going on. He found a cardboard box from the recycling bin and filled it with hundreds of pieces of paper of military battle scenes that he had meticulously drawn during the proceeding months. I had seen him draw day after day, but until he showed me the stack and explained its contents, I had no idea that they were each historically accurate scenes of Omaha Beach, Sainte-Mère-Église, and other WWII events. I saw the pride in his young face, as he waited for his hero to come home. My heart felt at peace when I looked at him. I knew my relationship with Ian, which was transformed by his near fatal accident over the summer, was stronger than it had ever been before. Maybe because Dad had been gone.

Beth Jackson

Thais simply followed me everywhere, all day. She stayed close but occupied herself by playing with her dolls and stuffed animals. As the hours ticked by, each of us seemed to pace around the house, not stopping in one place for too long. From chair to couch. Couch to chair. From room to room. The electricity in the air was palpable.

It was just after lunch when Colin called to say he was indeed coming home that night. The raw excitement we all felt was indescribable.

Ian told me, "This is a Christmas I will tell my children about. "

He then added, "This is the best day of my life. " I truly believed it was. Ian and I exchanged a hug in silence. And our wait continued.

In my exuberance, I went onto snapfish. com and ordered over three hundred Christmas cards to send to friends, announcing Colin's safe arrival home, four days before Christmas.

I also sent this e-mail to all our local friends.

> *Flight arrives Providence 11:50 p. m.*
>
> *Estimated time home 1:00 a. m.*
>
> *Flash mob in the dark, cold, rain, early morning hour for die-hards only!!! The timing and weather are actually quite funny in the context of all of this, so really, please don't feel obliged.*
>
> *For everyone else, feel free to just drop off a note for Colin on the front stoop anytime between now and then. . .*

My girlfriends all wanted to give him a grand flag-waving welcome. In the cold. With flashlights. One offered to bring cider. Another hot chocolate. They were not going to be deterred from sharing in this important occasion in our lives.

And I really wanted it, too. My emotions were starting to bubble over.

Yet, just when I most wanted to appear most beautiful for my husband, the enormous, honking, and painful fever blister that had first erupted during the hockey tournament before Thanksgiving, had now exploded in two distinct places across my top lip. Cleary, my body was spent. Exhausted. Stressed. Anxious. These blisters manifested my body's final surrender, the wave of the white flag.

I slathered white Abreva cream on my plump lip, now double its original size, and begged the image in the mirror to make the ugliness disappear before I saw Colin. Oh, how I just wanted to feel the softness of his lips with mine once more.

I walked over to my antique dresser, which did not match the rest of our bedroom furniture. It was the first thing we had purchased together as a married couple when Colin was on Active duty in Germany. Memories of that carefree time flooded my mind. I reached my hand into the middle drawer, through a pile of thick winter tights and cotton underwear. Eventually my fingers sensed a lacy texture and pulled out what I was looking for.

My eyes studied the small black thong that now rested in my hand. I hated thongs as they always crept into small places and reminded me they were there, but Colin loved them. And tonight I wanted to be as desirable as I could be, so I slid the black lace up my newly shaven legs. It had been months since I last shaved, and I was struck by the unfamiliar smoothness.

Last week I called Carrie, and asked her if shaving the bikini area was good enough, or if I had to get a bikini wax. Without hesitation, she replied, "Bikini wax. You are dating your husband again. "

Beth Jackson

I made an appointment at Arch Beauty in Newport and obliged a few days ago. My body was more exposed to the esthetician, who tore away at the hundreds of small hairs with a few bold throws of her arm, than it had ever been to my husband. After all the long, difficult months of this experience, I was good at holding my breath and did so in an effort to hold back the momentary pain. What I did not realize then, or during the whole time Colin was gone, was that holding my breath actually made it *worse*. The pain would have diminished if only I had known how to exhale.

I rummaged through the back of my closet to find a black push-up bra that made my saggy chest a bit more perky. Then my body squeezed into a long-sleeve black stretchy dress that had become too short to wear for work. With each wash and dry, the length of the dress crept up my thighs. But it was perfect for tonight.

I slipped two small diamond earrings into my pierced ears and a star-shaped ring filled with dots of tiny rubies onto my thin finger. Colin had bought me that ring after Thais was born. My blue topaz necklace hung in its usual place.

I pulled out my knee-high zipper black boots with two-inch heels that raised my frame to the same height as my husband, and I thought of looking into his dark brown eyes again.

Thais walked into the room and announced, "You look beautiful, Mommy!" My arms lifted her onto the white down comforter. The bed was neatly made an hour ago, but Charlotte had already nuzzled her way under the covers to make her den, and the pillows were scattered across the bed and on the floor. Thais slid her feet underneath the warmth as well and looked at me with the same beguiling smile as her Dad. I smiled back as my thoughts glided to the curves of his face. I was ready. The only thing left to do was wait.

The clock shone 8:28 p. m. I was so excited to have Colin home again, but I also wondered how we would all adjust to this other "new normal" of now having him back. *Had he changed?* Would he be part of the twenty percent that would have PTSD? *Had I changed?* Would we connect as deeply as before? Or had we grown apart? How would my relationship with the children change when he re-entered the scene? So many questions and unknowns swirled in my head.

I rose from the bed and looked out the bedroom window into the quiet darkness of the night. I could see a few lit windows at various neighbors' houses, but otherwise it was pitch black. There was a full moon, just like when Colin had left. Ten moons, nine full cycles. The side window of our bedroom was still cracked open from the night before, and I heard the faint sound of raindrops hitting the thick roof of our covered porch. I had thought about Colin's return for so long, with visions of a warm spring day under a vibrant sun and blue sky. Instead, the dark cool rain surrounded me. I wondered if this had any meaning, but I quickly pushed the thought away.

My fever blister throbbed once again and brought my thoughts back to the present. That lip could sure use one more day to heal, but I gritted my teeth at the disappointment that I could not control my imperfection. All I could do was finally surrender, and savor the expectation that I would soon be enveloped by my husband's embrace.

At 10:15 p. m. , the children and I left the house in my car. We were tired but so excited that Dad was finally coming home. Just minutes from the Providence airport, though, Colin called to tell us he missed his connecting flight. He mentioned there was another flight to Boston, but if he could not get a seat, he would have to fly out in the morning. *What should we do?* Should we start to turn back around and plan to come back in the morning? Or hope he could get a seat and start to head north up Route 1-95? Or just park somewhere? I did not want to turn north until we knew for sure, as that would just mean it would take more time to get back home at this already late hour.

So there I was. In a little black dress with a little black thong with black tights and black boots. Ready to welcome my husband home. But for fifteen minutes, I drove like a snail in the far right lane of the highway, not sure if Colin was indeed going to make it back tonight, or tomorrow morning. I started creeping on and off each ramp, looking for a well-lit parking lot or some other place to pull over and safely wait. But at each exit all I saw were rows of empty warehouses. An abandoned car. No lights. So I kept driving, slowly. On and off each ramp.

I began to wonder if I should wear the same clothes again if we had to go home and come back the next morning for Colin. I only had one black thong, you know. I thought about how one more night might help my honking fever blister heal a bit more, so I could actually kiss my husband when I saw him.

Colin then called back to say he was rerouted to Boston and would arrive in a few hours, so we turned back onto the highway and headed north. No need to wash the thong. I would just cover the fever blister with lipstick and hope he would not notice.

I called Karen and just started laughing. Really. Nothing was going to be easy about this return, and there was nothing to do but let go of control. Through my laughter, I asked her to send an e-mail to cancel the flash mob. We would be getting home way too late.

We entered Boston's Logan International airport parking and locked Charlotte inside the car. Of course we had brought her with us, as she was family, too. The air was chilly, and it was still raining. At this time of night, the rain, our footsteps, and some nearby construction work were the only noises we heard. We walked as a pack into the elevator and then into the airport terminal. Thais had fallen asleep in the car and was dead weight on my shoulder as we moved. We found the US Airways baggage claim area, since the check-in counters were already closed at this late hour. At first the customer service woman could not find Colin's name on the flight list. *Had he missed this flight, too? Did I hear it wrong?* The woman had to look three times, as she just kept shaking her head. I had no more energy left for yet another change in plans, and I just closed my eyes to momentarily shut out the world. Then she realized that it was past midnight, and she had to enter in the new date.

Phew! The woman processed our special passes to allow us into the gate area. As I carried my still-sleeping Thais, donned in PJs and shoes that kept falling off, she half mumbled that carrying her would help me be as strong as Daddy.

The boys were silent as we walked down the long corridor towards the gate, and the completely empty terminal echoed with the sound of our shoes against the cold ceramic tile floors. Chairs were already turned upside down on tables where the floors had been mopped. Lights were dimmed.

We still had an hour to wait for the plane's arrival, so we collapsed in the black vinyl chairs by the gate and just waited, quickly falling asleep, bundled inside our winter coats. I was worried that we would sleep through Colin's deplaning, though, so I set the alarm on my phone.

I dozed off, waking a couple of times with a startle.

At last, a US Airways employee walked down the quiet expanse towards us and announced, "The plane has landed!"

We quickly rose and gathered our signs. It was 1:24 a. m. My phone alarm went off just as I stood.

Beth Jackson

Four or five men exited the plane before Colin did. Then there
he was, walking off the jet way, back on home soil. Colin, my
love and our children's Dad. It felt like the world stopped as
nothing else around us or around the world mattered at that
moment.

Welcome at empty Boston Logan airport

The welcome was not quite what I had planned. I had envisioned a
standing ovation, but there was no one in the terminal to clap. Even
Colin's fellow passengers had no idea what was transpiring on this
otherwise routine flight from Philadelphia to Boston until they read
Karl's sign that said "9 Months in Afghanistan. Welcome Home,
Dad. "

I had envisioned tears rolling down my face, but it just felt calm.
The flash mob cancelled, we would just be driving back home as a
family of five plus dog in the early morning of December 22. Anti-
climatic, and somehow, just perfect.

At 3:26 a. m. in the dark, cool rain, our car rounded the curve
of our road. Up ahead, small lights glistened in the distance,
illuminating American flags. The driveway to our house was lined

on both sides with what seemed like a hundred flags that were lit by candle lights.

This absolute beauty in silence created a wave of emotion that rippled through my body. And the tears finally came.

A myriad of notes and welcome home gifts at the front door step greeted us. Once the children were in their beds, Colin and I made love. The same wonderful way we had months before.

***

We all slept in until after 11 that morning.

Karl made his batter for skinny pancakes to show Dad, and we all enjoyed a late, slow breakfast as a family. I had to pause and consciously count out five forks this time.

We learned that some of our friends had not gotten the e-mail that the flash mob was cancelled, and they had actually showed up at 1 a. m. at our house. We were sorry that we had missed the fanfare of those who came, but we were so grateful for their love.

While I was preparing dinner that night, the doorbell rang. Ian was closest and answered the door. I heard the man ask if his Mom or Dad were around.

Colin followed behind Ian towards the door. It was a man from our neighborhood that we did not know. He had seen the welcome home signs and asked Colin where he had been.

"Afghanistan," Colin replied.

Beth Jackson

"You are a hero," he said. The man repeated himself three times and handed Colin a bottle of champagne. He said thank you and left.

The next night, another neighbor whom we did not know repeated a similar scene. Champagne. Thank you.

The kindness of strangers continued.

Christopher from the local ABC new affiliate in Providence called on Christmas Eve. He wanted to do a story on Colin's return. He had left a voicemail message the day before and called back again that morning.

After listening to the voicemail, Colin had commented, "I don't want the publicity. It is not about me."

So when I answered the phone and Christopher was live on the other end, I told him, "As you can imagine, we want to spend time just as a family today. We would prefer if you do a story about all the men and women who are still serving over in Afghanistan."

There was a pause on the other end. I don't think Christopher was expecting my response. It did not fit his storyline.

"Merry Christmas," I continued joyously. And hung up.

On Christmas Eve night, we hosted 27 people for dinner. Neighbors and friends who did not have family nearby were invited, as always. My mom, dad, sister, and younger brother, who had already planned to join me in Colin's absence, came in town, too. And after we learned Colin was coming home, I invited additional close neighbors, along with their children and parents.

It was truly a Christmas we would never forget.

Epilogue: Learning to Breathe

Days later, there was Thais with one thousand beads to make necklaces, sitting on the carpet in her bedroom. She was still admiring the Christmas present. I could see it coming, but she was insistent on opening the plastic bag herself. Suddenly, the bag burst open, and the beads flew everywhere.

I called out, "Oh, no!"

Thais started to sob.

I took a deep breath. A week ago, I would have spent the next fifteen minutes cleaning up all the beads while Thais would have continued crying inconsolably.

Instead, I called down the hall towards Colin. "Col, can you please help Thais brush her teeth?"

A few seconds later, he walked down the hall and redirected her to the bathroom. Within seconds, she had stopped crying and was letting him brush her teeth. The drama was over.

I scooped up the beads, methodically. Scoop. Scoop. Scoop.

My heart felt truly lighter. My co-pilot was back.

***

In bed that first week home, I asked Colin to open the window. He did, but only a crack of one or two inches. As I lay in bed trying

Beth Jackson

to fall asleep with his arms wrapped around me, I started getting overheated. I asked him to move over to his side of the bed.

He laughed and said he was comfortable where he was.

I laughed back and said, "You are smack in the middle of the bed. Would you please move over?"

"But it is too cold next to the open window," he explained.

And so I started climbing over him to "his side," the right side of the bed. When I got there, I sat up and lifted the window up a foot.

"I will sleep on this side of the bed, then," I said with a grin.

"But that would be strange. Don't alter my universe. "

I acquiesced but silently thought about how my universe was being altered every minute since his return. It was strange enough having another human in my bed with me.

Within this short window of time since Colin was home, Charlotte also snuck her way back into our bed. In the blink of a night, Colin undid all his dad's training, and my continued effort to have the dog beside, not in, our bed. At first I was annoyed. I had a routine that was working just fine, thank you very much. I let it go. And moved back to the left side, my side of the bed.

***

A bowl fell onto the hardwood floor in the kitchen the next day. It made a loud breaking noise.

Colin was visibly startled. As was I. But neither one word nor additional sound was made. Just another day in a household of five.

In our bathroom, I started to notice a growing pile of dirty clothes on the floor next to the toilet.

I paused for a minute, wondering what was out of place.

Then I remembered. I had moved the dirty clothes bin into my closet off the bathroom shortly after Colin left. And I had not yet told him about that change.

"Hey Col," I called out from the bathroom. "I moved the dirty clothes bin into my closet. Next time can you please put your dirty underwear there instead of next to the toilet?"

"OK," he said, and he actually starting doing so.

Change was a simple thing.

Colin said the biggest difference was that he felt disconnected from an experience that none of us had. Like Rip Van Winkle, it was as if we had been asleep for nine months while he had this inconceivable experience in a totally different world.

But things here had changed, too. That afternoon as we drove on the way to Ian's hockey game, Colin commented, "this road was paved. "

Oh, yeah. I had forgotten. Colin was noticing all the little things that changed, things that had already transformed into normal in my everyday life.

***

Several days after his return I did not put on the blue topaz necklace.

That piece of jewelry had been my solace and comfort for what seemed like forever. A good luck charm. Superstition. It had worked. But that day I felt a bit buoyant as I chose to wear another necklace instead. I did not need to wear the blue one every day anymore.

I was liberated from fear.

But I still worried silently about Colin's full reintegration into our new life. Only later did I realize that it was me who had to reintegrate back into our marriage.

***

A week after Christmas, my family left town; Colin's mom and step dad arrived.

The next morning, we enjoyed leftover pancakes. Colin and I leisurely read the paper over coffee. Then Colin and his mom took the boys to run some errands.

I cleaned the house. Brought Christmas presents upstairs. Unloaded and loaded the dishwasher. Ran three loads of clothes in the washing machine. Ran a bath for Thais. Wiped down the counters. Swept the kitchen. Took down the stockings and Advent calendar. Took all the ornaments and lights off the Christmas tree. Dragged the garbage cans and recycling bins to the corner. Listened to music. Read books with Thais.

When the boys returned, I had them try on their ski boots. The five of us were going to go on a post-deployment ski trip in a couple of weeks. Karl's boots were too small. He needed new ones. Ian's fit just fine.

I then asked Colin, "Could you please take the Christmas tree out before you shower, or sometime tomorrow?" I made a concerted effort to add in "or tomorrow" and not give him an immediate honey-do request. I did not say it out loud, but I was thinking, how I wanted the tree removed before our cleaning lady came on Monday.

"No. I like the tree up," he remarked.

The plain, now undecorated tree.

"Fine! Karl and I will do it. We put it up when you were not here, anyway," I retorted.

Colin's mom overheard this dialogue and muttered under her breath, "That was harsh!"

I was out the door on my way to bring the now empty garbage and recycling bins back into the garage, when I heard her comment. I stopped in my tracks and walked back inside. I thought I had used a perfectly calm voice.

"It was not harsh!" I exclaimed. "Please don't critique me."

As I walked back outside to get the bins, I thought about what had just happened. I knew I had been in robot-mode for the past nine months. Just doing. Not stopping. No time to think. Christmas was over, so it was time to take the tree out. I was self-sufficient. Hear me roar.

Only days later when I described the scene to a friend did she help me realize that maybe Colin just wanted to revel in the holiday a bit longer. Maybe my tone did actually sound harsh. Maybe I had changed. *Was I still wearing my hard shell and mask?* With the holiday and family visiting, I had not actually had a chance yet to sit and relax and savor what was happening. I was too busy keeping busy. Still surviving. Looking back, I see that I was still emotionally numb, even to the man I loved with all my heart.

Beth Jackson

In that moment, though, all I wanted was a thank you.

A thank you for being a loving mother to our children, devoted wife to my husband, CEO of the household, bee-swarming solver, pee cleaner, and pool scrubber.

A thank you for doing my part in the service of the country by supporting my husband.

I was waiting for someone, anyone, to just say "thank you" - not just for my part in our family's sacrifice, but for loving Colin. But the thanks did not come.

A week later at Colin's welcome home party, as 90-some people gathered in our kitchen and living room, Colin's dad spoke of his pride that his only son had stood up and volunteered to serve our great country. He also thanked me for taking care of the children. Colin made a toast and thanked our friends for all of their help, and publically also thanked me. Too choked up, I was not able to give a proper toast.

On the back of our holiday card, though, three words below a picture of the children captured my sentiments.

Back of Christmas card

But then and even a year later, neither of us had still ever said "thank you" directly to each other.

***

One Month Later

Four weeks after Colin returned, we took that ski trip to Vermont. The connection Colin and I had built over two decades was wonderfully still in place, and we coveted this away time as a family.

The night before we left, though, Erin abruptly quit, leaving behind the house key and saying she would not return. Her reason was that she was just too overwhelmed by responsibilities at home.

The following morning, however, as I reached into the freezer to pull out cold packs to put into the children's school lunches, I noticed that several boxes of frozen appetizers were missing. And everything was moved out of place. Usually I did not pay much attention to the exact order of my freezer, but I had a general organization of ice cream and veggies on the top, meats in the middle, and the children's favorite foods on the bottom. And after recently trying to fit the many boxes of appetizers for Colin's welcome home party into the small space, I knew exactly what was in there. But that morning every single box had been moved to a new random location. And several were missing.

It suddenly all clicked. *Erin had stolen frozen food from us. Did she also take the gift cards? And the purse? And...* I was so shocked.

Right after school, we drove the five hours to Vermont and stayed in a dive of a hotel, which we loved because it had two large adjoining rooms, breakfast included, and an ice rink out back.

Beth Jackson

We skied. We skated. We laughed. We watched movies. We played cards. We enjoyed each other's company. We were just another family again. As the white fluffy cloud of my emotional protection started to dissipate, my tone with Colin slowly started to soften, too. The marathon was finally over, and I was recovering.

A few days into our ski trip, I got an e-mail from Erin explaining that she was bipolar and had a severe anxiety disorder. She stated that she was taking lithium and valium to treat the illness. She respectfully asked that I not contact her again about anything.

The information hit me like an ice axe. Cold. Sharp. Pain.

I was so upset that Erin had not previously shared this critical information with me when she was the caring for my three young children. I felt betrayed, again, and mad. The children's safety was my primary focus, and I had no idea of the depth of this caregiver's deception. This person that I had taken into my home and thought I knew was really just a stranger. I felt so exposed. But I felt sadness, too, when I thought about her illness and the angst it must cause her. And I even felt relieved to finally know that *my* mind was not playing tricks on me.

Just to be sure, though, when we returned from Vermont, I also fired our cleaning lady.

A week later, after months of no communication, our old sitter, Dana, must have sensed something. Out of the blue, she called and offered to babysit, as her treat, like a family member would, so that Colin and I could have a night out together.

The morning after, Thais told me, "Mommy, I love Dana. "

I realized that I did, too. It was that moment when I saw that my hard feelings, from the previous September when she had left us, stemmed from how much she had cared for me and my fear in losing her support. Forgiveness was a good thing. I was very grateful for her kindness, and I was glad that our relationship would continue.

***

A formal letter arrived addressed to me from the Under Secretary of Defense. It was a survey for Reserve spouses about how the family support services met my needs during the deployment. Laughter shook me as I studied the letter. So they clearly knew I existed.

I did complete that survey, with constructive suggestions. And on that day I made a vow to myself: I would make a difference for other women. To help them not feel alone.

"You look lighter," Karen announced to me one day when we saw each other at school drop off. The dark cloud that had been looming over me during the past year had lifted. I was my characteristically cheerful and exuberant self once again.

Karen also noted how Thais was back to being the bubbling little girl she first met. My daughter's body and soul glided through the air now, too, rather than grudging through life.

***

I went on a post-deployment escape with my sister to New York City. After I got over the guilt of leaving Colin with the three children and all the responsibilities that I handled alone for over nine months, I remembered that I needed to take care of myself. On my suggestion and invitation, Colin's mom also came in town to help him.

One night, Carrie keenly observed something I had missed this whole time. I had been holding my breath most of this year, in my attempts to hold on. But while I was losing faith given all the challenges of this experience, some force greater than my will was pushing and pulling the oxygen in and out of me when I could not.

Breathing was the one thing I was not very good at, but somehow, something had kept me alive, even if I was only taking in shallow gulps of air. That day, letting go and allowing myself to fully exhale, rather than holding on, became the core theme for this book, as I started to transform my journal into this journey.

Upon my return from New York, Thais ran up to me to give me a big hug. At first glance, I missed it, as her long hair was covering part of her face. But as soon as she pushed her hair back and tucked the long strands behind her ears, I saw it. Thais had cut off half of her hair and had given herself bangs. She cut the hair so short on top that little strands stood straight out from the scalp. In some places, huge chunks were just missing. Instead, a softball size wad of hair filled the trash bin in the corner of her room.

Thais cut off half her own hair

A smile crossed my lips as I just shook my head and let out a deep exhale.

***

Four Months Later

With my partner back, the children's eating habits were improving. Colin had the patience to sit at the table until each child ate his or her vegetables. Thais now drank milk at dinner again and ate baked chicken. She has not had cereal for dinner since December.

Thais still whispered to me every week or so that we should toast that Dad was home. The return was not a moment; it was an ongoing celebration of life.

Thais also had her dream fulfilled. All five of us and Charlotte took many walks on the rocks at the beach.

But normal was also real. Not always idyllic. After my first overnight business trip since Colin's return, when his mom was not in town to help, Thais told me that Dad forgot to brush her teeth and tuck her into bed. He was out of practice.

***

I went inside the bank for the first time since that day in December. I saw the bank woman who had comforted me and told her my husband was home. She shared with me that after I left that morning, she had walked into her boss's office and cried as well.

My eyes moistened and throat hardened as the emotions of her words were still very near. I thanked her for being there for me that day.

Beth Jackson

***

Ian's eye hurt one night as he tried to fall asleep. Unable to spot a loose eye lash or fuzz in his eye, I suggested maybe we try eye drops. In my bathroom, Ian pulled out that plastic bin, filled with all that expired medicine. He picked up the eye drop bottle and turned it to the back to read the label.

"Mom, this expired in 2004," he exclaimed. Eight years out of date.

"Throw it away," I said after a brief pause, and I gently exhaled as the plastic bottle bounced into the white wicker trash basket.

He pulled out a few more bottles of random medicine with dates from the last decade, and threw them out, too. He stopped, though, without completely cleansing my bin of expired goods. I was grateful. I was just starting my journey of letting go of control, and I needed a little more time.

***

On April 22, 2012, the U. S. -Afghanistan Strategic Partnership Agreement was announced. This agreement provided the long-term framework for the relationship between our two countries after the eventual drawdown of the U. S. forces in Afghanistan.

United States President Barak Obama and Afghan President Hamid Karzai exchange documents after signing the agreement in Kabul on May 2, 2012. Source: Wikipedia, image confirmed as in the public domain, as a work of the U. S. federal government.

After the announcement of this historic moment, Colin casually said to me, "That is what I worked on. I was the lead action officer, drafting the agreement with the Afghans. "

That was the first I had heard what my husband had actually done while he was away.

***

Six Months Later

Rummaging through a dresser drawer, I found the holiday DVD that I thought was stolen. Joy filled me, as I knew we could watch *The Little Drummer Boy* anytime we wanted next December. That discovery made we wonder, however, whether everything that was missing had indeed been stolen. But I decided not to relive those details. I had closed that chapter in my mind.

UPS still required that we sign for every package we received, so when we were not there, they left notes rather than packages on the front door. I had been too busy to call them to explain that they could just leave them on the front stoop again now.

A hospital bill from Ian's accident almost a year ago arrived in the mail. I had no idea why it took so long. But that weekend, Ian scored his first soccer goal of the season. His right leg, bolstered by two now strengthened bones, kicked the ball high above the goalie's shoulders to the right corner as his face glowed with pride.

My mom and I never really talked about the accident since those first 24-hours when it all happened. It finally struck me, now that I was returning to myself, that on the night of the accident, it was more of a crisis for my mother, caring for her injured grandson she so loved, than it was for me, away and desperate to get to his bedside. While I so appreciated the unconditional support and patience my mother showed me during my time of weakness, it wasn't until much later that I saw how ungratefully bitter I was at the time.

Six months after Colin's return, my mom finally scheduled the major back surgery she had been needing to heal the physical pain she had in her legs every time she stood. My mom had delayed this surgery during Colin's deployment, so she would be available whenever I needed her.

When I first learned of the surgery date, I told her I was coming to town, and she pushed back, saying, "You are too busy. You have a whole family to care for. And work. I will be fine. "

I replied, "You are a terrible patient, and for once in your life, please let me help take care of you. " I realize now that I had been a terrible patient myself, and I had not let her help take care of me. But my mom nevertheless had showed up for me over and over again, and if I had learned anything from my experience this last year, it was the importance of showing up.

And my mom let me help. When I flew to Michigan to care for her at the hospital and during those first days home after the surgery, I finally had the chance to switch roles with her. In her moments of vulnerability and fragility, I was there for her, so she knew she was not alone. Over the days we spent together, her ability to move her body progressed in advance of expectations. I was her cheerleader, and she was my mom.

***

We went to the Operation Military Kids Family Camp again this summer, this time with Dad and no wheelchair. Cara and her family came, too.

On the second night, just before bedtime as we all huddled around the TV in one of the common rooms to watch the Summer Olympics, my phone suddenly rang. It was our summer nanny and dog sitter. As I had instructed, she had left the doggie door from Charlotte's gated corner in the kitchen open to the yard when she went out for dinner. She arrived back ready to spend the night with Charlotte in our bed, but the dog was nowhere to be found.

A huge thunderstorm had passed through the area an hour before. There were loud claps of thunder and a deluge of rain. I suggested that our nanny check each bed and closet in the house, in case Charlotte had been able to hop the gate.

No luck. The nanny and several friends she had gathered began to roam the neighborhood, using their cell phones as flashlights under the pitch black darkness of the night. They knocked on doors to ask people if they had seen our dog.

No Charlotte. After an hour more, we agreed Colin would go home to help find her. It was already 10:30 p. m. at this point, and he was facing a 45-minute drive to get back.

Close to 1 a. m. , Colin texted me that he could not find Charlotte anywhere. That night, my sleep was restless at best.

In the early morning, Colin had no more news, even after walking and driving the neighborhood several more times. He ventured down to the beach, fearing that the coyotes could have taken her. I worried that, after she had waited for Colin to come home from Afghanistan, Charlotte finally had found her time to go away into the forest near the beach to die in peace. At the age now of fourteen, that would have been understandable. But the thought ripped my heart open.

After breakfast, as the camp continued with tug of war and parachute games, the children kept asking me where Dad was and if he had found Charlotte. How ironic it was that we had gone to the camp this time to share the experience with Dad, but he was missing it again.

After a call came with no news at 9:15 a. m. , I lost hope and started the process of accepting the worst. I was not sure if we would ever find her. My throat started to harden, and I realized how much I really loved Charlotte. She had been a force, a protector for me when I needed her. And now she was gone. A sadness swept my body.

A short while later, Colin texted me.

> *A neighbor across Sandy Point called. She found Charlotte in her back yard. I am going to get her now.*

A woman we did not know from across a busy road had found Charlotte, shivering under a bush behind her children's outdoor playscape. Charlotte was OK. My voice choked as I immediately shared the uplifting news with the children.

***

Nine Months Later

Since Colin's return home, I have only gone on two short business trips. My work-life balance seems much more in harmony as I have scaled back from overdrive to a normal full-time pace. My income is down by almost half, but it does not matter anymore. And somehow it all feels more stable.

Even though Colin is home now, flexibility in my life is just as important as ever, so I can find peace both in my work and in my personal life as an executive, Mom, and a wife. And have a little time left over for me.

It took months after Colin's return for me to gain perspective on my experiences and to notice how I changed. The thump no longer booms in my ear now, and I sleep better once again, without nightmares. I do admit, though, that I still have not turned off those Google alerts. The alerts are like a drug I need to gradually wean off. When I read of horrific war events and on days when there is no news of fatalities, I simply send notes of love to my new girlfriends who still have husbands over there. I also still have that worn piece of paper, the "orders," in my wallet. I don't know why I have not removed it, but I cannot yet seem to do it.

My body has filled out my clothes once again, and most of the smaller sizes I had purchased no longer fit. But when I share the story of Colin's return, my eyes still well up and my voice cracks. I think they will for a long time.

Beth Jackson

People have asked me if Colin had PTSD. I said no. He adapted right back into our lives, and frankly, he has been even more helpful and attentive than before he left. I think that perhaps I was the one that had a stress disorder given all the traumatic insanity swirling around my mind. But my numbness is now gone, and my naturally warm manner with Colin is finally back.

So as with most days since he has been home, I step over his smelly socks and chose to pick them up and put them upstairs with the dirty clothes rather than nag him to do it. Some things just don't change.

Oh, and our flagpole broke again. But even after Colin fixed it, hopefully for good, on a given day, and sometimes even twice a day when it's windy, I still hop up to pull down the furled flag.

One night in the early Fall, as I was walking by Colin's office, I overheard a few words of his phone conversation. "Just a few months... It could happen..." My mind immediately jumped to the assumption that he was talking about a future deployment, and I found myself holding my breath.

Later I learned he was talking about the book on counterinsurgency that he is writing, as a professor. My mind was just teasing me.

I know another deployment, while improbable, is always possible. I half jokingly tell Colin that I don't think I could survive it. Yet I remember telling myself that same thing after my second miscarriage. But, I endured.

***

This past year, I went from denial in my numbness, to anger in my bitterness, then finally to acceptance, in trying to fully embrace what I could not control.

I virtually held my breath for

HOLDING ON

9 months
1 day
21 hours
36 minutes

And it has taken me that long afterwards to breathe normally once again. But we luckily got a second chance on life, and these past eighteen months have truly changed me.

After being so consumed by my own crisis, I am softer, and learning to feel again. I am still practicing the depth of my breathing, though, particularly the exhale. I do feel that I am more empathetic than I was before, although I am still trying to teach my quick tongue to be quiet more often. I am humbled by those old and new friends that stood up for me, and I hope to be able to do the same for others in the future. I know I have become a better Mom, yet modeling patience may be a lifelong journey for me. And I am more committed than ever to nurturing our marriage and growing old together with my college sweetheart.

Colin and I went to our twentieth college reunion at the beginning of June where hundreds of our old friends descended. The clarity of time has shown me how we are all connected by our experiences, shared, concurrent, and disparate. I had my long moment of worry, utter exhaustion, and numbing fear. My friends have lost jobs, health, parents, and marriages. We all face challenges, and yet life moves relentlessly forward. With a little help from the sun, the rain, the bees, and let's not forget the air, the flowers keep returning, each time with stronger roots.

***

Ian has not said, "I love you," again since he did that one night in November 2011. But I don't need to hear it anymore. I know.

Beth Jackson

He did ask me if I would be his soccer coach next spring.

Thais, on the other hand, with bangs that now graze her nose in their slow path to grow back out, asked me to be her ice hockey coach again and then a few weeks later changed her mind. So instead of being on the ice with her and other five and six-year-olds, I will watch her winter season from the bleachers, practicing how to exhale. My story is really only beginning.

Acknowledgements

First, I would like to thank my sister, Carrie, to whom this book is dedicated. You helped save me in my darkest time of crisis. You also inspired me to keep writing, and after Colin returned, you helped me to look at my own weaknesses as I turned my journal into this book. Thank you for believing in me and the power of sharing my story.

I would also like to thank my mom, who gave more than she received from me during this experience. Your unconditional love of me, our children, and Colin means more to me than you will ever know. Thanks also to my mother-in-law for loving me like your own daughter. I am sorry to you both that I was so unappreciative. I thank you for all your love.

I would like to thank the wise military friends, whose numbers grew throughout this deployment. Anne, Meghan, Mykel, Margaret, Sharon, Gage, Rebecca, and both Lauras, thank you for your and your husbands' support. Cara, thank you for the sisterhood we shared and for making me feel normal. And especially Pamela, thank you for acknowledging me and my family. Words can never express my full gratitude.

I have been blessed by so many friends that offered to be early readers and give amazing insight and commentary to help me bring this book to life. Thank you to Molly, Laura, Nicole, Nicky, and my sister for being the earliest readers, before the story was even complete. Sabrina, Leah, Margot, Summer, and my mom, thank you for all your suggestions. And I am especially grateful for Karen and Patti, who read multiple versions, providing such thoughtful feedback and detailed edits each time. Christine Manory, thank you for capturing the beautiful image of my children that now graces the cover of this book. And of course my book club friends, I truly appreciate your overall encouragement and input on everything. I would specifically like to thank Susan Leon, my fantastic editor, for helping make the words more beautiful and concise, so women will eagerly share this book with others. And Brian McDowell, thank you for your pro-bono publishing and writing advice.

Regarding the deployment, I first started keeping a list of every little thing that someone did for me, the children, or Colin. But along with many other things that year, I did not have the bandwidth to keep up with it. Some of these gifts of kindness were included in this story, but many others were not. So I caution calling out specific examples and names of all who helped for concern of forgetting one. I just want to say thank you to all of my family and friends for all the individual and cumulative support that truly helped me endure. And thank you for the dozens of packages so many of you sent to Colin. Please know that from eyeglass cleaner to letters from the children's classes to a Hoagie Haven T-shirt from Princeton, he so appreciated of all of it. And a special thank you to my children's teachers, for loving my children so deeply.

As a marketer, I cannot help but acknowledge a few products and services for which I am so grateful. USAA, you are an incredible insurance company, and the Marine that first answered my call asking what I needed to do about our insurance during deployment made me feel so valued, when he responded, "Thank you, ma'm, for your and your family's service. I am honored to guide you through this process." Sesame Street, your deployment video was absolutely perfect. My daughter watched it over 30 times before and during those first weeks Colin was away. It treated a difficult topic so age-appropriately, helping her understand what was happening. Rebecca Christiansen, your book *My Dad's a Hero,* is also beautifully done. And Apple, thank you for the iPhone. Halfway through this deployment, I got an iPhone, and it truly changed my life. Rather than having to download pictures and videos late at night to send to Colin, I was easily able to send him clips of the children anytime, anywhere, to help keep us connected.

Colin, my true love and best friend, thank you for your patience and unconditional love as I readjusted to your return. I admire you more than you will ever know. And even though I never told you in person, I want to sincerely say thank you for your service, for keeping our children, me, and so many others safer. I look forward to growing old with you and solving the world's problems.

Lastly, but most importantly, I would like to thank my three beautiful and incredibly strong children, who have helped me become a better Mom. Ian, you taught me how to love more deeply. Thais, you taught me patience and the beauty of simple things. And Karl, you taught me how to always be a positive role model, even in the most adverse times. You three are the best gifts I have ever received. I love you all with all of my heart, which only continues to grow, especially now that it gets more fresh oxygen each day.

Join the conversation at www. holdingon. us

CPSIA information can be obtained at www.ICGtesting.com
Printed in the USA
BVOW001426160513

320916BV00001B/74/P